ELTON
TRUEBLOOD

ALSO BY JAMES R. NEWBY

Between Peril and Promise
The Creation of a Future: A Model for Spiritual Renewal
Reflections from the Light of Christ
Editor, *The Best of Elton Trueblood: An Anthology*
Editor, *Basic Christianity: Addresses of D. Elton Trueblood*

ELTON TRUEBLOOD
Believer, Teacher, and Friend

James R. Newby

1817

Harper & Row, Publishers, San Francisco

New York, Grand Rapids, Philadelphia, St. Louis
London, Singapore, Sydney, Tokyo, Toronto

FIRST EDITION

Library of Congress Cataloging-in-Publication Data

Newby, James R.
  Elton Trueblood : believer, teacher, and friend / James R. Newby—
1st ed.
      p.   cm.
  ISBN 0–06–252014–8
  1. Trueblood, Elton, 1900-   . 2. Quakers—United States—
Biography. I. Title.
BX7795.T75N49   1990
289.6′092—dc20
[B]   89–45749
                                                                CIP

---

90 91 92 93 94 RRD(H) 10 9 8 7 6 5 4 3 2 1

To the Company of the Committed
whose lives have been changed
because they have known
Elton Trueblood

Contents

A biography of a literary man, besides the common incidents of life, should tell us his studies, his mode of living, the means by which he attains to excellence, and his opinion of his own works.

——SAMUEL JOHNSON

Preface

Little did I suspect when I dined with Elton Trueblood in February 1973 that our meeting would lead to writing his biography fifteen years later. He was the guest at my parents' home in Wichita, Kansas, where he had been taking the leading role in the inauguration of Harold Cope as the new president of Friends University. At the time, my father was pastor of the University Friends Church, where Dr. Trueblood was scheduled to speak following our meal together.

I shall never forget the impression Dr. Trueblood made upon me—a young Quaker pastor from Nebraska—nor the topic that occupied our conversation together. "James," he said, "I want you to preach on the 'holy conjunction': *and.*" His important point was that the Christian life is a life of balance and conjunction—the combination of the clear head *and* the warm heart; the inner life of devotion *and* the outer life of ministry; the conservation of important traditions *and* the need to be open to new ideas. In the span of forty-five minutes over dinner, Elton Trueblood had initiated within me a course of thought that has continued to this day. At the time I was in the same condition as Walt Whitman, who said, "I was simmering, simmering, simmering. Emerson brought me to a boil." It was Elton Trueblood who brought me to a boil.

The biographer has the choice of writing about his subject while he is still living or waiting until after he has passed away. There are good reasons to wait and write about a person after death; the biographer can work on the life from a perspective that has a beginning and a physical ending. There are numerous advantages, however, to writing about a person while he is still influencing the world in which he lives and while he is still available to interview and clarify points with which the biographer needs assistance. I have chosen to write the life of Elton Trueblood while he is still living, and I am grateful that he has been available to help on matters that would have been very difficult to understand without him.

James Boswell said, "They only who live with a man can write his life with any genuine exactness and discrimination."[1] I have been Elton Trueblood's closest associate for the past ten years and an avid reader of his books all of my adult life. Although writing the biography of a person with whom one has been so close may cause some readers difficulty,

I would agree with Boswell that in order to have "genuine exactness and discrimination" there must be a close association between the biographer and subject. I have sought to present the picture of Elton Trueblood's life from the position of "detached affection," which is another way of saying I have tried to be "subjectively objective." But if admiration for one's subject disqualifies the biographer, then this particular genre of literature would be greatly impoverished, and I would be writing one less book.

A major literary project is never the product of only one person. In the words of Elton Trueblood, "Gratitude is the *one* thing that can never be overdone." As I consider all of the people who have helped in this major literary endeavor, I am filled with an overwhelming sense of thankfulness. James Todd, Jr., a generous and devout Yokefellow, provided me a beautiful lodge in the mountains of North Carolina for uninterrupted writing and study while I labored on this volume. Jane Owen, friend and encourager, graciously made "Mother Superior" house available to me in New Harmony, Indiana, while I worked to conclude this project. All of my colleagues at the Earlham School of Religion have been most encouraging and patient during the writing of this book, but an extra expression of gratitude goes to Professor Alan Kolp, who provided his own special encouragement when I needed it, and my dean, Tom Mullen, who first taught me the joy of writing when I was his student in seminary. For Jarrell McCracken, because of his enthusiastic response when I first sent him my proposed outline, and for Floyd Thatcher and Lonnie Hull, my thoughtful and most helpful editors at Harper & Row who have guided me throughout the writing process, I am very grateful.

I am indebted to the assistance of Kathy Barker, Melanie Kraemer, and her son Joe Kraemer, whose abilities at the word processor far exceed my own. With great struggle they were able to decipher my handwriting and make this volume readable. I am grateful to my family for their patience and encouragement. Without the help of my wife, Elizabeth, and daughter Lisa, I would not have been able to complete this work. I wish to thank the many people who have sent me material about their experiences with Elton Trueblood. It has not been easy to select and edit the numerous pages of material sent to me, because Dr. Trueblood has touched so many lives. Whenever a biography is written, it is done with the hope of including all relevant material on the person's life being examined. If I have inadvertently excluded material that others believe should have been included, I apologize. Finally, I thank the company of the committed Christians who are dedicated to the ministry of common life because Elton has, in some way, touched their lives. Out of gratitude to them and their faithful ministry I dedicate this volume.

January 1, 1989   James R. Newby
                                              Earlham School of Religion
                                                     Richmond, Indiana

Prologue

He looked cold against the dark grey sky. It was November, 1987, and it was typical weather for Indiana. Last year, twenty-eight out of thirty days in November were cloudy and wet. This year there was little difference. Today it was not only cloudy and wet but cold as well. A wet cold is the worst kind, especially if one is in his late eighties. Although he was wearing his hat, coat, and gloves, I could tell that the wind was cutting through him.

Elton Trueblood was making his daily walk (when he is at home on the Earlham campus) between his study, which he called Teague Library, and the international office of Yokefellows. As usual, his hands carried numerous letters to be typed by his secretary. Pausing at his rose garden, he looked down at the brown mounds of thorny stems that, in the spring and summer, bore beautiful roses. "We are in the melancholy days of the year," he told me yesterday at coffee. Perhaps as he looked at his once beautiful rose garden he was trying to remember how it looked in the summer, or maybe he was trying to envision how it would look in the spring. Today, it just looked ugly.

As he continued to make his way up the brick walk, he passed under an old oak tree that has now been cut back to the place where it is only a shell of what it once was. Each year since 1979 I have watched the tree trimmers take off a little bit more of what was once a beautiful and mighty tree. Today it only serves as a piece of wood on which an oxen yoke can hang over the walk. There is no foliage except for the poison ivy that winds its way around the trunk in the summer. And so it stands as a monument, with neither Elton nor the Earlham College grounds crew having the nerve to take it down completely.

As the door opens he is smiling. "Good morning, Kathy and Jim. How are you today?" His voice is always encouraging. He places the letters on his secretary's desk, takes off his hat, slips off his coat, and carefully puts them on one end of the couch while he sits down on the other. Elton Trueblood is a patterned man. This is a routine that I could perform blindfolded. He is now ready for coffee and fellowship with his staff. It is a time of reviewing events of last evening and discussing the schedule for the day. "Kathy," he said between swallows of coffee, "read to James my letter to Chuck Bennett." Dutifully, Kathy plucks out of the stack in front of her the letter addressed to Chuck Bennett and proceeds to read. "Do you approve, James?" Elton asks. "Yes, indeed, I do, Elton. It is just right." Elton Trueblood writes letters the way he writes sentences in his books—with great care and mastery of the English language. I can't recall an instance in nine years when I ever disapproved of what he wrote to anyone. And yet he has always asked my opinion. This is one of his great gifts. Elton Trueblood knows how to draw people out and make them feel included.

It was early in my seminary years when I first noticed Elton Trueblood's deliberate attempts to encourage and draw out his students. I was invited to his study to hear him lecture on the philosophy of religion, which was one of a series of "fireside chats" he would schedule with students from the Earlham School of Religion. There were only ten of us, so we really couldn't hide from his penetrating presence. Sitting in front of the fire in the beautiful walnut-paneled Teague Library, next to a man whose name was revered in my parent's home, was quite an exhilarating experience. For exactly one hour he questioned and drew each of us out, asking us to tell what we believe and why. At the end of our time together, he looked me straight in the eye and said, "James, I want you to soak yourself in the writings of Blaise Pascal, Samuel Johnson, and Abraham Lincoln." When Elton Trueblood spoke, I listened. Upon leaving his study that evening, I was ready to go wherever need be to find the writings of the three persons he mentioned. To this day I am still studying Pascal, Johnson, and Lincoln, the three men, I found out later, whose writing have influenced Elton Trueblood the most.

As he sat in the office on this cold November day, fourteen years after our first "fireside chat," he was still teaching, encouraging, and trying to draw me out. He loves mind games. "How many consecutive times can *that* be used in a sentence?" he inquired. Kathy and I looked at each other, trying desperately to construct a sentence using *that*. Finally, as in most instances, we gave up and asked Elton for the answer. "Five," he said, sitting up on the couch to make his point. "I know that that *that* that that person used is wrong!" He leaned back, folded his arms, and smiled a triumphant smile.

Elton likes nothing more than telling people something they have never heard before. He is a wealth of information, and he delights in sharing it with whoever is in the same room. These times of fellowship each morning are wonderful experiences. It is then I have the opportunity to pick the mind of Elton Trueblood, and he loves the chance to share what he knows. Teacher and student are both blessed.

Today's schedule is busy. At eighty-seven years of age he tries not to schedule much in the afternoon because he tires more easily. If a visitor comes in the afternoon, however, he is never rude. He is always the congenial host. At 9:00 A.M. today a man from Illinois is coming to talk about his manuscript, and after he leaves a woman is coming at 11:00 to talk about her manuscript. At 4:00, Elton has invited Bill Dennis, the son of a dear friend whom he has not seen for a year, to have tea at his home, and then he will have dinner with Bill's parents, David and Tresa Dennis. David Dennis is a former congressman whose most notable achievement was to sit on the House Judiciary Committee during the time of the "Watergate Hearings."

Making his way back to his library, Elton Trueblood takes the long way around so he can inspect the memorial garden. This beautiful little garden is situated on the north side of Teague Library. In the wall, behind a large brass plaque, are the cremated earthly remains of Virginia Trueblood, and this is also where the cremated earthly remains of Elton will be placed. He sits for a time on the teakwood bench, surrounded by the last remnants of flowers. Imprinted on the back of the bench are the words, "I will give you rest," from Matthew 11. Elton delights in the cadence of these five one-syllable words used together.

The garden was made following the death of Virginia Trueblood, and every visitor who comes to see Elton is asked, "Have you seen the memorial garden?" It is always a moving experience to have the grand old man lead you out to his garden and hear him talk about its construction. "Someday," he says, "all that is left of the physical Elton Trueblood will be behind that wall."

As a Christian philosopher, Elton Trueblood has never shied away from talking about physical death and is certainly not bothered with discussion about his own demise. At least once each week during our staff meetings he will say, "James, you are getting ready for me to die, and I like that." He is a realist who has never sugar-coated difficult subjects, and death is no exception. It isn't that Elton has a "death wish," but he knows that people living in their ninth decade do not have a long time left on this earth. With the passing of his beloved wife, Virginia, in September of 1984, this realization has become an ever more active thought in his day-to-day life.

Elton Trueblood's main vocation in life is that of writer, and so it is not surprising that he expressed his grief through the written word. In January 1985, after Virginia's death, he wrote the following poem concerning her passing:

"VIRGINIA"

The queenly one who honored me
By giving me her hand,
Became a traveller far and wide
By air and sea and land.

> She journeyed oft from north to south
> And also east to west;
> But now at last her journey's done,
> Her spirit is at rest.
>
> We built for her a royal seat,
> Amid a peaceful scene;
> But now the seat's unoccupied;
> Alas! There is no queen.

Following a few moments of meditation, he stands and walks back into his study, ready for visitors.

ELTON
TRUEBLOOD

1900–1922

THE HERITAGE OF JOHN AND AGNES

I think you're a Londoner, but you've been away a long time.

It was a damp, overcast day, the kind for which London is particularly noted. Elton Trueblood was strolling among the ancient graves of the "nonconformist" cemetery, called Bunhill Fields. Located just across from the famous Wesley Chapel, it is an important stop for any Christian who wants to feel the strong sense of fellowship with the saints of previous generations. Here lie the earthly remains of Susanna Wesley, Isaac Watts, John Bunyan, William Blake, George Fox, and many more.

While studying and meditating upon the ancient markers that protrude from the earth in a not very orderly way, Elton Trueblood was greeted by the caretaker of the cemetery. Following a brief conversation, the caretaker said, "Your speech puzzles me." In the Socratic style so familiar to his students, Elton responded to the question with a question. "What am I?" After a pause, the caretaker said, "I think you're a Londoner, but you've been away a *long* time." "That's right," said Elton, "over three hundred years!"

This brief encounter with the caretaker at Bunhill Fields is revealing, for it emphasizes the importance Elton Trueblood places upon his heritage. Of course Elton had not been away from London for over three hundred years, but his ancestors had. And in that close sense of affinity that he has always had with his heritage, Elton Trueblood was, indeed, telling the truth.

In the preface to his book, *The People Called Quakers,* Elton wrote about his Quaker heritage, which extends back to Arnold Trueblood, who died in prison in Lincoln, England, in 1658 as a persecuted member of the then infant Quaker movement. The first time the Trueblood name appeared in a historical record was in the Friends' *Book of Sufferings.*

John and Agnes Trueblood, Elton's direct ancestors from England, arrived in the New World in 1682 on the shore of North Carolina where Elizabeth City now stands. They had been married in Devonshire House, London, on July 31, 1679. By the time of their arrival from England there was already a strong Quaker community established. It was an area visited by George Fox, the founder of the people called Quakers, just nine years before the landing of John and Agnes. In his *Journal*, Fox describes the physical conditions of the area at the time of his visit as being "pretty full of great bogs and swamps; so that we were commonly wet to the knees, and lay abroad at nights in the woods by a fire. . . ."[1]

Elton Trueblood wrote of the Quaker community on the eastern shore of North Carolina this way:

The new colonists made progress with amazing speed, soon establishing both Meetinghouses and schools. The modern observer is bound to be impressed when he sees the site of the first public school of North Carolina, which is at Symond's Creek, fifteen miles south of Elizabeth City. The school was established in the vicinity occupied by my own ancestors near Little River, one of the streams with a broad estuary at its mouth. The ships in which these people arrived from England were very small and therefore could not contain much equipment for agricultural pursuits, but the people advanced rapidly in spite of severe handicaps.[2]

For more than a century, nearly all of the Truebloods of America lived just north of the Albemarle Sound. As with many Quakers in the southern region of the United States, however, Elton's ancestors decided to move to Indiana during the first two decades of the nineteenth century in order to help their liberated slaves. Believing that slavery is a sin, many Quakers of North Carolina were liberating their captive helpers. If the former owners did not make the effort to help these people find employment in a "free" state, there was always the possibility that they would be rounded up and resold.

For Quakers, one of the most enticing areas to settle on the westward trek was Washington County, Indiana. It is here that Caleb II, Elton Trueblood's great-grandfather, is buried, along with many of the former slaves he brought with him from North Carolina. To this day, Elton makes an annual pilgrimage to the little Blue River Friends Meeting and cemetery, located just three miles to the northeast of Salem in Washington County, Indiana. Here he can rekindle the important sense of tradition and the heritage to which he feels so close.

In the Blue River cemetery it is not easy to locate family graves, since, because of the Quaker belief that all of the children of God are one family in heaven, each person was buried in a straight line when he or she died. And so one must not only know the name but the date of death in order to locate the right grave. Walking along the row of grave markers one will find a marker for Samuel and Priscilla Trueblood, Elton's great-aunt and great-uncle. The story passed to each succeeding Trueblood generation is that Samuel and Priscilla loved each other so much that each prayed that if one would die, God would find it in his mercy to take the other as well. Both died of natural causes on the same day, February 16, 1906.

A familiar story told by Elton Trueblood about his great-grandfather reveals the tough stock from which this breed from Blue River came. John Harned was part owner of a saw mill. One day great-grandfather Harned's leg became entangled in the flywheel, which mangled the leg so badly that immediate amputation was necessary. He was a man of strong will, refusing an anesthetic, and being vehemently opposed to alcohol, he would not take any whiskey. His partner, Eli Overman, took the saw in his hand and began to amputate the leg. When he reached the marrow of the bone where the pain became intense, Eli began to cry, sensing the horrible pain that his friend must be feeling. John Harned looked up at his partner, stared him in the eyes, and with a stern voice said, "Eli, be a man!" Once the leg healed, John Harned made a wooden leg at his saw mill, and after that he was referred to as "Old Peg Leg" by the members of the Blue River community.

Every Trueblood now living in America is a descendant of John and Agnes. Though only two came to America, it requires a book of 280 closely printed pages to list their descendants over the past three hundred years.

CHILD OF THE HEARTLAND

Do you know what it is to be a boy who works the black soil of an Iowa farm with his head full of faraway things and then, periodically, to see crack trains of the nation speeding across his fair land . . . ?

In the mid-1800s, the land beyond the great Mississippi River was enticing to many in southern Indiana who were becoming increasingly crowded for acreage to raise produce. Oliver and Mary Trueblood, Elton's grandparents, sold their farm in Indiana and joined the westward trek of Quakers to Iowa. They arrived in Des Moines by passenger train on the evening of March 10, 1869. With the money received for selling their land in Indiana, they were able to purchase twice as much acreage (160 acres) in Warren County, Iowa, just to the south and east of Des Moines. Elton describes what their arrival in the "heartland" was like.

By the time Oliver and Mary reached Iowa, the train to Des Moines had been operating eighteen months, but the facilities were meager. With their five children, one of them only four months' old, they had to sit in the station all night, without a fire, their only food being that which they had brought with them on the train. In the morning, Oliver's nephew, Charles Trueblood, came to take the family south to Indianola where Charles was already established. In spite of having hot bricks in the sled, Mary, who was always frail, was terribly chilled upon their arrival at Indianola and had to be carried into the house. A few days later the Oliver Truebloods reached their new home on the prairie.[3]

The area in which the Truebloods settled was called Waveland, later to be named Motor. It was prairie for as far as the eye could see, with no trees in sight. One of the first tasks upon settling was to find a milk-producing cow for the little baby. That first summer the milk became contaminated and the baby died. "Think how they felt," reflects Elton, "There they were in a strange land, and they had to go out and bury their baby on the prairie when there was not yet a cemetery." The location of that little grave determined the location of the cemetery and the Quaker Meetinghouse.

Samuel Trueblood, Elton's father, was born in Washington County, Indiana, and was three years old when his parents moved to Iowa. He grew up working hard on the family farm and by the age of twenty-three had grown fond of a young Quaker girl named Effie Crew, whose family had migrated to Iowa from Chesterhill, Ohio.

In November 1889, Samuel and Effie were married. They began their life together in a small house on forty acres of land. Elton was born December 12, 1900, the fourth of five children. An elder brother, Oscar, had been born in 1891, and an elder sister, Blanche, had been born two years after Oscar. Another sister, Ethel, was born in 1897, and a younger brother, Clare, was born in 1906.

Blanche did not survive infancy. "The little girl brought wonderful joy to her mother," writes Elton, "making the blow of her death on July 27, 1895 almost unbearable."[4] Samuel and Effie kept a joint diary, but with the death of Blanche the writing came to an end. The last entry of the diary in Effie's handwriting was dated July 8, 1895, and reads, "Blanche took sick."

One cannot truly fathom the full extent of Elton Trueblood's life by just stating his age. But when we're told that in Elton's boyhood he knew people who could remember Abraham Lincoln as president, we can begin to understand how long this man has lived.

The most memorable and influential person in Elton's boyhood was Mary Harned Trueblood, his father's mother, and one of those who could, indeed, remember Lincoln as president. She was a recorded minister in the Society of Friends, a woman of distinction in appearance, and very conservative. She wore the plain clothing and spoke the "simple language" of *thee* and *thou*, so closely associated with Quakers.

Mary Trueblood enjoyed telling young Elton stories out of her past, such as the one about when Morgan's Raiders, the Confederate soldiers, came through Washington County, Indiana, stealing horses and food. She told him about feeding some of the soldiers in her own kitchen and about how her husband hid the good horses when they came so they only took old ones. It was fascinating for a young boy to hear stories out of a history book from one who had lived them.

The farm life was hard work. "I cannot remember any summer morning in my boyhood when I slept beyond 5:00 A.M.," recalls Elton. The work had to be done, and the whole family participated. Each of the farms in the community was self-supporting, raising their own meat and vegetables. The high point was that of threshing the grain in midsummer, when all of the farmers in the area would work together with no exchange of money.

In the winter, young Elton would often accompany his father to one of the coal mines along White Breast Creek. Since there were no trees to cut for wood, coal was the primary source of fuel for heat. They would leave the house by 4:00 A.M. and not get back with the load of coal until mid-morning.

The hard Iowa winters were never easy. The Trueblood children usually walked to school, which was about a mile and a half away. If the weather was really bad, however, mother Trueblood would hitch up the horses and take them. One time when young Elton was six years old, a blizzard came up so fast and hard that the teacher let the children out early to get home before it became worse.

He describes what happened next:

> My sister thought we could save time if we went across the fields, taking the hypotenuse of the triangle instead of the cubed sides. With each step I took I nearly fell, and I couldn't see a foot in front of me. I hung onto my sister's coat as she guided me across the field. I suppose she saved my life. We didn't know it at the time, but my father had hitched up the horses to the sled and started for the school to get us. Of course he missed us because we had taken the short-cut across the fields. He was terribly concerned when he got to the school and we had already left, and so he came back as fast as the horses could run and caught us after we got back to the road on the second leg of our triangle. I often think of this experience with gratitude toward my sister.

A good education for their children was very important to Samuel and Effie. Samuel was, for a time, chair of the school board. His responsibilities included not only securing good teachers but also providing a room in his home in which the teacher could live. The Trueblood children would then see the teacher in two situations, one at school and the other at home. The schoolhouse had only one room, which had many advantages. "The littlest ones were always observing the older ones in the class," says Elton. "I know why we have given up the one-room situation, but it is naive to suppose that the result is all gain."

The big change in Elton Trueblood's education in the early years came when he was nine. Samuel and Effie moved from the secluded Quaker community of Waveland to the outskirts of Indianola, sixteen miles east. This was done wholly because of school advantages. "It is hard to believe that two of Samuel and Effie's sons would have gotten degrees if they had not made this shift in their lives," says Elton. The move was made at considerable financial loss, since they had to pay more for the land near Indianola than they got per acre on the east edge of Warren County. They sold 160 acres and bought 120. Later, Samuel Trueblood sold twenty acres to help with college expenses for his children.

For the terms 1910 to 1912, Elton attended a one-room school just north of his new home. Like the one described earlier, it was supervised by a teacher who had all eight grades, leaving the students pretty much on their own. "Elton came up with the correct answers so often when there had been an argument about grammar, spelling, etcetera," reflects Elton's brother Clare, "that the teacher soon began asking him for the answers to things she didn't know."[5]

When he was fifteen years old, Elton's mother employed the services of a speech teacher. On the whole, the grammar in that part of the country at that time was not very good. So with the help of his parents and the speech teacher, Elton was given a higher standard in the use of language than was generally expected. This high standard has continued to this day, and you can be sure poor grammar will not be tolerated in Elton Trueblood's presence. I have had the uncomfortable experience of sitting in Elton's library when he has kindly, yet firmly corrected someone's speech. At first it can be an embarrassment, but if the person understands that Elton considers this a part of his ministry in raising the cultural standards of our society, it is more easily accepted. It is not, however, comfortable to be on the receiving end of a Trueblood lecture on the proper use of grammar.

The reading material in the Trueblood home consisted of the County and Des Moines papers, *Wallace's Farmer*, and the *American Boy*. The Horatio Alger books were very important to young Elton as he was growing up, and he can remember with great joy reading *Bound to Rise* and *Risen from the Ranks*. Each summer there was the opportunity to attend Chautauqua where lectures and classical plays were offered. One lecture Elton has never forgotten was delivered by Russell Conwell, entitled "Acres of Diamonds." Conwell was a Baptist minister and spellbinding orator who would give this same speech throughout the country. With what he earned in lecture fees, Conwell started Temple University in Philadelphia.

For another type of entertainment, Samuel Trueblood, Elton's father, would keep his children spellbound for great lengths of time with stories about himself or others in their Quaker community. One of his favorite stories was the one about how all of the men along the mail route decided they would each try to keep the postman talking for as long as they could as he traveled from house to house. Knowing how much the postman enjoyed conversation with those on his route, they didn't think this would be too difficult. It wasn't. When the sun went down the poor postman was only half finished with his rounds!

"There wasn't anything father liked better than a joke on himself," recalls Elton's brother Clare. One occurred at the Motor (Waveland) farm one rainy day. Sam Trueblood and two neighbors were in the barn lot playing horseshoes when they saw Billie Bales, a neighbor, approaching. Billie was particularly noted for his yarns which mixed some truth with a lot of fabrication.

When Billie pulled up at the barn lot, they asked him to stop and tell them a story, but he replied, "Sorry men, I don't have time today. I just came from Willits, her mother just died, and they asked me to drive to Milo and get the undertaker."

Billie then slapped his reins against the horse and rode off in his carriage towards Milo. In the meantime the three men all went home, changed into their "Sunday clothes," and then the three families rode over to Willits to offer their condolences. Once at the Willits' home they found Mrs. Willits in perfect health. They were left standing there embarrassed and wondering about the great laugh that Billie Bales was enjoying at their expense!

One of Sam Trueblood's favorite characters around the farm was a handyman who had very little education but would always try to use big words in his conversations. Once when he was fixing a cement foundation for a corn crib, a neighbor of the Trueblood's brought a wagonload of stones from a creekbed and asked the handyman to use them in making the base.

When the neighbor checked on the handyman later in the day, he discovered that the limestone had not been used. When questioned, the handyman replied, "Them is bastard limestone, and they won't inherit." In another instance, Sam Trueblood had heard that this handyman's wife had been injured in an accident, and so he inquired about her condition. In responding the handyman said, "And to make matters worse, she was practically pregnant." On still another occasion Sam asked about this man's mother-in-law, who reportedly was very ill. "How is she?" inquired Sam. The handyman replied, "She has been so bad they had to give her epidemics." Then Sam asked, "I know she is bad, but is she rational?" Said he, "Rational as hell; doesn't know a damn thing!"

In the summer of 1916, young Elton had his first opportunity to see his name in print. The local paper printed his essay on the significance of the Declaration of Independence. For his effort he received first prize. Here is a portion of the essay as it appeared on the front page of the August 24, 1916, county paper.

> The Declaration of Independence, to some unpatriotic and thoughtless people, is nothing but a meaningless and out of date scrap of paper. To the vast majority of American citizenship it stands for a Declaration of War upon some foreign foe. But to a few right minded and thoughtful people, it means the formal beginning of a new and hitherto unknown era of civilization.... One fact which certainly demands recognition is that Independence was not easily obtained, and the Declaration has had to be strenuously defended. This made the originators of it more fully realize its meaning. The American populace of today does not appreciate its rights because it receives them without any personal effort whatever. Possibly the most touching part of the Declaration is that in which the signers pledged to each other in support of the Declaration, their lives, their fortunes and their sacred honor. If they could pledge all this, in fact, all that any man can have, in support of the Declaration of Independence, it certainly meant a great deal and it ought to mean as much to us today.

In the early years of the twentieth century, the most important characteristic of living in the heartland of America was the close connection between the life of religious faith and the life of work. This connection has not been lost on Elton. "There was no discussion of the work ethic because none was needed. We all worked hard." The religious life was also basic. "It was centered in the Meetinghouse, and we were never absent when the doors were open," reflects Elton. It was a community in a time when hard work and strong religious convictions went hand in hand.

The two big events each summer were Yearly Meeting, a time when Quaker congregations gathered for a week of inspiration and business, and the threshing of grain, when all of the farmers came together and traded work while the women cooked large meals for their hard-working men. Each family in the community was both owner and worker of the land, and the farms were largely self-sufficient. The Truebloods raised and butchered their own meat. There were always vegetables and fruit to be canned, since they were never without a big garden and orchard. This was also true of all of the others in that rural Iowa community.

Today many of the roads around Motor, Ackworth, and Indianola are no longer dirt, yet they are still unpaved. Occasionally they receive a treatment of gravel, usually in the fall and spring. The Trueblood home is no longer standing, and the one-room schoolhouse has long since disappeared. The old Meetinghouse, the last thing in the area to go, was finally replaced with a new one in 1986.

Yet even with all these changes, the countryside and way of life around Waveland, which became Motor, is not markedly different than when Elton Trueblood was a boy. The children still do farm chores, and the Quaker Meeting is still a social center for the community. Going to Des Moines remains an exciting venture, and the talk is still of crop gain or loss and the weather. In this land the seasons remain strikingly different—a time to sow and a time to reap, as well as intermediary times to plan and think about the season to come. In the basics of the human condition, the way of life in central Iowa is the same as it was at the turn of the century when Elton Trueblood was born one cold winter night.

The graves of grandfather Oliver and grandmother Mary, and parents Samuel and Effie, rise along the fence row that divides the Meetinghouse property with the farmland that borders it. They are continuous reminders of the pioneers who first came and settled this one-time prairie of rolling hills and waving grass. Today the planted corn and soybeans are the predominant summer view across the countryside, and even a few trees stand against the ever-widening horizon.

Things change slowly in this area. There is a sense of stability—a belief that the elements and the changes in technology, the threat of a world-wide economic catastrophe, or even the farm foreclosures that grow more numerous cannot sway the traditional way of life that makes this Quaker community so clearly different from an ever-changing American landscape. It is rural, Quaker, clean-spirited, and not very exciting by the standards of most. Families still sit down together for meals, and the "preacher" and his or her family are still invited over to a parishioner's home for Sunday dinner.

The inhabitants in and around the Motor community know who they are and what they are. Their lives have a clearly understood sense of meaning, which seems to elude so many in modern urban American, especially those who live on the "fast track" associated with each coast. A child growing up in this part of the heartland is provided a strong base in life and thought, which a more mobile and urban setting cannot provide. To this day Elton Trueblood is a farmer at heart—a lover of the dirt and life forces that make rural America the strong, disciplined, and fiercely independent society that mark its existence.

It was indeed a good life for a boy, one that was disciplined, orderly, and devout. Iowa, in the early years of the twentieth century, was still very much on the frontier, and one can sense in talking with Elton about his childhood that this frontier spirit is still an important part of who he is. It is the belief in possibilities and the feeling that if one just works hard enough any dream can come true. He is fond of saying, "Be careful what you dream, it may come true."

For Elton, the limitless frontier state of mind was especially to be found in his educational pursuits. He worked hard on the farm, but as his brother Clare has attested, at times Elton was "off reading a book" instead of doing some chore. Books opened young Elton to a world that he had not yet visited, but there was no doubt in his mind that someday he would. As he considered the instruction at Indianola High School and the "splendid training" he received, Elton has said, "I never doubted for a minute that I would go on to advanced work as far as I could go. Later when I took degrees at Harvard and Johns Hopkins it was not the least surprising to me because I'd always expected to reach as high as I could." The disciplined, visionary spirit that was so a part of his boyhood has been a sustaining presence throughout his life.

Many years later while living in California, Elton thought about his life in Iowa and wrote about his love of trains and what they meant to a young boy of the heartland:

> Ships thrill me, but never as trains do. No ship that ever sailed looks finer than does the Denver Zephyr. I grew up near a branch line of the C.B and Q. Dear reader, if you do not know what those magic letters stand for I am sorry for you. . . . Do you know what it is to be a boy who works the black soil of an Iowa farm with his head full of faraway things and then, periodically, to see crack trains of the nation speeding across his fair land—coming from afar and going further? Do you know what it is to be a little fellow who loves geography and hears a train caller announcing stations that reach across the continent with San Francisco as the end of the world where the West stops and the East begins?

In 1917, Elton graduated from Indianola High School. An anonymous friend captured Elton's studious intensity in verse:

The Debater, 1918

Here's to the boy whose hand goes up first!
He must state his opinion or sure he would burst.
He's good at debating and orating too,
Though little in stature, he's *True blood clear thru.*

Under his picture in the annual for that year one finds these words:

YMCA Cabinet; Older Boys Conference; Debate Team 3, 4; Forensic Club 4; Commencement Program. Always absolutely sure he is absolutely right. A brilliant student. Never uses a short word when he can use a long one. Staunch Quaker. Thinks 99.9% of the people in the world are narrow minded — he and W.J.B. excluded. Has good opinions on everything. "All great men are dead and I'm not feeling well."

These are the descriptions of a young, hard-working and driven student who had little patience for sloth. His formal academic pursuits would continue upon his entrance to William Penn College, the small Quaker school of Iowa. For the next year after graduation, however, Elton worked at home on the farm, and when his father could spare him, he worked for a farmer a few miles away. Since he was only sixteen (the youngest member of his class) when he graduated from high school, he needed the year to grow physically and also to earn money for college expenses. In September 1918, Elton Trueblood enrolled at William Penn College.

WILLIAM PENN COLLEGE

The little college, sixty years ago, did not have much money, and it had very little prestige; but it had a unique power, the power of expectancy.

"Scoop" Trueblood, 1919

Elton speaking before his fellow
students on the campus of William
Penn College

By no means the least of the assets of a college is her ideals. Penn College
prides herself upon her ideals. It is our purpose to develop the most symmetri-
cal men and women, mentally, morally, and physically. To reach this highest
development demands a clear mind, a noble soul, and a sound body. The
object of all regulations and restraints is to call forth the nobler traits of
character, and to develop on the part of students, industry, self-culture, true
courtesy, and generosity, the qualities which are most likely to insure the
greatest success in life.

These words are found on the Penn College calendar of 1920 and exem-
plify the purpose of the school during the time Elton was a student. Penn
College was fifty-five miles east of the Trueblood farm, located in
Oskaloosa, Iowa. It had been established by Iowa Yearly Meeting of Friends
in 1873 as a school for Quaker young people but also for all who valued the
ideals of Quaker education. When asked why he chose Penn as his college,
Elton says, "The fact that it was the college that belonged to the Quakers of
Iowa. That was the controlling reason. My sister was there ahead of me, and
it was just assumed that it would become my school as well."

It was a professor at Penn from whom Elton Trueblood was taught one
of his most important disciplines concerning writing and which he has
used throughout his writing career. The professor, Edgar Stranahan,
taught his students that *content precedes order*. Thus, at the beginning of any
writing project one should not be concerned with correct order, but

should, instead, write down as rapidly as possible all of the ideas he has on the subject, and the order will follow. The point is to get it down before you lose it.

Writing for publication was a constant interest of Elton, and the idea that he might even write a book was something he was considering and even worked on during his college years. On February 18, 1922, Elton recorded the following in his diary:

> I have been thinking about my future today, Feb. 18, and feel now that I want to make writing a profession. I should like to get on the editorial board of some magazine. This would give me a chance for the writing of books, etc. It would give a chance for lecturing and I could talk in the meetings for worship as the spirit might lead.

In her diary, Pauline Goodenow, later to become Pauline Trueblood, wrote about young Elton's book-writing ideas. "We talked about writing a book parallel to the *Life of Christ*. I wish he would do it." In a later entry in her diary, Pauline wrote: "We left the recital and spent our evening on Reynold's porch. Elton let me read parts of his book. I am so glad he did." Elton was twenty-one years old when he dreamed of this possibility. He would have to wait fifteen more years to see his first book in print.

His most influential professor while at Penn was William E. Berry, from whom he learned classical Greek. He was one of the few professors at Penn who had a Ph.D., and he was a very good classical scholar. Although he had studied Latin in high school, Elton found Greek more difficult. He would rise every morning at five during his tenure in this course and study until breakfast. He wrote, "Already I realized that I was a morning person, and though I had not yet heard the maxim, 'Never use prime time for the second-rate tasks,' I knew that I needed to use the time of my greatest intellectual energy for whatever was most difficult."[6]

Another important course in Elton's educational life was a course in English composition taught by Anna Eves. In her class he was taught the discipline of writing an essay of six hundred words each week, and handing it to her on Monday morning. This lasted for nine months, all of his freshman year. He learned a most important lesson in this weekly exercise — the truth that *people learn to write by writing* and by accepting the criticism of those who care enough to require you to write.

At the beginning of his second year in school there was a large influx of male students who had just returned from service in World War I. (Elton was never drafted since he was only seventeen when the war ended.) With all of the new male students on campus, a good football team looked like a reasonable possibility, and so Elton tried out for the squad. His nickname was "Scoop" Trueblood, and in the homecoming program of 1919, he was referred to as a "hard tackler" and one who "runs strong interference." The coach, "Biffy" Lee, was a former player at Notre Dame and had arranged for Notre Dame's second team to play at Penn on

November 27, 1919, Penn's homecoming. Sadly, Penn lost 27–0, but playing even the "second string" of a team with the national recognition of Notre Dame was a real privilege for little Penn. In reflecting on his college football career, Elton has written, "I find it difficult to explain the precise value of intercollegiate football, but I know that it helped me immensely. The toughness of the discipline, the necessity of going on in spite of fatigue, and the comradeship with teammates made a real difference in my life."[7]

Elton's serious relationship with Pauline Goodenow began during the school year of 1919. Pauline came from the small town of Union, Iowa, and was a Quaker girl. Her ancestors, like those of Elton, had moved to Iowa from Indiana, and her grandfather, like Elton's grandmother, was a Quaker minister. Although it is clear from reading her diary that Elton's studies always came first, he was nevertheless with her frequently for dates to plays, concerts, and picnics. In his college memory book there is a place to list the "Theaters, Lectures and Entertainments," and the name of the girl he took to each occasion. Before October 1919, Elton's dates were varied, with such names as Esther Whitely, Esther Jamison, Laura Templeton, and Edith Jones listed. After October, however, the name of Pauline Goodenow is mentioned consistently.

The meticulous notes in Pauline's college diary give the reader a glimpse into the fun side of Elton Trueblood. The entry for January 13, 1921 reads, "This afternoon Elton and I went skating again on the reservoir. . . . I am just discouraged at learning to skate. My left foot turns over all the time. . . . Elton is more patient than I thought he would be, but I suspect he gets provoked inside."

The next day Elton took Pauline to a football party. She recorded what happened when they left: "Nearly all the boys fell off the porch because it was icy. Elton made me eat two mouthfuls of snow. I'll have to get even some way." On Sunday evening of the next week Pauline wrote about Elton taking her to Christian Endeavor but leaving before the church service to go back to the dorm: "Elton got to talking about orthodoxy quite earnestly. I just love him when he gets all worked up over some such subject, and I like for him to believe the way he does. But I don't see what vital difference it makes so long as one is good, lives up to convictions, and trusts the Lord."

During his sophomore year at Penn, Elton was feeling the need to expand his horizons beyond his native state and had considered transferring to Earlham College in Richmond, Indiana. He had discussed this possibility with Pauline, and she wrote, "I think it will be the best thing ever for him to go there. I wish I were to be there too, though it will be better for him if I don't." In the end he stayed at Penn to finish his undergraduate work and didn't go to Earlham until twenty-five years later, not as a student, but as a professor of philosophy.

There were periods in Elton and Pauline's relationship when she felt he was not as attentive to her as he should have been. On a Sunday night

Elton and Pauline at William Penn
College, 1920

in 1921 she wrote, "I haven't seen Elton since Thursday night and don't feel like I want to. I called him at noon and told him not to come out tonight. I said it was because Gladys [a roommate] was sick, but that wasn't the real reason. The real reason is that he thinks he can go with whomever and whenever he pleases, and I'm showing him he can't be so sure about me. This is one of the days when I don't think he is very necessary to my happiness." The next Wednesday, however, she wrote, "Tonight I wanted to call Elton and ask him to go walking with me after supper. Of course I didn't do such an improper thing."

Elton was a studious academician during his college years, but his hard study did not get in the way of some pranks. One night, with the college president's permission (not knowing it was a prank), Elton and three other boys were allowed to look for, and hopefully capture, an imaginary man who had been seen by some imaginary girls lurking around the women's dormitory. Pauline recalled what happened:

> The girls all over the dorm were frightened. Our room was full of folks looking out of the window. I had learned about this prank by the boys, and so I told Gladys what I knew in order to enjoy the situation completely. Once when they were slipping under the window she poured a gallon of water out but didn't hit anyone. Then one of the boys ran out to the end of the garden with the other boys pursuing him like he was the man who had been seen around our dormitory. He turned and pretended to shoot at the boys, and the boys shot back. They all ran down the road not to be seen again. All of the girls were frightened and didn't sleep all night.

On another occasion, "the greatest escapade yet" according to Pauline's diary, Elton and four other boys were able to sneak some ice cream away from the "Commercial Students." In order to get it, they had to climb the fire escape. Pauline wrote, "Then Elton phoned out to get a bunch to come down to the cellar so they could all have a feed. I hated to say they could because if we got into trouble it would be all my fault. But it sounded like so much fun that I couldn't resist the temptation. So they came out with four bricks of ice cream. . . . It was a lot of fun." This incident became *the* prank during the four years Elton was at Penn and was frequently referred to in his college memory book by his friends.

On at least one occasion, Elton didn't leave the women's dormitory on time. Pauline recorded what happened next: "Elton came after supper and stayed until it was so long after 7:20 P.M. that he had to slip out the back door. He couldn't get out because the door was locked and he had to open a window and then we sat on a box in the entryway and enjoyed the situation." There they sat until they thought the coast was clear, and then "Elton made a dash for the cellar and kicked over a bucket. . . . Finally Elton discovered that the door that opens out from the third unit had a key in the lock so he went out that way."

Elton's college diary depicts a young man who was not only studious but also in touch with his feelings. In July 1921, he recorded these insightful words:

> All history is a great story of human struggle. Sometimes it is bright and sometimes very dark. The element of love is the connecting thread of light that burns through the ages. It flickers but it does not go out. It is burning dimly today. But, actually, it *is* the eternal. It, alone, can never die. When we once experience real love we know that it can never pass away. This whole story of the upward struggle seemed to pass in vivid form before my eyes one evening as I sat by a bonfire behind my brother's store in Ames [Oscar owned a shoe store]. It was the most beautiful experience of my life.
>
> A few weeks later I was thinking of human suffering. I thought of some of the calamities that befall people and I wondered how such people could ever be happy. Suddenly, it flashed upon me that, though they could never be happy while thinking of their own welfare, they could be by enjoying the happiness of others. It is a very simple idea and very old but it came to me with the vividness of something entirely new. But the fact that it is commonplace does not detract from its truth. As a rule there are no panaceas but this comes as near being a sure cure for unhappiness as could be imagined. "Enjoy the happiness of others."

The debating club was a very important part of Elton's college life. He was on the debate team all four years at Penn and participated in numerous public speaking contests. In 1922, he was awarded the first prize in the state extempore speaking contest. Pauline wrote about her impression of Elton as a debater, just following a meet: "His debate was perfectly great. I was just as proud of him as his mother would have ever dared to be. . . .

Elton debates just as easy as though he were President. I believe he will be President someday!"

During these years on the debate team at Penn, Elton learned the great value of speaking without notes. To this day he rejects the use of notes for public speaking. "They are a barrier between the speaker and the audience," he says. I have never been with Elton where he has used any form of notes for public speaking, and yet he encourages a great deal of note-taking before the actual speech. He always arduously prepares for a speech, making many notes of ideas, and then develops an orderly way of presentation. Sometimes he has even taken the outline with him in his coat pocket. To my knowledge, however, he has never taken the notes out of his pocket for help. "There are only two reasons why a person would use notes for a public speech," he says. "One is that the person is not well prepared, or, secondly, the person is a coward." The debating team at William Penn College helped him learn how to prepare thoroughly and then to be brave when facing an audience.

Also at work in Elton is the Quaker belief in the direct leading of the Holy Spirit. Full manuscripts or notes, he believes, can get in the way of such "leading," and can hamper a person from seeking guidance from the Living Christ. If a manuscript or outline is written to be delivered, so the logic goes, then the speaker will feel that it must be delivered, whether or not it is the message he or she is "led" to give. For Elton, more so than most public speakers, openness to the leading of the Living Christ and close interaction with those gathered to hear him is basic to a good presentation. It is this conviction that accounts for his practice of speaking with absolutely no "crutch," be it a manuscript, podium, or pulpit, all of which he feels separate speakers from God and audience.

As he reflected on his experience at William Penn College, Elton wrote:

It is my sober judgement that the little Quaker College in Southeast Iowa provided me an excellent preparation for my public career. We were sufficiently small for each one to be needed and to be recognized as a person, but we had sufficient strength to provide what Whitehead later called the "vision of greatness." The important thing about Penn College sixty years ago was its vision of wholeness. I do not remember any suggestion of the necessity of having to choose between intellectual integrity and spiritual vitality. We did not have an athletic sector, segregated from the remainder of the academic community. . . . The little college, sixty years ago, did not have much money, and it had very little prestige; but it had a unique power, the power of expectancy.[8]

This "power of expectancy" was ignited in Elton Trueblood by excellence on the football field, on the intercollegiate debate team, or in the academic classroom. He was taught, in the words of the 1920 Penn calendar, to develop "a clear mind, a noble soul, and a sound body," all of which prepared him for his future life as a whole and his ventures in higher education in particular.

Elton had met his future wife, and since it was necessary for her to stay in her native state to teach school in order to pay off school debts, he could not take her with him as he left for his next chapter at Brown University in Providence, Rhode Island. He did not, however, forget her. Graduation came on June 7, 1922, and afterward he immediately left for New England. Throughout his final year at Penn, Elton had struggled about his life's vocation. "The idea of settling down into the limitations of any certain occupation doesn't appeal to me," he wrote in his diary. "I should like to be a professor, an editor, a preacher, and a dozen others all in one. However, my desire in each case is identical. What I really want to be is a *prophet*."

1922–1933

EASTWARD BOUND

I feel lonely and homesick tonight as I sit in the station waiting for the train to Providence. But, when I think of the millions less fortunate than I am, I know I must brace up and be a man.

Before his graduation from William Penn College at the age of twenty-one, Elton Trueblood had never been out of the state of Iowa. In his senior year at Penn the invitation had come for him to be the pastor of the Woonsocket Friends Meeting in Woonsocket, Rhode Island. This was a perfect arrangement since it provided him the opportunity to study at Brown University, a short distance away in Providence. The pastorate paid a hundred dollars per month. The headline of the article in the Indianola, Iowa, paper announced the appointment: "21-year-old Indianola Boy Called to Pastorate In Rhode Island." In the company of Forest Comfort, a classmate from Penn, Elton left Des Moines by train for the East.

The first stop on the journey was Chicago. One can imagine what a sight this major city must have been to an Iowa boy who had never seen a city other than Des Moines. The large museums were a special treat for Elton, who had vowed to make the trip east as educational as possible.

After Chicago came Detroit, and from there the two boys traveled by boat across Lake Erie to Buffalo, then on to Niagara Falls. Following a day at Niagara, they took the train to Albany and then another boat ride down the Hudson River. Forest Comfort stayed in New York while Elton proceeded on the final segment of his journey by train to Providence and then to Woonsocket.

In his diary, Elton noted his feelings concerning his first visit to New York City and his feelings of loneliness as he left his friend and awaited his train to Providence:

> Tuesday evening, June 27, 1922 — I have just made my first visit to New York. A man tried to get me to ride in a horse carriage from the wharf to the Grand Central Station. If I had done so, I fully believe I might have been robbed or beaten. My heart goes out to innocent people who are thrown in bewildering

surroundings. Within a few hours I have seen the palatial residences on the Hudson and the squalid tenements of the city. The only hope of recovery lies in the Christian religion. To make the kingdom of God a reality should be the compelling motive of every life. If the kingdom were here there would be no slums and innocent people would not be left to the mercies of thieves.

I feel lonely and homesick tonight as I sit in the station waiting for the train to Providence. But, when I think of the millions less fortunate than I am, I know I must brace up and be a man. Instead of giving up to the loneliness I must be strong enough to help someone less fortunate if need be.

Elton's world was rapidly expanding. He had left the small Quaker agricultural community in Iowa for an industrial center in the East. Although self-assured and most capable, he did experience homesickness and loneliness. At Woonsocket, he immediately launched into his work as a pastor and in the summer of 1922 was able to build a Young Friends program that began with twenty-five members and grew to seventy-five.

Even though his college sweetheart remained in Iowa to teach while Elton went east, plans for their eventual marriage were made before he graduated from college. On the night following his senior class play, Elton and Pauline had sat on the banks of the Des Moines River and planned their marriage for two years in the future. This would give Pauline time to work as a teacher and pay back her college expenses, and it would give Elton a chance to get started in graduate school. It was a difficult time of separation. As with all of Elton's life, however, it was a well-planned period of time in which both Pauline and Elton had personal goals to complete.

Woonsocket Friends Meeting provided Elton with a group of people with whom to share his ideas and the disciplined structure for him to prepare a "message" each week. His first sermon at Woonsocket was entitled "The New Apologetics" and was delivered on July 2, 1922. Portions of this important sermon have been preserved. The young pastor began:

> It is now common knowledge in religious circles, that many of the most eloquent defenses of religion are being made by those whose chief interest and occupation is outside the field of theology proper. One of the finest examples of this general tendency is to be seen in the work of professor W. P. Montague of Columbia University. Suggestions of his point of view are to be found in various places, but it appears most explicitly in the article he contributed to Volume II of *Modern American Philosophers* and in his recent book, *Belief Unbound.* . . . One feels that he is reading not arguments brought forward to support a point of view already held, but an actual search for truth which follows the argument wherever it leads.

We can capture from just a few words the cerebral, academic side of Elton. I am sure he had a Scripture text for this message, but he certainly did not consider it central to what he was saying. The "philosopher" was developing in the young man, and he was beginning to see that the field of "theology proper" was not the only field in which one could study or defend a religious view of the world.

In the fall of 1922, Woonsocket Meeting began the process of recording Elton as Friends Minister. They submitted his name to New England Yearly Meeting as one who "had the gift for ministry." Elton describes a meeting he had with a leading Friend who was appointed to interview him to make sure he was theologically sound. In his diary for November 11, 1922, Elton wrote:

> John of Worcester was appointed to interview me to ascertain my fitness to be recorded a minister. He began at once to apply the regular tests. Did I believe in the Virgin Birth? etc. Of course I said such matters were not essential. He reported adversely to my being recorded. The other members of the meeting refused to accept his report. I really felt sorry for him. He was doing what he thought was right. But how big a fool does a man have a right to be?

In the recording process, a Friend asked Elton his belief on a certain theological point. Elton responded in written form:

> I consider that our Friend's question is a perfectly legitimate one. It is right that you should know what I believe and I welcome this opportunity of informing you. I realize, however, that the present is not the time or the place for a debate on abstract theological issues. And, moreover, even if this were the time and place for a theological debate, I have little faith in that method. Consequently I have attempted to reduce my religious faith to the simplest form of statement and to couch it in words that cannot be misunderstood. My statement is this: "I am endeavoring to the best of my knowledge and ability to live and teach the religion of Jesus." For the present, at least, this statement is final. I shall say no more. It needs no elucidation. If you see fit to record me as a minister on that basis I shall be very glad. I could be recorded no other.

He was recorded as a Minister among Friends on May 12, 1923.

Elton continued to write articles and submit them for publication. The *Penn Chronicle* was an important outlet for this creativity, and his alma mater was glad to print whatever he sent. "The Faith of Jesus in Men" was one such article, showing Elton's development toward being a "philosophical anthropologist."

> It was in direct opposition to the general current of thought; but His faith in the underlying goodness of humanity became so great that he was actually forced to breast the tide of popular feeling and "to preach deliverance to the captives."
>
> It is easy to see how all his subsequent teaching flowed naturally from this basic conception. . . . His recognition of the worth of little children seemed strange to His associates, but it was an integral part of His whole conception of life. Time after time He was advised to pass by persons considered hopelessly debased, but none was too low to receive His considerate attention and help.
>
> A true acceptance of this fundamental concept of Jesus changes the whole

basis of life. It cuts straight across the implications of the trite statement that it takes all sorts of people to make a world." It takes only one sort of people to make the sort of world toward which Jesus was looking—a world in which everyone is brought to the highest of which he is capable. The great principle underneath the teachings of Jesus is actually revolutionary. In the end, it would do away with poverty, with subjugation of backward peoples, and with all tyranny of every kind.

Two of the books he read before his entrance into Brown University in the fall were *Sartor Resartus* by Thomas Carlyle and *The Philosophy of Loyalty* by Josiah Royce. In recent years, Elton has enjoyed the opportunity to return to these volumes that have had a prominent place on the shelves of his study, Teague Library, at Earlham, and go through them again. A great enthusiast of marking in his books, he has been able to study the notations he made at age twenty-one and recall the progression his thought has taken over the years to the present.

Many of the connections at the Woonsocket Meeting have lasted throughout Elton Trueblood's life, and he truly enjoyed his ministry there. He wrote to Mrs. Carl McGrew, a close friend in Motor, Iowa, about his experience,

> I am leading an enjoyable life as a Quaker minister in New England. I have visited most of the large cities such as Boston, New Bedford, Fall River, Worcester, Springfield, etc., and I am in Providence every week. Woonsocket is a city of more than 40,000 people, but it is very different from Iowa cities. It is full of mills, factories and tenement houses, and it has sections where English is rarely spoken. More than half of the people are French Canadians. I cannot understand their language at all. My work, however, is entirely with the American people and we have an enterprising church.

BROWN UNIVERSITY AND HARTFORD SEMINARY

When I came to New England I was inclined toward a Unitarian view, but now I have found my Lord and Master.

Brown University was Elton's choice for graduate study because of its close proximity to his pastorate in Woonsocket. He could attend classes at Brown three days a week and still accomplish his pastoral duties. During this year at Brown (his *only* year there), President Faunce asked Elton to join the Brown faculty and teach at the University of Shanghai as the representative of "Brown-in-China." It was a "heady" offer for a twenty-two-year-old student and one the young man had to consider seriously. He wrote to Pauline Goodenow in Iowa and asked her, "If I accept, will you become my wife and travel with me to China?" In her response she said that she had stayed up one whole night trying to reach a decision, and when she did, it was yes. Upon the receipt of her letter, Elton had concluded that he needed more time as a student, thus declining President

Faunce's generous offer. It also allowed Pauline and Elton to stay on course with their prior decision to wait two whole years before marriage.

His final seminar at Brown was on the synoptic Gospels. Each course taken had enlarged Elton's thought and deepened his faith. He owed a special debt of gratitude, however, to a Dr. Fowler, who helped Elton move toward a more Christocentric faith. Elton wrote in his diary, dated May 8, 1923:

> I owe Dr. Fowler of Brown University an unpayable debt. When I came to New England I was inclined toward a Unitarian view, but now I have found my Lord and Master. The personality and the spiritual insights of Jesus have so gripped me that I can no longer maintain a coldly intellectual attitude toward him. I care no more for theology than I ever did, but my thinking is certainly Christocentric. I do not know what I was shying at before; I objected to thinking of him as an incarnation of God. Now it seems so simple. I think, however, that the whole trouble was my conception of God. I still thought of God as a glorified eastern potentate and of course Jesus wasn't an incarnation of that. But, if God is the eternal Spirit of Love, Jesus was that in Flesh and Blood.

Throughout the summer of 1923, Elton's enthusiasm for the Christian faith swelled within him. In diary passages dated July 10 and 14, he recorded,

> The past few months have, I feel sure, been very important ones in my spiritual life. For once, I have had something under my skin, bursting to get out. I have seen the glory of the Christian message and I am most anxious to tell it to others. It is no longer a matter of intellectual assent with me. From the very nature of the case Christianity cannot be satisfied with intellectual assent, it is fundamentally a matter of sacrifice and daring. To be a Christian is to *believe* that Jesus revealed God and believe it so strongly that it makes a difference in all of the relationships of life. It is to bet one's life that God is Love. It is to believe that Jesus is to be taken seriously. It is to accept a faith that dares to be tried. It follows, therefore, that a religion which serves as a pastime or opiate, demanding no sacrifice or change in manner of living, is not Christianity. Christianity is a glorious adventure, but there are many who call themselves Christians who do not know the meaning of the word. They sit in ease and luxury and when they are asked to make some sacrifice to match that of missionaries, for instance, they say they aren't interested. . . .
>
> I have been trying to put into words just what it is in the gospel that grips me so strongly. Yesterday I wrote the following which satisfies me for the present, "The gospel is simply the news that, in the midst of this world of pain and contingency, there lived one who was entirely victorious and who, thereby, proved for all time that, in spite of the 'ocean of darkness and death,' there is an 'infinite ocean of light and love,' which has, and therefore can yet 'flow over the ocean of darkness.' He proved that, not only God, but also man, is essentially Love."

The most important practical lesson while at Brown came during Elton's interview with President Faunce about the China position, which was quite unrelated to the topic at hand. In the midst of their conversation, the president suddenly stopped talking, took a notebook from his pocket, and started writing. "Not able to know the reason for the interruption," writes Elton, "I simply waited silently until he finished writing and had returned the notebook to his pocket. Then he said, 'I hope you can forgive me for this seeming discourtesy of stopping our conversation. The reason for this interruption is that, suddenly, I had an idea, and I learned long ago that I have to put down ideas when they come, if I do not wish to lose them.'"[1]

From this brief experience in the president's office, Elton was taught a practice he has never forgotten, and that has, indeed, become an integral part of his life. Often I have heard him say, "The six most important words in my life are *Put it down* and *do it now!*" Every morning of his life since this experience at Brown he has made sure that he has small pieces of paper and pen in his pocket before he leaves the house. "Ideas are my capital," he says, "and if I don't write them down when they come to me I am likely to lose them." This practice has led to keeping a writing pad and pen next to his bed at night, so when an idea comes before or during his sleep, he can immediately get up and write it down. He has learned that if he waits until morning he is likely to forget it.

The unexpected way in which this invaluable practical tool became so much a part of Elton's daily discipline is reminiscent of the time when I was visiting David Tyler Scoates, pastor of the Hennepin Avenue Methodist Church in Minneapolis, Minnesota. As I entered his study he welcomed me with the startling statement that his life had been changed at a seminar Elton Trueblood once led at the Yokefellow Institute.

Knowing that I would be writing his biography, I was anxious to learn what it was in this Trueblood seminar that had changed his life. He explained that he was standing with Elton outside the seminar room during one of the coffee breaks. He said he asked Elton, "How do you find time in your busy life to write all of your books, as well as maintain a family life and your teaching load, as well as the demands of your speaking schedule around the country?" In response, Elton took his datebook out of his pocket and showed David Scoates the secret. For one year in advance, Elton had crossed out certain days, hours within the day, and even some weeks, which, he explained, are set aside for writing. "If I didn't do that," Elton said, "then those hours would be filled with other things. Nature abhors a vacuum, and so my secret is to fill my calendar *first*."

David Scoates went home from this seminar and soon forgot everything else said except this idea of the crossed-out datebook. Accepting this practice as his own, he soon deepened his life by becoming the controller of his hours, rather than letting events control him. What both the Trueblood and the Scoates episodes teach us is the truth that life-changing experiences can often come in unexpected ways. As Elton has reminded us, "All of the best things in life are unexpected, and all of the worst things in life are unexpected."

Brown University has been a special place in the life of Elton Trueblood since it gave him his first real opportunity to study in a large and
prestigious eastern university. It was certainly different from the somewhat protective atmosphere of the small Quaker school in Iowa. Both
styles of education were important to the young man. The small classes at
Penn, and certainly the one-room school at Waveland, were different
experiences from what he had at Brown, but Elton was prepared for the
challenge. Years later he would return to Brown University, this second
time not as a student but as chief religious information officer of the
United States Information Agency. There he delivered the Colver Lectures, which became his book *Declaration of Freedom.*

After only one year as a student at Brown, Elton left. His departure
was for one reason: to study with Alexander Purdy at Hartford Seminary.
Purdy was a brilliant New Testament scholar and a Quaker. The change of
school did not mean a change from his pastorate at Woonsocket. Every
Friday evening he would travel by train from Hartford back to Woonsocket, and then on Sunday afternoon he would return to Hartford. Each
Sunday Alexander Purdy would speak at Moses Brown School in Providence, and so he would stop and pick up Elton at Woonsocket and take
him by car to Hartford. This gave the student valuable additional time
with his professor.

Hartford Seminary was a popular school for young Quakers studying
for the pastoral ministry. Since there was no Quaker seminary at the time,
Quaker ministerial students would tend to go to a school with Quaker
influence on the faculty. With the esteemed Alexander Purdy on the
faculty, Hartford became an important place for Quakers to study. Years
later, in retirement, Alexander Purdy came to help the new Quaker seminary get started at Earlham, teaching New Testament and Quaker
Thought. This was a happy arrangement for Elton, since it gave him the
joyful opportunity of being with one of his favorite professors as a colleague on the Earlham faculty.

In the spring of 1924, Elton left Hartford before the end of the term
and traveled to England for the London Yearly Meeting of Friends. He
served as a representative of American Young Friends in the activities in
England surrounding the three-hundredth anniversary of the birth of
George Fox, the founder of the people called Quakers. It was to be his first
of many trips abroad.

FIRST TRIP ABROAD AND MARRIAGE TO PAULINE

*In the presence of the Lord and before these Friends, I take thee Pauline Claire
Goodenow . . .*

The headline above the article in the Indianola, Iowa, paper read,
"Will Spend Summer In Europe: Indianola Boy Goes On Important Mis-

sion." I suppose the importance of Elton Trueblood's "mission to Europe" depends upon one's perspective. It was, indeed, an exciting opportunity for the young man, who sailed on May 10, 1924, from New York City on the ship *Adriatic* and arrived in Liverpool, England, on May 16. He went directly to the London Yearly Meeting, which, in this particular year, was being held at Llandrindod Wells, Wales. Following the sessions of Yearly Meeting, he traveled to Birmingham to become a student at Woodbrooke, the Quaker school among the cluster of Selly Oak colleges in that predominantly industrial city.

During this summer term of 1924, Elton became acquainted with Dr. Rendel Harris, a most important figure in the development of his religious and academic life. Anyone who has had any contact with Elton knows how much his teachers have meant to him. As an academician himself, his teachers have been his models. "All of my life I have been a learner," he said at the beginning of his address before the 1988 Yokefellow conference. "Every one of my teachers is now dead. I cannot thank them face to face, but I can express to you my gratitude."

Rendel Harris is one of those for whom Elton is grateful. A Quaker, he was a member of the first great faculty at Johns Hopkins University. He was a scholar of the finest order, who could speak sixteen languages fluently. What so attracted Elton to Rendel Harris was not just the fact that he had a good mind, but that he combined his intellectual integrity with a sincere piety. "What amazed me," says Elton, "was that when a group of students was in his house, it would always end in prayer. He would turn and kneel by the chair in which he was sitting, and pray like a child. . . . He was not ashamed to be pious, and I determined that I would not be ashamed." In the life of Rendel Harris, Elton witnessed a holistic life that did not choose between thinking and praying. He learned, experientially, about the "Holy Conjunction."

The first time at Woodbrooke College not only brought Elton in touch with great teachers but also provided the opportunity to study with students from many different backgrounds. In an article telling about his experience, Elton wrote,

> While diplomats are arguing about the possibility of the League of Nations, we who live at Woodbrooke have become quite accustomed to seeing a true league of nations in actual practice. Here in our settlement and in the greatest harmony live Norwegians, Danes, Germans, Hollanders, Swiss, Americans and representatives of several other countries. . . . The realization of the artificiality of accepted divisions of the human race grows on one with tremendous force until he is almost ready to say that they are entirely meaningless.

Elton's first trip abroad lasted for three months, after which he returned to the States in mid-August. He had left his fiancée behind during this time of study and had only been with her occasionally since his days in William Penn College. But they had planned and worked

together, at great distance, for the day when they would be married. A letter from Pauline Goodenow to Elton just prior to his departure for
England told of her anticipation:

> There is so much to say in this last letter you shall receive in America from
> me, and yet much of it will be left unsaid for lack of words to express deep feel-
> ings.... If there are any times when you are lonely [on board ship] just walk
> the deck, look at the stars and know that I shall be thinking of you.... Three
> more months before we can say those happy words written in quotation marks
> in our marriage certificate.... Let us remember through these remaining
> weeks of separation the verse from Proverbs, "a merry heart maketh a cheerful
> countenance: but by sorrow of the heart the spirit is broken." We have joy out
> of all proportion to our deserts now but still do I ask more; that you may have
> every opportunity for enjoyment and service open to you and that you may
> come back dedicated anew to the crying need of the hearts of humanity and
> that you may find a surer way of reaching them than ever before.

Elton Trueblood and Pauline Goodenow were married under the care of
the Woonsocket Friends Meeting on August 24, 1924. The wedding took place
at the home of Joseph Estes, after the manner of Friends. The local paper, the
Warner Gazette, recorded the event:

> A striking contrast to the fashionable weddings of today was that of Miss
> Pauline Goodenow of Grinnel, Iowa, and David Elton Trueblood of Woon-
> socket.... It was an old-time Quaker wedding, marked with utmost simplicity
> as are weddings of Members of the Friends Society.
>
> A Meeting of Friends was called for Sunday afternoon at the Estes' home.

Young Elton Trueblood

The newlyweds on the campus of
Wellesley College

Ten besides the bridal couple assembled and the regular service opened at 4:00. During the service Miss Goodenow and Mr. Trueblood arose and plighted their troth. Another period of silence ensued after which Joseph Estes arose and read the marriage certificate, which was signed by witnesses. The service continued and closed in the usual way. . . .

Following the service the bride and groom were served a luncheon on the lawn in their honor. According to the paper, it was believed that the Trueblood-Goodenow wedding was the first Quaker wedding to have taken place in Warner.

The traditional Quaker vows Elton and Pauline repeated to one another are as follows: "In the presence of the Lord and before these Friends, I take thee [David Elton Trueblood/Pauline Claire Goodenow] to be my [husband/wife] promising with divine assistance, to be unto thee a faithful and loving [wife/husband] so long as we both shall live."

Upon his return from England, Elton had accepted the call to become the executive secretary of the Friends Meeting in Roxbury, Boston, Massachusetts. This position offered the young couple a parsonage and a small salary and the opportunity for Elton to continue his studies at Harvard Divinity School in Cambridge. Immediately following the wedding, Elton and Pauline left for Boston. When they arrived at their new home they discovered it was not quite ready for occupancy, and so they continued their honeymoon by taking an overnight steamer from Boston to Portland, Maine. Upon their return to Boston the parsonage was ready for them, and it was their home from 1924 to 1926.

HARVARD UNIVERSITY

I began to understand what it meant to experience "emotion recollected in tranquility."

Elton Trueblood's transfer from Hartford Seminary to Harvard Divinity School occurred for the same reason that he had transferred from Brown to Hartford—the opportunity to study with a particular person. In this case it was the dean of the Harvard chapel and seminary and Harvard Divinity School, Willard L. Sperry. "From the beginning the dean took a close personal interest in me," Elton has written, "and finally became my tutor, criticizing my papers in a regular and meticulous fashion."[2]

Willard Sperry was a Rhodes scholar at Oxford University who had grown to love and appreciate the one-on-one tutorial system of learning. Each week Elton wrote a paper for him, and after Sperry had read it, he sat with the young man and went over it, showing him where he was clear and where he needed help in clarification. During one whole semester they read together the long poems of Wordsworth, going over every line of *The Prelude* and *The Excursion*, with Elton making notes and then engaging in dialogue about what had been read. "This effort differed from anything

I had experienced in my academic life up to that time. I began to understand what it meant to experience 'emotion recollected in tranquility.'"[3]

It was Sperry who helped Elton appreciate more fully the idea that
because of the written word one can "choose" one's own companions. "He
made me realize that through the magic of the written word I could be
just as close to Plato as the students at the Academy in Athens, and maybe
closer because I have *all* the *Dialogues*," reflects Elton. This idea has been
one of the most important for him and has led him to the realization that
as twentieth-century Christians we know more about Jesus Christ than did
some of the disciples, because we have the Gospels, and many of them did
not. Elton is fond of quoting Abraham Lincoln when he was asked what
he considered to be the greatest invention of humankind. The president's
response: "The written word."

During his last semester of work with Willard Sperry, the dean said to
Elton, "I think you can be a writer, but if you are going to be a writer you
need to soak yourself in the great models. They are as available to you as
to anyone in the world."

With the encouragement of Sperry, Elton began to "soak himself" in
the writings of William Hazlitt and Olive Schreiner. He was attracted
most of all, however, to the works of Dr. Samuel Johnson. "Johnson has
affected my style more than any other one person," Elton has noted. To
this day he keeps all of the collected writings of Samuel Johnson in a
bookcase next to his chair in his bedroom. A week does not go by that he
does not read a portion from the pen of the great Englishman himself or
what his biographer James Boswell has written about him. As an example
of the great style of Johnson, Elton is fond of reciting from memory Johnson's words at Iona, recorded in Boswell's *Tour of the Hebrides* of 1773: "Far
from me and from my friends, be such frigid philosophy as may conduct
us undifferent and unmoved over any ground which has been dignified by
wisdom, bravery or virtue. That man is little to be envied, whose patriotism would not gain force upon the plain of Marathon, or whose piety
would not grow warmer among the ruins of Iona!"

In lifting the vision of his own students, Professor Trueblood often
repeats these words and encourages them by saying, "You don't have to
engage in slovenly talk. You can express yourself this way. What you need
are models." For Elton, the model of Johnson was, like Rendel Harris, a
model of wholeness. Samuel Johnson did not separate his intellect from
his devout faith. To help the world know the devout and religious side of
Johnson, Elton edited his written prayers for publication twenty years
after being introduced to him by Sperry.

With his enrollment in the divinity school at Harvard, Elton was able
to take courses in any of the university departments at the graduate level.
And so with his work with Willard Sperry on a one-to-one basis and
Sperry's chief course, "The Art of Preaching" (helping Elton to tie for first
prize in the Harvard preaching contest his senior year), Elton partici-

The three Trueblood brothers with their father, 1923

pated in courses in English literature and philosophy. He enrolled in courses entitled Seventeenth-Century Religious Literature, Thomas Carlyle, Poetics, the History of Gothic Architecture, and the Philosophy of Hegel, all of which served as important supplements to his theological studies.

Dr. Bliss Perry taught the course on Thomas Carlyle and was another professor at Harvard who had a profound impact on Elton's style. There were two hundred men in Perry's class every Tuesday and Thursday, and after each lecture they all applauded. "This was not perfunctory," reflects Elton, "but occurred because Perry's rule was never to teach a class that was not his very best."

The secret of professor Perry's excellence was in his discipline of preparation. One evening, Elton attended a student gathering in the Perry home. At 9:00 P.M. the professor excused himself because, he said, "I must go and get ready for tomorrow's lecture." His daughter, who was in

In Boston with young Martin,
1926

the room with the graduate students said, "Oh, Dad, you don't need to do that. You have taught that course a long time." Perry responded, "No, if I don't study tonight, it will not be good enough tomorrow."

This example of Bliss Perry's disciplined style gave Elton a model for his own teaching. "If I was to be a good teacher," he said, "I was determined to make that model my own." All who have ever sat under the tutelage of Elton Trueblood can attest to his fresh and exciting teaching style, the reason for such success being that he determined early in his life to do his best on every occasion.

Pauline Trueblood became very ill in December 1924. She was pregnant with their first child, and the doctors were concerned that either the mother or child would be lost. "The terrible winter. . . . wore on," Elton has written, "as everyday I went both to my classes at Harvard and to the New England Hospital for Women and Children."[4] Pauline eventually gained enough strength so that her mother could take her back to be nursed in Iowa until after the baby was born. Elton remained in Boston, traveling to Iowa in July to be there for the birth of their first son, Martin, on July 26, 1925. He was named after Dr. Martin Luther Hooper who had been the Trueblood family physician in Iowa and had delivered Martin. As soon as Pauline was strong enough, the three Truebloods traveled back to Boston.

During their third year in Boston, the Truebloods helped the Roxbury Friends Meeting combine with the Cambridge Friends Meeting. This allowed the Roxbury Meeting to sell their property, and led the Truebloods to seek housing in Cambridge. They found an apartment at 945 Massachusetts Avenue, with the combined Meetings for Worship being held in Andover Hall on the Harvard campus. With the move to an apartment, a new practice was begun in the Trueblood home. Elton recorded the pattern in his diary: "We have started the practice of having morning worship after breakfast, and going to another room for it. So far it looks as though it would be great. Our schedule is breakfast at 7:30 and worship at 7:50, thus beginning our day's work at 8:00."

In February 1927 their apartment was robbed, and it so happened that the thief was the same man who, the next night, was to steal from the family of Herbert Hoover, Jr., son of the future president and a student in the Harvard Business School. This contact with the Hoovers through the mutual sorrow of being robbed was the beginning of a long and meaningful friendship between the Hoovers and the Truebloods. Thus Elton knew the son as a neighbor in Cambridge before he had any contact with the president who was later to become his neighbor on the opposite coast at Stanford University.

While sitting in the courtroom awaiting the arraignment of the young man who had robbed them, Elton was troubled by what he saw. As he thought about it that evening, he wrote, "It was very disheartening to sit in court and see the sad wrecks of humanity. I even feel sorry for the poor boy who robbed us. He is the loser in every way. I want to learn his history and have a good talk with him."

This passage from his diary indicates the beginning of a profound concern for those who have broken the law of the land and who are, or who soon will become, prisoners. Years later, in 1955, Elton was to found the Yokefellow Prison Ministry, which is presently active in prisons and jails around this country. His empathy for those behind bars was shared when he once addressed a group of prisoners and prison ministry professionals at Lewisburg Federal Penitentiary. His opening line was, "My fellow prisoners, caught and uncaught!" He went on to say that he was among the uncaught.

On another occasion this deep concern for the incarcerated found expression when Elton was asked to address a prayer breakfast sponsored by the mayor of Indianapolis and the governor of Indiana. I happened to be in the office at the time when the call inviting him came from Indianapolis. He took his calendar from his pocket and looked at it; he politely told the person on the other end of the line that he had a prior engagement and could not accept. When he had hung up the telephone and sat back down on the couch, I said to him, "Elton, this was an opportunity for you to address a major gathering of important people in Indianapolis, including the mayor of that city and the governor of the state. What can be more important in your date book than that opportunity?"

Slowly he said, "James, I have spoken before mayors, governors, and even presidents for much of my career as a public person. On the date they wanted me in Indianapolis, I am scheduled to visit a man in the local jail who has asked to see me. At my age I need to use my energy where I feel it will do the most good. I believe that I can be of more help to that young man in jail than I can be to the assortment of business people and politicians at that breakfast." Never again did I question Elton's wisdom concerning his schedule and the use of his energy.

Elton Trueblood continued to dream about writing a book for publication. In his diary dated February 14, 1927, he wrote,

> It seems to me that there is a place for someone who can approach Quaker literature from the viewpoint of a literary critic. Is there a peculiar Quaker style? Which literary form has best expressed the Quaker idea? This would make a good book with chapters on Fox's *Journal*, Penington's *Letters*, Barclay's *Apology*, Woolman's *Journal*, Penn's epigrams, etc. This would be a novel approach. Not much history should be given. Whittier might be included.

His diary during these student days at Harvard is devoted largely to ideas concerning book possibilities or thoughts on various topics, rather than personal events. Headings for different sections include: Security, Ministry, Disappointment, Belief, Inner Light, Revelation, Progress, and Creation. There are some exceptions to this rule, however, such as a personal meeting he had with Bishop Slattery of the Episcopal church on

March 3, 1927. The bishop was hopeful that Elton could be persuaded to become an Episcopalian. Elton wrote,

> Today I have been to see Bishop Slattery and have had a good talk with him. He assures me that the Episcopal Church is comprehensive and that it needs the Quaker spirit. In it I believe I can realize "both/and." . . . I can have "Quakerism plus." I shall go to see him again. . . . There is no reason why my idea of a minister as a servant cannot be worked out in a regular ministry which has the authority of tradition behind it.

On March 14, eleven days later, Elton's mind has changed, due in great part to the persuasion of Pauline. "If I should [join the Episcopal church] it would seem to the world that I had broken with Quakerism, no matter what I might say." For a time Elton considered the possibility of becoming a pastor for a church in the country, convinced that the more tranquil, unhurried rural life would provide him the atmosphere necessary to think and write. His model for this idea was Richard Hooker, who gave up a city pastorate for a country parish in England, which gave him uninterrupted time for writing.

In the spring of 1927, many options were presented to Elton as he pondered his future course. He had graduated from Harvard Divinity School with a Bachelor of Systematic Theology degree in 1926, and had stayed in Boston the following year to continue his noncredit studies in Plato and other subjects of interest. Now, however, he was feeling the need to begin a new chapter. One of his possibilities was an offer from President Raymond Binford of Guilford College, Greensboro, North Carolina, to become professor of philosophy and dean of men. He accepted the position after studying his options and recorded his decision in his diary: "I have agreed to leave Boston and go to Guilford College. . . . The prospect allures me. . . . I shall try to meet people on the basis of essentials." As he considered his first college teaching assignment, he reflected on his model: "In my teaching my model is that of Bliss Perry. I find that I can repeat almost word for word his lecture on Emerson. This is a great tribute to his teaching ability. The great thing is to be interesting and lure the student to study. . . . I must be true to my own style and not go off into oratory."

President Binford was clear and to the point with his new dean of men when he expressed to him via letter that there were some at Guilford who considered Elton "too aggressive and opinionated." Obviously concerned, Elton responded to this criticism in his diary, "I certainly do not intend to merit this reputation and must try still harder to avoid it. I have enjoyed the opportunity of expressing my attitude toward Jesus which has been called out by Binford's letter."

In the fall of 1927, Elton, Pauline, and Martin moved to the Guilford College campus to begin a new life. He was twenty-six-and-a-half years old. Elton had made the decision to focus on teaching at a college, rather than becoming a pastor in a parish. His apprenticeship was over.

PROFESSOR AT GUILFORD

[He] was a great favorite with the students — an advisor, father confessor, and the most important person on campus.

Guilford College was founded by the Society of Friends in 1837. When the Truebloods arrived on campus in September 1927, it was still six miles out in the country from Greensboro, on Friendly Road. Today it has been surrounded by a growing and thriving city that is a part of what has been called the tri-city area, encompassing High Point, Winston-Salem, and Greensboro. "The college was a well-respected institution with about four hundred students equally divided between men and women," Elton wrote later. "We were assigned the use of a small house on the wooded campus close enough to the dormitories to bring us into contact with the students at all times."[5]

One of the new classes that Elton taught at Guilford was a course on the Christian classics, modeled after a course Willard Sperry had taught at Harvard. "It was a delight to see how eagerly the young men and women from the farms and towns of North Carolina accepted the challenge of the ideas of such people as St. Augustine, Thomas à Kempis, and Blaise Pascal. The way in which the written word transcends both time and space filled my mind with a sense of wonder."[6]

This great interest in the classics has been an important part of Elton's life and teaching ministry. It has set him at odds with contemporary society's mood and its emphasis upon the new. I have often heard him say, "One of the greatest dangers of contemporary thought is its chronological snobbery. Truth is truth regardless of when it was produced. It is unfortunate today that many people will choose a book *not* because of the truth between the pages but by the date it was written."

His diary during this time is filled with ideas. The summer of 1928 was a prolific time when he wrote numerous articles for publication. "In Praise of Fear" went to the *London Friend*, and "Modern Heresy" was sent to the *Friends Intelligencer*. "A Quaker Look at Protestantism" was mailed to *Harper's*, and "The Literary Prelude" was sent to the *Atlantic Monthly*.

He was also thinking about his belief system and wrote on August 14, 1928,

> I have only one article in my creed; it is this: I believe there is something in the outside world which corresponds to the creative, loving, striving spirit which I feel in myself and recognize in others. I know that is a belief and cannot be proved. It is a valuable assumption and explains much, though it would not be fair to say it explains all. It doesn't really cope with the problem of evil, of course. It is simply the best fraction of apparent truth available to me now.

A year later an entry in his diary indicates his growing Christocentricity. "I am more and more a Christian. . . . I believe Chesterton makes the best apologetic for Christianity that there is. It is attractive because he is humorous and totally lacking in the Sanctimonious Spirit."

Clare Trueblood, Elton's brother, had come to North Carolina to live with them as a way to cut down expenses and to give Clare a college experience to his liking. He had been enrolled at the University of Minnesota but had found the large school impersonal and lonely. He was also needed around the house because Pauline had become seriously ill with what was diagnosed as pernicious anemia. In his diary, Elton wrote, "Pauline is terribly anemic. She must not do any work. The outlook is not bright. I have just taken her upstairs and put her to bed. . . ." In his autobiography he has noted, "With the advantage of hindsight I see now that the pace of living which seemed reasonable to me was really too much for my young bride, whose courage always tended to obscure her physical weakness."[7] Because of Pauline's illness, the preparation of meals and care of Martin fell mainly to Elton and Clare. In his personal family history, *Footprints*, Clare has written how the problem was eased, "Elton eventually got one of the mountain girls to move in and take over the household duties in return for room and board. This girl, like many of the students had come from a poverty-stricken background and had very limited funds. By living with us she was able to stay in school."[8]

Clare was a student in many of Elton's courses. As he thought about his brother's expertise in the classroom, Clare wrote, "Elton taught psychology and philosophy and kept the students on the edge of their seats. His course in psychology was so popular they had to hold it in the auditorium. He constantly amazed us since he could finish the summary sentence each session just as the bell rang. . . . [He] was a great favorite with the students—an advisor, father confessor, and the most important person on campus."[9]

Joseph Cox who now lives in the Friends Retirement Center across from the Guilford campus, was in Elton Trueblood's first class at Guilford. He has laughingly called Elton "my patron saint." When asked if he could remember anything special about Trueblood the teacher, he said, "I remember him as an encourager. A fellow student once said to me that Elton Trueblood has the ability to make you think that you are the smartest man at Guilford next to him!"

As Pauline's health improved, the Truebloods invited students to their house on Sunday evenings. Sometimes they would have forty or more students in their living room for what was called the "Heretics Club." There was no limit on what could be discussed. The group varied from week to week in the hope that all of the Guilford students could be entertained before the year was over.

This practice of inviting students to their home was one that Elton and Pauline, and later Elton's second wife, Virginia, were fond of doing and something they did wherever they lived. The informality of an evening discussion in Professor Trueblood's home was a wonderful, uplifting experience. In later years, Elton and Virginia limited their invitations to a few students, but it included a dignified dinner. The receipt of such an invitation always guaranteed an enjoyable and interesting evening.

My first invitation to the Trueblood home for dinner on the Earlham campus was during my student days at the Earlham School of Religion. There was delightful predinner conversation with two or three other students and spouses, centered around a beautiful fire in the fireplace. Elton would seek to draw us out, asking each of us about our studies and always able to supplement a new thought or idea that we had not yet considered in relation to any given topic. Later we would gather around the table for dinner, before which Elton would read a portion of Scripture and offer a prayer of thanksgiving. Everything was orderly and done in exquisite taste, with Virginia serving as the gracious hostess, and Elton raising our standards of conversation. These were experiences that would become etched on one's mind and a style which students would seek to emulate.

In the fall of 1928, Herbert Hoover was elected president of the United States, and Elton Trueblood was in his second year of teaching at Guilford. The new year of 1929 began with great enthusiasm for the new president, and Quakers were especially pleased to have one of their own in the highest office of the land. As he reflected on this fact, Elton wrote, "Quakers are in great danger now that a Quaker is in the White House. Is it like Christianity at the time of Constantine? Quakerism was formerly a despised sect, but now, 275 years after its origin it has one of its Members in the place of supreme power. . . . Many are far too proud of the fact." The concern that Elton expressed was legitimate, since it put Quakers in the awkward position of trying to remain faithful to the peaceful teachings of Christ, while supporting one of their own as president of a large and powerful nation. The question was, "Would the witness of the Society of Friends be stifled?" Of course, it was not, but the concern was real.

On September 22, 1929, during this first year of the Hoover presidency, Elton was asked to speak at Irving Street Friends Meeting in Washington, D.C., the home Meeting of the Hoover family while they resided in the nation's capital.

Writing to his family in Iowa, Elton shared this account of the experience:

> I had the experience of a lifetime yesterday. I actually preached to the President of the United States. . . . Early in the morning the policemen came and put up "No Parking" signs. Later they put up ropes to avoid crowding about the doors. Then a secret service man came and looked all over the building for bombs or any other source of danger. His name is Colonel Starling and has been the personal attendant of the last two Presidents. I was glad to meet him.
>
> It looked for a moment as though I should miss my chance for the President and his wife were five minutes late. Just as we had about gotten disappointed, they came. Everyone stood until they were seated. They had a whole seat to themselves. The President looked very tired, but I made him listen. Wash-

ington Friends said I was the first one who had been able to make him listen attentively. Mrs. Hoover is a charming looking woman.

Seated on the "facing bench" (the front seat in a Quaker meeting where the ministers sit facing the congregation) Elton witnessed a delight-ful exchange between the president and Mrs. Hoover. As the offering plate was being passed toward them, the president was frantically searching throughout his suit pockets for some money. Quietly, and with dignity, Elton saw Mrs. Hoover inconspicuously place a ten dollar bill in the presi-dent's hand just before the plate reached him!

On Tuesday, October 29, 1929, the stock market plunged. The head-lines in the *New York Times* read, "Stock Prices Slump $14,000,000,000 in Nationwide Stampede to Unload." At the time, Pauline Trueblood was pregnant with their second child. She was becoming stronger each day, mostly by eating nearly raw liver and taking liver extract. Elton's busy schedule of teaching and administrative work continued, and they looked forward to a possible Christmas or New Year's baby. Arnold Trueblood, the second boy, just made it into the new year, being born on January 2, 1930. He was named after the writer Matthew Arnold who was so admired by both Elton and Pauline.

With the crash of the market in October, the Depression was soon to follow. Exactly one week following Arnold's birth, the faculty members at Guilford College were told that they would all have to cut their salaries in half in order for the school to keep its door open. This was a terrible blow to a young professor and his family, especially when it was not easy to sur-vive on what he was making *before* the salary was cut in half. Wanting to continue his education by working toward the Ph.D. degree and in need of an appointment that would support his family financially, Elton True-blood handed his resignation to President Binford and waited for a new position to appear.

BALTIMORE QUAKERS AND JOHNS HOPKINS

Yesterday I dared to have another interview with Lovejoy. He is a fine tonic for me.

The position of executive secretary of the Baltimore Yearly Meeting of Friends became open, and the committee in search of a new executive invited Elton to become a candidate. At the time of his interview he took his first son, Martin, with him and, according to Elton, "he won every heart on the committee." The decision was made to accept the offer, which gave him an office at Homewood Friends Meeting, just across from Johns Hopkins University, the opportunity to enroll in the Ph.D. program, and a salary of three-thousand dollars, plus the use of an automobile.

In the summer prior to starting his new chapter in Baltimore, Elton worked for Fall Creek Friends Meeting near Indianapolis. This opportu-nity gave him the freedom to do some studying in the Indianapolis Public

Library. He recorded in his diary, dated June 26, 1930, just how appreciative he was for such study time: "I am in the Indianapolis Public Library. I have a most unrestrained sense of the joy of living. I suppose it is because I have been reading about R.L.S. [Robert Louis Stevenson] I want to keep the youthful spirit. . . . I want to impart to others some of the sense of constant wonder and joy which are mine. Libraries often have this effect on me. It is glorious! Again I say, 'Thank God for Andrew Carnegie.'" A few days later Elton writes that he was back at the library, looking into the possibility of making Albert Schweitzer the major topic of his work at Johns Hopkins, "Yesterday I spent some time in the Indianapolis Library with the usual result. I am very enthusiastic about the A.S. [Albert Schweitzer] project. There seems to be no genuine study of him in print."

In the fall of 1930, Elton, Pauline, Martin, and Arnold moved to a home on the northern edge of Baltimore. Martin was enrolled in the Friends School and was driven to the school on North Charles Street each morning by his father, who then proceeded to his office at Homewood Friends Meeting. One of Elton's first tasks was to organize a luncheon club at the university for the undergraduates. Because he took a leading role in this organizational work, the university cut his tuition in half. The name of the club was "The How to Be Religious Though Intelligent on Wednesday Club." It was an immediate success with lasting results. To this day one of the luncheon participants of fifty-eight years ago, Keith Conning, is one of Elton's close friends and his son, Keith Conning, Jr., serves on the board of Yokefellows International.

The Trueblood love for luncheon clubs began with this one at Johns Hopkins and has lasted until today. Later, at Stanford, he established a luncheon club, and then at Earlham he began a Yokefellow Luncheon Club that is still very active with at least eighty to ninety persons coming every Thursday noon to First Friends Meeting for a simple lunch and brief message by one of the participants. Because he was in London on numerous occasions later in life, Elton was asked to join the Authors Club, and he was most active in the Chit Chat Club in San Francisco, which was made up largely of Stanford and University of California professors.

As a student at Johns Hopkins, Elton's one and only mentor was Arthur O. Lovejoy. "Yesterday I dared to have another interview with Lovejoy," he wrote on October 3, 1930. "He is a fine tonic for me. He will correct my looseness and superficiality." Professor Lovejoy was one of the most respected men in philosophy at the time that Elton became his student. He was a former president of the American Philosophical Association who had founded the History of Ideas Club. He was an extremely formal man who took three years before he addressed, "Mr. Trueblood" as "Elton." "He scared his students to death," reflects Elton. "No one ever thought about being a smart aleck in one of his classes." In the words of another student, "He seemed like Zeus on Mt. Olympus." "With his eyes upon you," wrote yet another student, "you would weigh your words twice before uttering them. His presence discouraged laxity of thought, intellectual bravado, and facile talking."

One particular occasion stands out among many memories of Elton's time under the tutelage of Professor Lovejoy. It was a meeting of the History of Ideas Club. When the seats around the large oval table were filled, students gathered on the floor. Lovejoy was at one end of the table and Dr. William Welch, noted professor of pathology at Hopkins and last of the "Big Four" in the medical school, was seated at the other. The whole evening was spent in dialogue between these renowned scholars. "There may have been some opportunity for discussion," says Elton, "but those of us who were students kept our mouths shut! We didn't want to appear foolish in the company of those two great men."

Each week, beginning with his second year, Elton wrote essays for Lovejoy. "He seemed to take a special interest in me when he learned that I was a Quaker. Having served at the university since 1910, he remembered the time when many of the Board of Trustees were Quakers and was aware, of course, that Mr. Hopkins was one himself."[10] Once again, Elton was experiencing the wonderful educational opportunity of regularly writing papers and having them criticized "one-on-one." It was a pattern of education that began for him with Anna Eves at William Penn College, continued through Willard Sperry at Harvard, and now was an important part of his doctoral work at Johns Hopkins under the direction of Professor Lovejoy.

Rendel Harris, whom Elton had met many years earlier at Woodbrooke in England, was another reason for the excellent academic reputation of Johns Hopkins. While visiting him in 1939, Elton asked the aged professor what he considered the secret to the greatness of Hopkins. "Simple," he said, "we all attended each other's lectures." They were humble scholars, open to learning from one another.

Besides his work at Johns Hopkins and the various duties that occupied his time as executive secretary of the Baltimore Yearly Meeting, Elton was a family man. Young Martin provided his father with a great deal of humor. On November 10, 1930, Elton recalled the following incident: "This morning Martin and I said the 23rd Psalm together. At the end he suddenly said, 'Daddy, I don't want to dwell in the house of the Lord forever. I'd like to go outdoors sometimes!' This was a great moment in my life."

On another occasion Martin said, "Daddy I love you better than anybody else in the world." When his father asked him what made him love his father so much, he responded, "God did!"

During a particularly rainy period, Martin told his father, "Daddy, let's get a long ladder and pull the sun down close so that it will be sunny all the time." His father responded, "It is too far away." To this Martin said, "I have seen it when it has been very close to the ground."

Martin was Elton's "kindergarten philosopher" and an absolute joy to his father. "In our three years at Baltimore, and the following three years at Haverford," wrote Elton, "we were very proud of our two little boys and spent as much time with them as our duties would allow." In 1964, Elton dedicated his book *The Humor of Christ* to Martin, with the inscription, "To Martin, who knew when to laugh."

Elton's first visit to the White House occurred in 1930. The Irving Street Friends Meeting in Washington was a part of the larger organization of Friends Meetings called Baltimore Yearly Meeting, of which Elton was executive secretary. "I considered the President and Mrs. Hoover to be my parishioners," he recalled later. Not one to be shy, and a great proponent of what he calls "holy boldness," Elton went to the White House to make a pastoral call on Mrs. Hoover. When he was escorted into the Hoover's private residence, the butler asked him to place his card on the silver tray, so that he could be properly introduced. Not anticipating the need for a calling card, Elton had none. In its place he scribbled his name on a scrap piece of paper he found in his pocket and placed it on the waiting tray! He was admitted, and, as he recalls, he had a delightful visit with the First Lady.

This idea of "holy boldness" has been a part of the Trueblood personality for years, but the idea of the availability of prominent people really began to develop in his retirement years when he had more time to nurture new friendships. While in England studying after his retirement from Earlham, Elton asked to see J. B. Phillips, whose translation of the New Testament had become such a meaningful addition to the Trueblood library, as well as to millions of others. Not only was J. B. Phillips delighted to see him but expressed gratitude for the opportunity to share ideas together. Dr. Phillips told Elton that he rarely had visitors because people assumed that he would not be available.

The same bold style led him to visit with Dr. Radhakrishnan while on a tour of India, "largely because he illustrates so well the platonic pattern which combines political responsibility with philosophical vocation." He explains his approach, "While we were in New Delhi, I addressed a note to the former President of India at his home in Madras, saying we wished to call on him.... When we reached our Madras hotel, we found a note from Dr. Radhakrishnan, inviting us to tea at his home. We enjoyed greatly the subsequent conversation...."[11]

Elton discovered that, regardless of how prominent the person is in the world, he or she still needs fellowship and an opportunity to discuss ideas with other persons. Time and time again, whether it be presidents, senators, governors, or respected teachers such as Edith Hamilton, Paul Tillich, or Albert Schweitzer, Elton would boldly take the initiative of contact when he wanted to enlarge his circle of acquaintances and friends. "If you want to see someone," he tells his students, "then do it!"

The experience at Johns Hopkins helped Elton to know how much he didn't know. Though he had been verified in his already vast storehouse of knowledge and abilities at communication, he was learning the paradox of education—the more you know, the more you realize how much you don't know. "While at Hopkins," he reflected in his 1988 address to the Yokefellow annual conference, "I felt as though I was walking among giants." He was helped to clarify his own thought and develop a love of logic. He writes,

> The common enemies of the philosophy department were vagueness, ambiguity, equivocation and confusion. In one sense the constant topic of all the teaching was the title made famous years earlier at Hopkins by C.S. Peirce, "How to Make Our Ideas Clear." Under Lovejoy's tuition, clarity became my professional goal, whether in written or spoken communication. I realized that there is little chance of making clear to others what is not clear to ourselves.[12]

Part of every meeting with Lovejoy included three questions: (1) *Is it true?* (2) *Does it follow?* (3) *Can you think of any exceptions?*

In 1933 after three years in Baltimore, Elton was informed by Rufus Jones of Haverford College that there would soon be an opening in the philosophy department. On Christmas Eve, five years before this opening, he reflected in his diary on his interests and where best he could share his ideas. "I find that my deepest and most abiding interest is always in the story of human thought. . . . I am interested in the interplay of ideas in the same way that a chemist is interested in the interplay of atoms and electrons. I suppose my greatest favorite is the field of Quaker ideas." And then in thinking about possible places to study, write, and teach, he wrote that he would like to be at Haverford College or Swarthmore College in what was at the time, the center of Quaker thought. This, of course, was largely due to the fact that the most widely read Quaker of the time was Rufus Jones of Haverford.

Before he accepted the appointment, Elton was encouraged by Rufus Jones to come to the campus and visit. "I knew that the work would be difficult," wrote Elton, "since it would be necessary to teach courses of which I had had no previous experience, and also to finish my Hopkins dissertation at the same time, but the prospects were alluring, chiefly because Haverford standards were high."[13] In September 1933, the Truebloods moved to Philadelphia to begin a new chapter.

1933–1936

TEACHING AT HAVERFORD

The greatest single advance in my teaching career during my Haverford Chapter came in the field of logic.

Elton Trueblood's first year of teaching at Haverford was Rufus Jones's last year. The two had met ten years earlier at New England Yearly Meeting of Friends, in June 1923 at Moses Brown School in Providence, Rhode Island. Elton was the young pastor of Woonsocket Friends Meeting, and Rufus Jones was the best known and most widely-read living Quaker, producing over fifty books in his lifetime. At the time of their first meeting, Rufus Jones was sixty and Elton was twenty-three.

It was from Rufus Jones that Elton learned that if something is worth saying, then it can be put in the language of ordinary, thoughtful people. In all of his thirty-six books, Elton has sought to maintain this focus in his writing. He has said, "I would rather be quoted in 'Dear Abby' than in the *Philosophical Journal!*" This concern he owes to the influence of Rufus Jones.

A true story from the experience of Rufus Jones helped him to understand the importance of simplification of style. Early in his career, Rufus had sought to impress people with "big" words. He would fill his speeches with wonderfully complex verbiage like *eschatological* and *epistemological*, and sometimes he would even throw in *apocalyptic*. At the conclusion of one of these "heady" speeches, an elderly Quaker woman arose from her seat and said, "Our Lord said, 'feed my lambs' not 'my giraffes.'"

It was Rufus Jones who first introduced Elton to the larger college and university communities by suggesting that they invite him to speak in their chapels. The elder statesman of Quakerism had far more invitations to speak than he could possibly fulfill, and so knowing of Elton's gift in using the spoken word, he would confidently suggest his name. The first such invitation was to speak at the chapel of Mt. Holyoke and then Wellseley, followed by Smith, Dartmouth, Yale, and Princeton. He became so popular on the college and university lecture circuit that he had very soon spoken in all of the Ivy League schools, as well as most of the other colleges up and down the east coast.

Rufus Jones was a man who loved humorous stories. And it was, per-haps most of all, this sense of humor that so infected his junior colleague in the philosophy department at Haverford. I have often heard Elton say, "I don't trust the theology of any person who doesn't laugh." What Rufus Jones knew, and what Elton was learning, was that humor is often the only way to respond to the human condition. Already Elton was very apprecia-tive of G. K. Chesterton's humorous approach to religion, and so the humorous spirit of Rufus Jones was naturally infectious.

His work at Haverford consisted of teaching Introduction to Philoso-phy and Logic and sharing the teaching responsibilities for two courses with Rufus Jones. One of the classes, a seminar for seniors who were con-centrating their work in philosophy, met in Rufus Jones's upstairs study. "The first semester, taught by Dr. Jones, dealt with Kant, while the second semester, which I taught, dealt with Hegel," writes Elton. "I had a splendid opportunity to watch Dr. Jones' technique and to try to understand the secret of his power. Part of it I soon saw, was his authentic friendliness. He really cared about the senior men, and they could not fail to know that. They are mature men now, and they may not remember much of the *Critique of Pure Reason*, but they can never forget Rufus Jones."[1]

Another class jointly taught by Elton and Rufus Jones was *Ethics*. In this course the junior colleague would read all of the papers, and Rufus Jones would lecture. This particular course was required of all seniors and was recognized as the "capstone" of their college studies. Reflecting on the input of Rufus Jones as a professor and his larger-than-life presence on the Haverford campus, Elton has written, "His teaching reminded me of the apocryphal answer of Professor Alfred North White-head to a student who inquired what courses he offered: 'I have three courses,' he is reported to have said, 'Whitehead I, Whitehead II, and Whitehead III.'"[2] If Rufus Jones was teaching the course, the topic was a secondary matter. Whatever the assigned topic, the major impact on the student's life would come not from the material presented, but from the life of the presenter! He was a man who, as Thomas Carlyle said of his wife Jane, "had the gift of calling for the best qualities that were in people."[3] When Elton's first book, *The Essence of Spiritual Religion*, was released, it was dedicated to Rufus Matthew Jones.

Although Elton's course work at Johns Hopkins was completed, the dissertation still hovered large over his head. Not only was Elton having to prepare for courses he had never taught before, but he had to travel monthly to Baltimore to work with Professor Lovejoy on his dissertation. At one time, Elton seriously considered making Albert Schweitzer the sub-ject of his doctoral work and corresponded with the great missionary doc-tor about this possibility. A letter from Albert Schweitzer (in his own handwriting) to Elton tells of Schweitzer's acceptance and encouragement of such a project.

In seeking help for this study, Elton wrote to his former professor,

Edwin Moore of Harvard, hoping that Moore's personal relationship with the missionary doctor would be enlightening. Moore responded by encouraging Elton to pursue research in Schweitzer's thought and ministerial activity. The professor from Harvard was especially interested in learning more about *why* Albert Schweitzer would give up so much in his life to become a doctor in an isolated village in Africa.

In the end the decision was made not to pursue a dissertation on Albert Schweitzer. Elton's studies with Arthur Lovejoy had broadened his thinking far beyond the works of one man to the theme of philosophical anthropology. The exact title of his dissertation was "The Differentiae of Man." Elton has written about how he fastened onto this theme:

I had come to see that the most important fact which we know about our universe is that, at one point, it has persons in it. Without conscious intent, I had become a philosophical personalist, and I wished to learn, as much as is possible, what a "person" is. Professor Lovejoy encouraged this line of study, partly because it was congenial to his own thinking.[4]

Throughout the fall and winter months of 1933–1934 the dissertation was written. By April, it was almost finished, and Dr. Lovejoy had been kept thoroughly informed of its progress during their monthly meetings. Pushing Elton a bit more, the professor wrote to him on April 2, 1934, urging him to do some more thinking about his last chapter. He was concerned about Elton's busy schedule, and hoped that his suggestions were not the counsel of a perfectionist. On May 1, 1934, following Elton's changes, Lovejoy wrote that he and his colleague, Dr. Boas, were ready to recommend to the Board of University Studies that his dissertation be accepted. He concluded that the extra effort on the last chapter was well worthwhile.

The recommendation to the board follows:

We have examined the dissertation of Mr. D. Elton Trueblood, "The Differentiae of Man, and Historical and Critical Study of Theories concerning the Uniqueness of Man in Nature," and recommend its acceptance in partial fulfillment of the requirements for the degree of Doctor of Philosophy. The author gives evidence of a competent philosophical grasp of the issues pertinent to the subject he has chosen, has surveyed and discussed discriminationally a very wide range of relevant literature, and on the basis of his analysis of these theories has presented a well considered conclusion of his own. The historical portion, particularly that dealing with the early modern period, is, necessarily, not entirely complete, but in spite of some *lacunae* the dissertation gives, on the whole, a more comprehensive and methodical critical review of modern, and, especially, of recent reflection on the problem than any treatment of it with which we are acquainted.

His written examinations were scheduled to be conducted on Friday, May 12, and Saturday, May 13, and his oral examination took place on May 22. The following day he was sent this note from the university registrar:

My Dear Mr. Trueblood:

Your name has been recommended to the President of the University by the Board of University Studies for the bestowal of the degree of Doctor of Philosophy. Detailed directions for the Commencement Exercises are enclosed.

Responding to a letter of gratitude from Elton, Dr. Lovejoy expressed his gratitude for the opportunity of working with Elton, and the satisfaction he had received in watching his student develop the gift of reflective inquiry.

With the successful completion of his dissertation, and the awarding of the doctor of philosophy degree in June 1934, Elton and Pauline took their family to a farm near West Grove, Pennsylvania, for the summer. It was a well-deserved time of rest and recuperation, when Elton could be with his loved ones for a prolonged period of time. "The boys roamed the countryside with their dog, Socrates, and Martin learned to swim in the nearby creek. I was glad that for a while they could have an unhurried father."[5]

The following academic year at Haverford began without the large presence of Rufus Jones, who had retired and was spending the year in England. However, Douglas Steere, who had been on sabbatical, returned, and together with Elton they taught all of the philosophy courses. In reflecting on his personal growth during this time, Elton wrote,

The greatest single advance in my teaching career during my Haverford Chapter came in the field of logic. I soon became convinced that the study of logic, including scientific method, is one of the most important steps in the development of trained minds . . . what I learned by my teaching of logic at Haverford College had enduring effects in my subsequent teaching at both Stanford University and Earlham College.[6]

It was during this year that a most important invitation came from his old professor at Harvard, Willard L. Sperry. During the summer of 1935, Dr. Sperry was to be in England, and he asked Elton if he would be willing to serve as acting dean of the Harvard chapel while he was absent. Without hesitation, Elton accepted. Not only would it give the professor from Haverford the great opportunity of reaching the minds of a new group of young people, but it would give him the glorious opportunity of uninterrupted time for writing. Elton Trueblood's dream of writing a publishable book was about to become a reality.

THE CHAPEL AT HARVARD

In the midst of our confusions of today here is a clear voice which is pretty sure to be heard.

In June 1935, the Truebloods took up residence in Cambridge, occupying the home of Henry J. Cadbury, the Quaker scholar and professor at Harvard Divinity School. Elton's major responsibility was to conduct the morning worship each day, Monday through Friday. While occupying Dr. Sperry's desk in Memorial Church, Elton wrote every day following the chapel worship enlarging in written form what he had said earlier in the service. It was a pattern that he would practice for the rest of his life. Each of his books were sermons or lectures first. What he had learned was that he could judge the acceptability of his thoughts by sharing them by way of the spoken word before he attempted to put them into written form.

What became *The Essence of Spiritual Religion* is, in fact, the enlargement of the talks he gave in the daily chapel service at Harvard. With the unmistakable influence of Rufus Jones on his life and thought, Elton wrote twelve chapters with such titles as "Spiritual Religion and Belief," "The Spiritual Inwardness of Jesus," "The Spiritual Nature of God," and "Worship in Spirit and Truth." In this first volume from the pen of Elton Trueblood, we also discover his first serious discussion of the ministry, which is chapter 11, entitled "The Abolition of the Laity." A sentence from this chapter that goes to the heart of one of Elton's main concerns and that has been central to his own ministry is this: "A full understanding of the Christian message leads us straight to the position that *all Christians are ministers* and that the mere layman is nonexistent."[7]

Not even knowing the name of the religion editor at the publishing house of Harper, Elton sent his completed manuscript to New York. Before the Truebloods had left Cambridge to return to Philadelphia, he had a letter from Harper & Brothers stating that his manuscript had been accepted. Willard Sperry's foreword to this work was most important, since it opened doors for the young Trueblood that could not be opened otherwise. At this time not many in the religious and academic community knew Elton Trueblood, but they all knew Willard Sperry. In part, Sperry wrote,

The work of a man to whom the Quaker tradition is native . . . but who recognizes the values inherent in the Catholic position. The book is at once a personal witness and an adventure in generous imagination. Its contents will commend themselves both to the layman and to the scholar. . . . My relation with Mr. Trueblood goes back to the days when he was working with us at Harvard; it has been continued and matured during the intervening years, and I am happy to commend what he has written to all those who, like myself, look to the birthright Quakers to speak to us with peculiar pertinence in a day when both our creeds and our moral codes need reexamination and restatement.[8]

Rufus Jones added his praise of *The Essence* with these words:

I have read Dr. Trueblood's forthcoming book on *Spiritual Religion* with profound satisfaction. It has depth and insight and beauty and style. In the midst of our confusions of today here is a clear voice which is pretty sure to be heard. He is reinterpreting with telling words and in fresh ways many old truths which often seemed to be no longer *alive* and *current* because they were wrapped in congealed words and phrases. He has set them free and given them marching power once more, which is a notable service.

The reviews were encouraging.

The Presbyterian Tribune: "Before he finishes the book the reader is convinced all over again that the Religion of the Spirit is not the private possession and responsibility of special ministers, but rather is a challenge to all men and women. . . ."

The Christian Century: "The outstanding quality of this book is its fairness and insight. Though the author is a devoted member of the Society of Friends, and the pages are dedicated to Rufus Jones, yet there is evident throughout of a sincere appreciation of the spirit of organized Protestantism, and a sympathy with much that is Roman Catholic. . . . The book is sound, easily read, and provocative of thought. . . ."

The Churchman: "Professor Trueblood has given to us a fine interpretation of religion as essentially spiritual. . . . It is an exceedingly penetrating discussion, and we cordially acknowledge our indebtedness."

Church Management: "In 1935 his summer chaplaincy at Harvard attracted the thoughtful. In this book the young scholar has given proof of his power both to think and to write clearly. . . . It would seem as if a rare and gifted writer on the faith has begun his course. His readers will hope for a steady succession of books through the years."

Religion in Life: "Many who have been reading the writings of Rufus M. Jones for a generation or more have wondered who would take his place in the years to come. Clearly it would not be an easy place to fill. He has spoken out of the great Quaker tradition, giving continued emphasis to a mystical type of religion. He has enlarged and enriched his spiritual inheritance through his own philosophical research and experience.

"Then we heard about one of his students, who was appointed as Assistant Professor of Philosophy at Haverford College (more recently appointed as Chaplain of the University and Professor of the Philosophy of Religion at Stanford University). Evidently here was the heir apparent. Naturally great expectations were aroused. The admirers of Rufus Jones have been waiting to hear and read what this young man had to say. Those who have heard him know that he speaks with a strange insight and pertinence, even 'as one having authority.'

"There have been articles here and there. Now comes this book, the first. . . . The book is dedicated to Rufus M. Jones, to whom the author acknowledges that he owes a great debt. Elton Trueblood, however, is not the echo of any teacher. The reader quickly feels that the author is venturing out on his own, and is not bound by the limitations of an inherited faith or even by the positions of greatly respected teachers."

The summer spent in the chapel at Harvard was one of those "unequal times" that Elton talks about, where more happened in a brief concentration of days than sometimes occurs in months or years. He not only produced his first book, but because of this interim experience his name was brought before Dr. Ray Lyman Wilbur, the president of Stanford University, who was looking for a chaplain and professor of philosophy. Elton met with him in Philadelphia on his thirty-fifth birthday, December 12, 1935. President Wilbur encouraged Elton to travel to Stanford during the semester break at Haverford and deliver the sermon in the university chapel on Sunday. Elton consented to do so, traveling alone by train across the country. This was his first trip west of Nebraska. At the conclusion of his visit, Dr. Wilbur told him that the appointment was his if he wanted it.

EDITOR OF THE *FRIEND*

Friends have great literature of the past, but with this we must not rest content. There are . . . new applications to be made.

In the October 10, 1935, edition of the *Friend*, J. Henry Bartlett announced a change of editor for the oldest Quaker publication still being published.

> Continuity has been the outstanding characteristic of the *Friend* in its one hundred and eight years of history . . . changes in editor and in editorial staffs have kept the pulse of progress beating. It has been a case always between editors and subscribers of action and reaction. A live clientele of readers demand a widening outlook as well as deepening insight. . . .
>
> The variety in editors of the *Friend* is interesting. In one particular, however, they have been alike. They have been Friends, and whether birthright members or not, they have been of the order described as convinced Friends. Their convincement has inspired their editorship. They wrote what they had seen and known and what they handled of the word of life. Quite as certainly as we have been sensible of this in the recent past under the leadership of Olive R. Haviland [the outgoing editor], shall we find it true under the new incumbent, D. Elton Trueblood. Happily he needs little introduction to readers of the *Friend*. He has written for our paper and for others now and again during the past ten years. . . .
>
> In the Society of Friends . . . our new editor has had very wide contacts. On this account he would seem very particularly to have come to this responsibility at a critical time. Reconciliation is not the catchword of the hour merely, it is of the lost essence of Christianity itself. There can be no higher call than that of gathering the scattered sheep in the Society and out of it. The *Friend* is more than ready to dedicate its resources to that high aim and to welcome one who is so fully equipped and has the call to this undoubted opportunity. . . .

Elton Trueblood's first editorial as editor of the *Friend* was entitled,

"Religious and Literary," which was a focused essay on the *Friend's* subtitle, "A Religious and Literary Journal." In the editorial he stressed his hope for the journal.

> Friends have great literature of the past, but with this we must not rest con-tent. There are new implications of our basic premises to be pointed out, new applications to be made. New expositions of spiritual religion are required if we are to hold our faith intact in the midst of current turmoil. The *Friend* stands squarely for the production of new thought and expression in our day on a level which serious men everywhere are bound to respect. . . .

The editorial position was not a full-time duty but one that Elton Trueblood could handle along with his work as professor of philosophy at Haverford and later as professor and chaplain at Stanford. It was of par-ticular joy to him because of the opportunity to employ the written word to reach people with his ideas. Editorials such as "Vocal Progress," "Ideal Uses for Vacations," "Children in Divine Worship," "The Paradox of Christmas," and "The Authority of Christ" flowed from his pen.

In the "dust bowl" summer of 1935, Elton traveled to Iowa and Nebraska to visit relatives. While in Nebraska, he was anxious to visit the country of Willa Cather, the novelist, whom he considered to be one of the greatest writers of the time. In the July issue of the *Friend*, Elton wrote a moving editorial about his experience, which he entitled "The Lord's Song in a Strange Land." This is, perhaps, Elton's finest editorial and will give the reader a beautiful example of his style:

> Until this summer I had never been in Nebraska and I was eager to make my first visit count for as much as possible. I knew in advance what I most wanted to see, including the magnificent capitol building at Lincoln, easily the finest State Capitol in America. Most of the state capitols are poor copies of the great structure in Washington, but the Nebraska building is unique. A sin-gle shaft rises out of a broad, low base, symbolic of the broad prairies. My deepest interest, however, was not in any building, but in a stretch of country lying north and west of Red Cloud, the country in which Willa Cather lived as a little girl and of which she wrote so powerfully in her early novels.
>
> My interest in the country near Red Cloud is great because I share the opinion of those who believe Willa Cather's fiction is the finest now being pro-duced in America. She went to Nebraska as a little girl about a half century ago, going from the finished civilization of the Shenandoah Valley to the new life of the Great West. Many of her neighbors were struggling immigrants from central and eastern Europe and of these she wrote later with great insight. Those who have read *My Antonia* cannot easily forget the picture of a Bohemian girl whose life was beautiful, though the background was bare. I wanted to see the rolling hills, the great stretches of wheat land, and mingle a bit with the present descendents of the hardy pioneers. . . .
>
> As I looked over the hills, and stopped at the little Scandinavian Church where so many of the tombstones told of birth in Sweden and Denmark, I tried to visualize the country when the first sod houses were built. What struck

me most was the reflection that each family brought more than covered wagons, more than plows, more than simple furniture; each family brought a *pattern of life*. For the Bohemians it was one pattern, for the Russians another, for the Danes another, and for the old Americans still another. The conviction grew upon me that Miss Cather's power comes from a single theme, the theme that a pattern of life can be maintained even in an alien setting.

It is hard, as the Psalmist tells us, to sing the Lord's Song in a Strange Land, but Miss Cather has given us a brilliant succession of stories to show that it can be done. . . .

All lands have seemed strange to the singers of the Lord's Songs. It is of the essence of life that it is forever facing new issues, and life is meaningless apart from genuine novelty, but hope lies in the fact that there is an enduring Song that can be sung, however strange the land. The most important thing we can do is to keep alive an ideal pattern of life in our day that we may be able to pass it on to our sons, who will also live in a strange land. We know little of the world our children will face, but of two things we may be sure: first, it will seem strange and baffling; second, it will be a world in which men can still live for ideal ends.

As editor, Elton was always searching for new ideas, themes, and authors he felt could contribute to Quaker thought in particular and to Christian thought as a whole. One such person was Thomas R. Kelly, whom he had met years earlier while a student at Hartford Theological Seminary.

Thomas Kelly had been known within the Society of Friends as a bright young scholar, who had done much of his scholarly work on the philosophy of Emile Meyerson. He had been teaching at the University of Hawaii when Elton accepted the position at Stanford University. The vacancy in the philosophy department at Haverford when Elton left was offered to Thomas Kelly, and he accepted it at once. The Philadelphia *Evening Bulletin* announced the news: "Dr. Thomas R. Kelly, of the University of Hawaii, has been named assistant professor of philosophy to fill the vacancy *caused by the death* of Dr. D. Elton Trueblood." This misprint became the basis of any number of jokes about Elton's demise, which, of course, had been "greatly exaggerated." Since Elton was able to remain as editor of the *Friend* under his new appointment at Stanford, he kept a very important Quaker connection that helped him stay in touch with the work of people like Thomas Kelly.

"In the late summer of 1937," writes Elton, "we returned from California to the Philadelphia area for the Friends World Conference, which was held at Haverford and Swarthmore, and which I had the privilege of addressing. This gave me an opportunity to converse with my successor, with whom I had not previously had much direct acquaintance. This contact in 1937 was an important step in the unfolding of the drama because it opened the way for the publication of essays which later, in book form, made Thomas Kelly famous."[9]

In the spring of 1938, Elton solicited his first article from Kelly for the *Friend*, entitled "The Eternal Now and Social Concern." This article expressed Kelly's radical change from secular philosophy to religious experience. A year later this was followed by "The Simplification of Life." The Thomas Kelly writing the articles was not the one who came to Haverford in 1936 but one who had been, in his words, "shaken by the experience of the Presence." Through a humbling academic failure at Harvard (Kelly did not pass his oral examination for the Ph.D.) Thomas Kelly turned inward, and it was as a result of this self-introspection that he became "acquainted with" the Living Christ.

Douglas Steere, Kelly's colleague at Haverford, remembers the change in this Quaker philosopher and how he was "shaken by the Presence." In the biographical memoir introducing Kelly's book *A Testament of Devotion*, Steere writes,

In the late autumn of 1937 after the publication of his book, a new life direction took place in Thomas Kelly. No one knows exactly what happened, but a strained period in his life was over. He moved toward adequacy. A fissure in him seemed to close, cliffs caved in and filled up a chasm, and what was divided grew together within him. Science, scholarship, method, remained good, but in a new setting. Now he could say with Isaac Penington, "Reason is not sin but a deviating from that from which reason came is sin."[10]

In his biography of his father, Richard Kelly describes this divine-human encounter in the following way:

There is no exact record of what happened in the following weeks, but it is certain that sometime during the months of November or December, 1937, a change was wrought within the very foundation of his soul. He described it as being "shaken by the experience of the Presence — something that I did not seek, but that sought me." The inner awakening of an "Awful Power" surged within him. He later confided to a friend, "It is an awful thing to give oneself to the Living God...." Stripped of his defenses and human self-justification, he found, for the first time, a readiness to accept the outright gift of God's love, and he responded with the unlimited commitment to that leading."[11]

The articles first solicited from this "changed" man for the *Friend* eventually became a book entitled *A Testament of Devotion*, one of the most widely acclaimed books of Christian devotion ever produced. Since 1941, it has remained in continuous print with Harper & Row. Unfortunately, Thomas Kelly died on January 17, 1941, and never saw his devotional classic in print. It was put together posthumously by his friend and colleague Douglas Steere.

Elton's work with Thomas Kelly and the consequent production of *A Testament of Devotion* was, perhaps, the most enduring experience of his entire career as editor of the *Friend*. As he prepared for his next chapter at Stanford, it was important for him to maintain this place in Quaker publishing and academic circles, and this he could do if the magazine board agreed to allow him to remain as editor, though living on the West Coast. The board agreed, especially since Elton's associate editor, Richard Wood, would remain in Philadelphia. All seemed to be falling into place for a coast-to-coast move.

1936–1945

THE MOVE TO STANFORD

The future is full of promise. There is verily set before our friend an open door which no man can shut.

Elton Trueblood has never been a sectarian Quaker. Always he has sought to apply the basic teachings of Friends concerning spiritual religion to the larger Christian community. He realizes that a religious movement serves little purpose if its main attention is focused inward on what is good for the sect, rather than *outward* on what is good for the world. His decision to leave the sectarian atmosphere of Philadelphia Quakerism for the "larger" academic community was made with this ecumenical understanding of Friends in mind, and by keeping his position as editor of the *Friend*, he was able to maintain his Quaker identity, which many sectarian Friends felt he would lose by taking the Stanford chaplaincy.

Augustus T. Murray, a man with impeccable Quaker "credentials" and himself a Stanford faculty member, wrote an article during Elton's second year at Stanford entitled, "Our Quaker Chaplain." This article helped put to rest the growing concern that Elton had deserted the Quaker fold. "Doubtless many Friends heard of his coming to assume the chaplaincy of a great university with some misgivings," Murray wrote.

> They realized that it might well prove for him the opening of a life-work fraught with immense promise and with almost boundless opportunities for service; but they may well have wondered whether a concerned Friend could feel free to accept such a position, and have regretted that his action would remove him from the Quakerly activities of which Haverford is so naturally a center.
>
> It was the writer's privilege to talk over with our friend the prospect of his coming to Stanford before his decision had been reached, and to seek to make clear to him the problems he would meet and the opportunities for service which would be open to him. It was plain that acceptance of the position would entail the sacrifice of some cherished hopes, separation from loved friends, and remoteness from centers of Quaker influence; it was for our friend himself to decide whether or not there were compensating advantages.

I did not seek to influence his decision, much as I hoped he would come to us. I sought merely to be the interpreter of an existing situation. . . .

Under the guidance of our friend the services of our chapel have been definitely enriched. There is about them no touch of ecclesiasticism. No one is led to feel that the chaplain is attempting the impossible task of worshipping in his place, or that on his own part listening to the sermon and to the organ music and the singing of hymns makes of him a worshipper. The atmosphere of the chapel is one of reverent group worship, and the moments of silence which follow the sermon and precede the prayer are a new and rich means whereby this spirit finds expression.

So too in the thoughtful discourses delivered by our friend there is nothing that suggests traditionalism. The problems of the religious life in this critical age are frankly faced and the basic truths, so fundamental in Quakerism, are stated and interpreted with candor and convincement. A prominent member of our university community said to me not long ago, "I never go to church unless I know that Dr. Trueblood is going to preach, and then I never fail to go." These discourses, to many of which one loves to return in memory, are happily delivered without notes.

The life of a college chaplain is a busy one, and it would be a hard task to enumerate the manifold claims made upon his time and energy; but Elton Trueblood has in addition continued his work as editor of the *Friend*; has visited meetings of Friends in central and southern California; has met groups of other denominations and interpreted to them the Quaker view of life; and our little group of Friends has held its meetings for worship at his house twice each month.

The future is full of promise. There is verily set before our friend an open door which no man can shut.

The Trueblood family moved to the West Coast during the summer of 1936. The presidential campaign was in full swing, with President Franklin Roosevelt running for a second term against Governor Alf Landon of Kansas. The Quaker, Herbert Hoover, had been defeated in 1932, and he had taken up residence with his wife, Lou, on the Stanford campus. The Trueblood's settled in a home near the former president at 747 Delores Street, and they soon became good friends.

The Stanford move had been a major one that was, in the words of Augustus T. Murray, "The opening of a life work fraught with immense promise and with almost boundless opportunities." When Elton had become convinced that they should go to Stanford, he discussed it with Pauline, and upon her concurring, they had sent a telegram to President Wilbur telling of their acceptance of his offer. "All that we did in the next few months pointed to the largest shift which we had ever made," Elton later wrote. "We felt at home at Stanford from the first day. We had good neighbors, the nearest being Dr. Edgar E. Robinson, chairman of the department of history."[1]

His closest relationship on the Stanford faculty was with Dr. Hardin Craig, professor of English and renowned Shakespearean scholar. Elton played golf with Dr. Craig nearly every week. Since he was twenty-five years older than Elton, these times of relaxed conversation were important to the junior faculty member, who greatly respected his elder colleague.

Elton's relationship with President Ray Lyman Wilbur grew very close during his tenure at Stanford, so that he treated Elton almost as if he were a son. Dr. Wilbur had been the secretary of the interior in the Hoover administration and was a former president of the American Medical Association. "Ray Lyman Wilbur towered above the others at Stanford, both physically and intellectually," Elton has written.

When I visited his office, all was business. Normally he went on signing checks while he listened to my proposals. Always when he finished, he gave me an answer, so that I was never in doubt. Once he stopped to explain his method. "I have many decisions to make," the Lincolnesque man said, "and some of them are wrong. But I have learned that there is something worse than a few wrong decisions, and that is indecision."[2]

The headline of the article in *Forward* magazine announced the Trueblood agenda: "Religion Wakes Up at Stanford." "It seems a paradox that Dr. D. Elton Trueblood, Chaplain and professor of philosophy of religion at Stanford University, occasionally finds the Stanford chapel, one of the most beautiful chapels in the country, a hindrance in his work at the University," the article begins. "Too long has the chapel, with its picturesque mosaic front . . . been simply a tourist sight. 'We've got to kill the idea that it is a tourist center.' Dr. Trueblood says. 'I want a place of living importance, not something just to look at. . . . '"

During the Trueblood years the Stanford Chapel did, indeed, become a "place of living importance." Once again a luncheon club was established by the chaplain, where students could come and have lunch for twenty-five cents and listen to an informal lecture. There was no membership, and all students were welcome to attend.

Elton strengthened the religion department, adding courses and attracting serious students who truly wanted to study religion and who were not just "looking for 'courses' to fill in their program." What Elton sought to do throughout his tenure in Palo Alto was to fulfill what Mrs. Stanford had in mind when she built the chapel—to make it the center of campus life. Physically, it clearly occupied the center of the campus, and Elton sought to make it the spiritual center as well.

Another dimension of the spiritual revitalization of the university under Elton's leadership was the bringing to campus of well-known religious leaders. One such person was Professor Reinhold Niebuhr, who came to Stanford to deliver the West Lectures in 1944. Dr. Niebuhr was fifty-one years old at the time and had "reached the apex of his national reputation." The theme of Niebuhr's lectures was "The Children of Light and the Children of Darkness," which later became the title of a book. He spoke entirely without notes.

As mentioned earlier, Elton never speaks from notes, a practice learned as a debater, and he is always working to get his students to speak in the same way, often using the example of Reinhold Niebuhr to make his point. Once Mary Cosby was on the Earlham campus to address the students. Mary is the co-founder, with her husband, of the Church of the Saviour in Washington, D.C. Elton sat up front with her. As the students were gathering, Elton leaned over to Mary and inquired, "Mary, you aren't going to use notes are you?" To this Mary replied, "Yes, Dr. Trueblood, I am." "Why Mary!" Elton retorted with a twinkle in his eyes, " I never use them, and Reinhold Niebuhr never used them, why must *you* use them?" With a smile and in her beautiful Georgian accent, Mary Cosby responded, "Dr. Trueblood, your well *is*, and I know Dr. Niebuhr's *was*, very deep — ever so much deeper than my own. Please forgive me for 'using notes.'" Whether Elton did forgive her, I do not know. I doubt it. It was, however, the best response to one of Elton's standard questions of a speaker that I have ever heard.

The impact of Reinhold Niebuhr's thinking on Elton was great. What Niebuhr helped him do was to take *sin* seriously. Elton's first contact with the professor was in 1929 when Niebuhr spoke before a group of Friends who were startled by Niebuhr's ideas.

"Already he had renounced the kind of liberalism," Elton wrote, "which talks of the natural goodness of man. He had come to see that no philosophy can stand unless it comes to terms with the profound idea of sin."[3] Many of the Friends of Philadelphia in 1929 still clung to the idea of "the natural goodness of man," which is why Niebuhr was so upsetting to them. For the most part, and to their credit, Quakers continue to look upon the bright side of human endeavors for examples of the utopian, Christlike world that, in the words of George Fox, "would take away the occasion of all wars." They emphasize, again in the words of Fox, the "ocean of light which flows over the ocean of darkness."

What Niebuhr helped Elton and his Quakerism to face was how sin "in the precise sense of self-centeredness and the struggle for power, enters into every human situation and is, therefore, something with which we must always reckon."[4]

When Elton was only thirty-three years old, ten years before Niebuhr's visit to Stanford, he had already found such thinking attractive and related it to Quakerism in an article for the January 1934 *Friends Quarterly Examiner*:

> During the past year, religious thinking on this side of the Atlantic has been greatly stimulated by the wide reading of Reinhold Niebuhr's *Moral Man and Immoral Society*, a book which presents a theory of man which is far from flattering. Thus the theological tide is beginning to turn.
>
> The reason for the continued existence and occasional vigor of the doctrine of Original Sin is that it attempts to account for a fact, the fact of our glaring imperfection. There is, in human life, a surprising contrast between

our ideals and our actions. Something, it would seem, has gone wrong and continues to go wrong with the inner life, not simply of a few men, but of all men everywhere. Often we know exactly what we care most about, but we continually fail to apply ourselves consistently to it. We catch a glimpse of what we might become and, before nightfall, we have been unfaithful to the ideal so warmly espoused. . . .

The doctrine of Original Sin is not an explanation, in the sense that the evolutionary and Socratic theories attempt to be explanations, but is rather the acceptance of a fact. The fact of a radical contradiction or illogicality is recognized in human nature, and far from being explained away, is held to be permanent, deep, and original. This discrepancy goes, so the doctrine holds, not merely to the basis of human nature, but to the very basis of the world. It is significant that the Hebrews, from whom the essence of the doctrine was inherited by Christians, had the genius to see that human sin is one of the elementary mysteries, like life, or love, or death. These all belong together, and they do appear together in the early chapters of Genesis.

There is no great reason why Quakerism cannot include the idea of Original Sin in its system, and probably the only reason we have ever failed to include it has been the unfortunate confusion in some minds caused by the failure to distinguish between the ancient Christian doctrine and the extremely distorted version of it taught by Calvinist theologians. We would seem to be on firm ground if we maintain, on one hand, that all have sinned and are sinners by nature, and, on the other hand, that there is a light which enlightens every man.

It was during this visit to Stanford that Reinhold Niebuhr prompted Elton to consider Abraham Lincoln as a theologian. "In a planned discussion a professor asked our visitor who the most original theologian of America might be; and, without any hesitation, Niebuhr replied, 'Abraham Lincoln.'" This response led Elton to engage in a long study of Lincoln's religious thinking, leading eventually to the writing of a book in 1972 entitled, *Abraham Lincoln: Theologian of American Anguish.*

On December 4, 1938, a third son, Sam, was born to Elton and Pauline in the Stanford University Hospital. For a long time there had been concern that Pauline would never be strong enough to have more children. The warm climate of California, however, was most agreeable and served as a tonic. Her health steadily improved. Sam was named after Elton's father, and when he wrote his book, *The People Called Quakers,* he dedicated it to "The two Samuel J. Truebloods between whom I stand."

In May 1939, Elton was invited to deliver the Swarthmore Lecture at the London Yearly Meeting of Friends. He had been saving his free academic quarters, and so the decision was made to go in late December and return early in June. He arranged for Pauline and the baby to spend the winter months at Carmel, while he took Martin with him to England. Arnold stayed with the Blake Wilburs (Ray Lyman Wilbur's son) so that he could continue his schooling in Palo Alto.

As he reflected on his departure for England, Elton told of the sorrowful good-bye in his diary dated December 16, 1938: "This has been one of

Woodbrooke College faculty and staff, 1939; Trueblood is third from left, second row

the blackest days of my life. Imagine how hard to leave a twelve-day-old son, Samuel, and a wife only lately returned home from the hospital. She was very brave. Dear Arnold, usually so sturdy, had an attack of illness. He waved to us from the study window."

The trip east was by train and went well, with a stop in Iowa to visit family. Elton's father, Samuel, had died in November 1938, and so he had the hard experience of visiting the grave for the first time on December 19. "It was good to see Mother, but so hard to find Father gone," Elton wrote. "We went to Motor and saw the grave. It was an overcast, chilly day. I'm glad we went."

In England, Elton became a fellow of Woodbrooke, the Quaker college in Birmingham that he first visited as a young Friend in 1924. His studies in 1939 were devoted to seventeenth-century writers, with a special emphasis on the Quaker theologian Robert Barclay. Twenty-eight years later, following his retirement from Earlham, he was finally able to complete the scholarly work that began that winter of 1939.

In April 1939, Pauline joined Elton and Martin in England, taking with her young Richard Wilbur as a companion for Martin. The baby was old enough to be left with a nurse, thus giving Pauline a chance to travel across the Atlantic for the first time. Keeping meticulous notes, Pauline wrote about her ship, the *President Roosevelt*, finally reaching land:

> After a stormy voyage the President Roosevelt dropped anchor at Cobh, Ireland, early in the morning and one day late. The sun rose over the rim of hills which almost surround the harbor and the green ring of land, under its rosy light, seemed a glorious symbol of all that solid earth means to human kind. The water was quiet in this sheltered circle and the engines were at rest for the first time in eight days. The passengers for Ireland and the freight were loaded onto the tender while the passengers for England and the continent rested in the respite from wind and waves and the strain of the engines and walked the sunny decks, wishing heartily that the voyage could end here for them, too.

About eight o'clock we were slipping out of the gateway of the harbor into fog again, and our minds prepared for twenty-four more hours in the channel. It was here that I was pleasantly surprised to find the sea calm and the boat steady. The day passed slowly. After lunch I took a nap. The signal for the life boats brought me to my feet, and, without thinking much, I carried out the necessary preparations almost mechanically fully believing that the summons was a serious one. Once in the lower halls I realized that my own sleep had fooled me and that the alarm had been for a sailors drill. I was glad to discover what my behavior would be in an emergency.

Most anxious to see her husband and eldest son after weeks of separation, Pauline described her feelings upon reaching the dock at South-hampton:

We knew we could not land before eight, but even so I found myself ready to go ashore before six-thirty. I had awakened at five-twenty and even though I hate being ready far in advance of the time to do a thing I was ready and already irked by my imprisonment when I knew Elton and Martin were so near me. I was standing on the after deck looking wistfully over the docks and thinking that they must be getting their breakfast and feeling as impatient as I did when I heard something which made me turn and in a moment of recognition I was in Elton's arms and Martin's smiling face was just behind. I was surprised beyond any hope I could have had. An hour and a half of weary waiting had been exchanged for a happy interval where minutes did not count. We had breakfast together on the boat and talked. Martin had been awake at five and looking from the hotel window saw by the boat funnels that I was there at last. They had spent two nights waiting there, since the boat was late in, and they had come eagerly, early, hoping that they might manage to get permission to go aboard. The officials were kind and we had a happy beginning of my visit in England.

The Truebloods were in England at a time of heightening tension in Europe. In 1936, Germany had moved into the Rhineland, and in 1938, it invaded and annexed Austria. On March 15, 1939, just days before Pauline sailed for England, Hitler had invaded Czechoslovakia. A letter to Pauline from Elton just two days after the invasion tells of his concern:

Of course you know as soon as I do, by the papers, of events in eastern Europe. They are terrible and everyone here is consequently sad. I have talked with several, however, who are unanimous in saying they think you run no risk in coming here this spring as I run no risk in staying. I am afraid you are a bit puzzled as to what you ought to do. It will not surprise me if I get a wire from you asking advice.

During their meetings at Woodbrooke in April, much of the talk was about Germany. Pauline wrote, "All through the tenor of the meetings was a sense of strain because of the state of affairs in Germany and all of Europe. The news was reported so that those unable to listen to the 'wireless' would not miss the most recent information."

A special treat during this time in Birmingham was an invitation to dinner at the home of the Quaker chocolate manufacturer, Edward Cadbury. Pauline recorded the experience:

> At twelve-forty Edward Cadbury arrived with his Rolls-Royce and chauffeur to take us out to his home in the country for lunch. We passed along the highway by the Lickey Hills where Cardinal Newman is buried. Edward Cadbury's mother owns an estate opposite these hills and his brother owns another very near. We went on out to the end of the tram line and then began to ascend the hill finally coming out on top at an elevation of one thousand feet. The woods and hills in this area were bought by the Cadbury brothers and they have given a great tract to the city of Birmingham for park land. People flock here from the city on weekends and holidays. It is beautiful country easily accessible to city people.

Toward the end of the English journey, the Truebloods went to the home of Professor Rendel Harris for tea. As mentioned earlier, it was from Harris that Elton learned that in many things of philosophical and theological importance, one does not have to choose, thus providing Elton with the spark of insight leading to his understanding of the "holy conjunction *and*," as well as his emphasis on "clear thinking" *and* the "warm heart."

This is Pauline's description of their visit.

> On Sunday we were completely lazy and sat in the sunshine instead of going to meeting. In the afternoon we went to the home of Rendel Harris for tea. We found him in the spacious lawn at the back of his home sitting in his wheelchair. He is eighty-eight years old now and is so emaciated and weak that he looks more dead than alive. One eyeball has been removed about four years ago. His white beard gives a distinguished look to his very kind face and he has a spirit which shines brightly through the frailty. When he began to talk with us we were ready to make allowances for this once brilliant man. So blind that he could not see us he asked after our comfort and made sure that we each had tea by direct questions. His cup was put in his hands and then he could manage it though it looked most precarious.
>
> Dr. Harris talked so brightly and wittily about his years in America at The Hopkins and at Haverford. He told of his last lecture at the Selly Oak Colleges. He spoke of his essays which had not been published and seemed to chafe under the limitations of his poor body. He had had his companion read Elton's Swarthmore Lecture to him though it had been published but four days and he had recognized the opening quotation as words of his own. He had taken especial pleasure in the title subject of the lecture and felt very kindly toward Elton for his emphasis on religious experience. It was a lovely thing to see the old man and the young man talking together so sympathetically about the same places, persons and ideas.
>
> As we were leaving Rendel Harris said he thought he might fly to America when he was ninety for we had made him very homesick for a sight of Haverford again. I thought we had tired him and his mind was slipping but then I realized I had been taken in, for he continued, "This visit shall be accounted to

you for righteousness." I have always taken that to mean, you have done the right thing. And so we left him chuckling over his clever turning of an otherwise pious remark.

Shortly thereafter, with the outbreak of World War II, the old professor was killed by a bomb.

On June 2, 1939, the Truebloods returned to North America on the RMS *Antonia*, which departed from Liverpool, with stops in Greenock, Belfast, and Quebec, before reaching the final destination of Montreal. Elton and Pauline had hopes of visiting in Philadelphia and Iowa before returning to Stanford, but the ship was delayed because of fog. Since Elton felt committed to attend Stanford's baccalaureate and commencement, they had to forego all other plans and go directly home to California. When the ship finally docked in Montreal, they boarded the Canadian Pacific train for the trip to Chicago and then on to California, arriving just in time for commencement.

Concluding the journal of her first trip to England and home again, Pauline wrote of the happy reunion with her baby following commencement:

> In the evening we left the boys with Ariel Oliver in our own house since she was leaving with her parents the next morning. (They had lived in our house while we were away.) This made it possible for us to go on down to Carmel that night to see our baby. Elton had not seen him since he was twelve days old. We arrived just as Samuel was finishing his ten p.m. bottle. He was not in the least afraid or shy, but came to us all smiling and happy. He seemed quite different from the little baby I had left three months ago. Then his hair was dark, now it was light. He seemed ever so big. How wonderful to come home to a happy healthy baby. Monday Elton paid the Carmel bills. We packed our car and left about ten o'clock. We were home in time for lunch. Now with our family reassembled and settled in our own home again we could look forward to a quiet life once more. Traveling is over for the Truebloods for a long time.

The focal point of the trip to England was the Swarthmore Lecture at the sessions of London Yearly Meeting, entitled "The Trustworthiness of Religious Experience." Elton challenged his listeners to take seriously the funded religious experiences of the ages as essential in understanding God. He said,

> The value of this evidence lies in its cumulative effect. Agreement about one thing might conceivably be attributed to coincidence or to the similarity of the observers, but as the area of agreement widens with the progress of critical intelligence, the hypothesis of coincidence becomes harder and harder to uphold. The most reasonable explanation of the agreement is that men of all ages are reporting what is true.

The lecture was published in England in book form, expanded in this country by Harper & Brothers, and issued under the title *The Knowledge of God*. The reviews were encouraging.

Journal of Religion: "The professor of philosophy of religion at Stanford University has written a spirited defense of religious experience as a means of gaining religious knowledge. It is an important book."

Religion in Life: "This is a book that deserves to be widely read, and its message to be widely and vigorously preached—especially at the present time!"

Christian Century: "A contribution of exceptional timeliness and value to contemporary Christian apologetic."

The Christian Science Monitor: "Dr. Trueblood in this volume has presented his case so convincingly that none may dispute his conclusion. In this day of doubt and denial it comes as a clear, strong breeze to sweep away the misty arguments of error. It was the fool who said in his heart, 'There is no God.'"

The San Francisco Chronicle: "With the coming of Bennett to Pacific School of Religion, Diller to Mills, and Trueblood to Stanford, our region stands second to none in vigor of theological thinking. This expansion of Dr. Trueblood's 1939 Swarthmore Lecture merits serious attention everywhere. . . . Trueblood has strengthened the case for faith in ultimate reality beyond ourselves."

The Truebloods settled into a more relaxed and patterned life once back at Stanford in their own home. The events in Europe, however, were far from relaxing. During a "fireside chat" in September 1939, President Roosevelt stated, "When peace has been broken anywhere, the peace of all countries everywhere is in danger." On April 9, 1940, Germany attacked Denmark and Norway and then marched into the Netherlands, Belgium, and Luxembourg. Winston Churchill became prime minister of England in May, and soon after, France fell to Hitler. Late in 1940, Elton was asked by Reinhold Niebuhr to write an article on "vocational Christian pacifism" which was the only pacifism Niebuhr respected. Elton did write a celebrated article for the *Atlantic Monthly*, which was published in December 1940, entitled "The Quaker Way." In his position at Stanford, Elton had to take a stand regarding the Quaker view of war, and he did. Because the article is important in understanding Elton's position at this critical time, I reprint much of it here:

> Opposition to war is only one of many "testimonies" which seem to Friends to be of equal importance and to stem from a common root. Opposition to all oppression, to racial prejudice, and to all kinds of slavery—these are quite as important in the slowly developing Quaker way of life as is the opposition to war. What, then, can a Friend do if faithfulness to one of his "testimonies" means unfaithfulness to another?
> The Friends must seem inconsistent to many people. Worse than this, they may seem to be people who evade their responsibilities. "You are merely let-

ting other people fight your battles for you," is one easy remark. If we hold that war is sinful, how can we keep our self-respect when we profit by the protection which the armed forces give, but in which we will not share? The problem can never be avoided and never fully solved. If we refuse to fight we seem to aid Hitler, and if we try to stop Hitler in the only effective way he can be stopped we weaken the fight for peace. . . .

Friends do not pretend that their renunciation of war has destroyed their powers of moral judgment. There is no logical inconsistency in condemning what is patently evil and, at the same time, seeking to overcome this evil in other ways than the ways of military power. The Quaker tradition of active good will is as far removed from isolationism as it is from militarism.

The Quaker opposition to war arises, not from refusal to face reality, not from the nature of the issues in a particular war, and not from fear of physical death, but from a conception of how the world is to be remade. The Quaker position entails an entire way of life, to which conscientious objection to war is incidental. It is a way which seeks to overcome evil with good, not in isolated cases, but as a consistent and enduring policy. If every person has, at least potentially, some kinship with the divine nature, our task is to treat persons in such a way as to draw this out and depend upon it. Though the record of Friends is far from perfect, it is a fact that a long-time effort in overcoming international strife by the development of active good will has been undertaken through many years. The record of Friends in reconstruction and child feeding during and after the World War is well known. This program was continued by means of intervisitation and the establishment of centers of friendliness in European capitals. . . .

Realistically, we cannot fail to see the predicament of a nation made up of all kinds of people, most of whom are not pacifists at all. For such a body of men there is not the requisite discipline to make active pacifism possible. Since the nations have not adopted the long-time pacifist method, which we believe will succeed, the attacked nations now have only two practical alternatives: to defend themselves by arms or to succumb to the invader. Since they let the door go shut, they have now no single good choice. The only practical thing that statesmen can do is to take the choice of evils. Adherence to the Quaker way does not make it impossible to see that there may actually be a choice of evils, and that the submission to invasion at the hands of those who will destroy freedom may be the worst of all possible choices.

We are often asked whether we are willing for the entire nation to follow the Quaker way. We are willing and eager, and it is likely that, if the entire nation had adopted our way, there would now be no war. But we recognize, at the same time, the need of time. Friends, to be logical, need not maintain that the sudden adoption of non-resistance after war has started will succeed. Certainly we do not suppose that our love for an aviator, though we have never done anything to make him know it, will keep him from dropping bombs on us. We do not believe in magic. Love must be tangible to make a difference, and in most cases it cannot be tangible unless it is part of a long-time program. The Friends have reason to avoid condemnation of those in charge of affairs of state who are faced with invasion that will destroy the liberties of their people. We do not condemn them for their failure to change programs overnight, but at the same time we hold that they ought not to condemn us or ask us to abandon our way. We plead for a mutuality of tolerance in these difficult matters.

We are working for the long future, and unless in the various nations, there are bodies of men who maintain a perfectionist standard, it is not likely that the ultimate goals will be kept in view. The nations as a whole, though it takes the way of war, as America is now doing in its war preparation, should welcome our conscientious objection, founded as it is on a rock of principle.

We continue to be extremely opposed to oppression; we continue to try what seems to us a better way of opposing it; but we are not bound for that reason to condemn those who oppose it in the only way they see that they can. I realize there are people who will suppose that there is something inconsistent about this, but I am inclined to think that it is only those who miss the profound truth of the dual nature of moral demands who make this judgment upon us.

All of us are living through days of strain, knowing full well that a hair's breadth of mistake may be disastrous for much that we hold dear. We shall be making no mistake if we encourage each serious and patriotic group to be loyal to its own vocation.

The year following the publication of this article was devoted to writing a book in Elton's major field of expertise. The book was entitled *The Logic of Belief: An Introduction to the Philosophy of Religion.* It was released in 1942 by Harper and met with good reviews. The *Christian Evangelist* found it "readable philosophy. The book is clean, comprehensive, and reads like fiction — a style rarely found among technical philosophers." The *Christian Century* said, "The author has set his hand to a task that could easily have been exacting and dull. That the result is both exciting and exacting is as much a tribute to the author as to the perennially interesting subject matter of religion." And the *Churchman* wrote, "The simplicity, clarity and sincerity of this book will commend it to readers of all degrees of ability."

Once again, Elton had produced an important contribution to the genre of philosophical literature. He had yet to produce, however, a book that would capture the attention of the general reading public, as opposed to academic readers. He was beginning to study the works of C. S. Lewis, and strengthened by Lewis's style, two years following the production of *The Logic of Belief,* he would strike the responsive chord he sought with *The Predicament of Modern Man.*

On April 30, 1941, Pauline gave birth to a daughter, Elizabeth Claire Trueblood, in the Stanford University hospital. She was named for Elizabeth Jones, the wife of Rufus. In a note to her new daughter, Pauline told of being in the delivery room and expressed her joy that Elizabeth was a girl:

I had wanted you to be a girl, but I fully expected a boy. Three times I had heard the word boy and I thought I probably couldn't have a girl. I could hear you crying so I knew you were alive and strong. Neither the doctor nor the nurse said whether you were a boy or girl and as soon as I could recover the use of my tongue, I asked them. The nurse said, "A girl," and I said "Not really!" It seemed too good to be true because it meant that I had everything I wanted; a husband, three boys and a girl. That makes a very good family, and I felt lucky.

Eight months and seven days after Elizabeth's birth, the Japanese attacked Pearl Harbor. Four days later, Germany and Italy declared war on the United States. To help the Stanford students cope with the effects of war on their young lives, their chaplain wrote a message entitled, "To Stanford Students in a Time of Strain." It said,

> The clock has been turned back, and again there is a war generation, to which you belong. For some it seems remote, but for others it means profound discouragement. As you seek, in study, to learn something of the order of nature and man's life on this planet, the whole enterprise will often seem futile, because you will realize that young people like yourselves, only less fortunate, are dying on battlefields or enduring cruelty in prison camps.
>
> There are two things of great importance to keep in mind in such a time. The first is that your responsibility is for the future. Though you can do but little about the present calamity in human civilization, you can dedicate your powers to a better order in coming years. The one mood we must avoid is that of indifference. Some day this war, like all which have preceded it, will be over, and there will again be a chance for world opinion to share in the formation of a peace that is lasting. Your present task is to develop your powers, so that you may be effective when your opportunity comes.
>
> The second thing to keep in mind is that men and women must have resources on which to draw, if they are to take their right places in critical days. Often, when hard problems are faced, people suddenly realize that they have had no spiritual preparedness. The experience of millions is evidence that the one unfailing resource is faith in the Living God. The love of God is broader than the temporary plans of men. Faith in the Living God has outlasted other crises, and it will outlast this one.
>
> Seek in these days to nurture your faith by private prayer, by public worship, and by fellowship with those of similar mind. Try to have a sense of your oneness with suffering humanity everywhere, and seek reverently to know your own destiny.

Elton's life at Stanford was an extremely rich one. The war made some things difficult, and his time was more and more devoted to addressing, from a Christian perspective, the conditions of a civilization in upheaval. He thoroughly enjoyed his visits to San Francisco and the regular dinner meetings of the Chit-Chat Club, as well as his continuing work as chaplain of a great university. He had a lovely house and a beautiful garden that he dearly loved to tend, and his neighbors were all pleasant and devoted members of the university community. One neighbor, however, was very special. He was a Quaker, like the chaplain, and he had served as president of the United States.

FRIENDS OF THE HOOVERS

Mr. Hoover always dressed immaculately as he took his daily walk and looked very much the carefully dressed ex-president.

"The Hoovers, regularly took a morning walk, usually coming past our house," wrote Elton. "They were always dressed impeccably and the former president always carried a walking stick. I was surprised at the innate shyness of a man who had seen so much of the world. With a few he would talk familiarly, but invariably he fell into silence when others entered the room."[5]

During one of the Hoover's morning walks, Pauline Trueblood witnessed an interesting episode. "They made it a practice to take an early morning walk around the hill," wrote Pauline in her journal.

> I was ill and having my meals in my room. Sitting up in my bed with my breakfast tray one morning I observed Mr. and Mrs. Hoover walking down the hill across the street on our neighbor's sidewalk. There was a mass of amaryllis in bloom in the nearest border of plantings. These delicate lilies are something of a miracle in appearance as they rise on long strong stems out of the packed crust of the dry earth without a leaf to give them any contrasting color; just long brown stems with large pink lilies in a mass of color. Mrs. Hoover saw them first and her California heart was moved by this scene so typically Californian. She stopped entranced and soon had Mr. Hoover's attention on the lilies, too. She stood for a moment and then feeling too near for a good general effect she stepped out into the middle of the road followed by Mr. Hoover where they admired the lilies again. Then they continued on their morning constitutional.
>
> No sooner had they passed out of sight than our neighbor came stealthily out of a nearby clump of trees and shrubs and walked down to observe his lilies from the spot where the Hoovers had first stood on the sidewalk and then he went out into the road and looked again as the Hoovers had done. He had on his disreputable garden clothes and I supposed that he had hidden in the shrubbery when he saw the Hoovers approaching. Mr. Hoover always dressed immaculately as he took his daily walk and looked very much the carefully dressed ex-president. I didn't blame my neighbor for hiding though I knew they had known each other for many years. Mr. Hoover never made his neighbors feel at ease in his presence. He couldn't have made a cordial experience out of meeting his neighbor while gardening when he was on his morning walk. But my neighbor was pleased that the lilies had been enjoyed by Mr. and Mrs. Hoover. Soon I saw him cutting a great sheaf of the lilies and I thought the Hoovers were about to be presented with a gift.

One of the great annoyances of being a neighbor of so famous a man was the constant flow of tourist traffic in search of the former president's home. The Hoover house was not easy to find, and any number of times the people who lived up and down the street would be asked for directions. The closer one go to the house the more difficult it was to see. It so happened that one of the best views of the Hoover home was from the guest room at the Trueblood's, which gave Martin and Arnold a great idea for making money. While playing out in the yard, they had often been asked by tourists where the Hoovers lived. On occasion, the tourists would give them some loose change for their directions. Martin and Arnold's big idea was to charge tourists a certain sum to go up to the guest room in their house to view the Hoover house! Their mother kindly, yet firmly, had to dampen their enthusiasm and say no.

Early in their Stanford experience, Rufus Jones was invited by Elton to speak in the university chapel. When he arrived in Palo Alto, the Hoovers asked the Truebloods and the Jones over for a dinner party. "All during dinner," writes Pauline, "Herbert Hoover had nothing to say. He looked down at his plate and ate. Everyone else was having a happy conversation and Mrs. Hoover was conducting the dinner with grace and charm. . . . After dinner the men went to Mr. Hoover's study and they reported later that Mr. Hoover had opened up and entertained them with many interesting stories."

The first Hoover funeral that Elton conducted was for Herbert Hoover's sister-in-law, Mrs. Ted Hoover. The burial was to take place on the other side of the Santa Cruz Mountains by the ocean. The Hoovers invited the Truebloods to ride over with them. Their butler, Boris, was driving. "Mr. Hoover sat in front with Boris," relates Pauline, "and said practically nothing." The Truebloods were seated in the back with Mrs. Hoover who provided lively conversation. After the service was completed, they ate a lunch and then started back to Palo Alto. On the return trip, the former president began to talk.

> He listened to a particular news report on the radio which he made it his practice to hear. This turned his mind to world affairs, and he began to tell us of his visit to Germany and his private conference with Mr. Hitler. We were interested and surprised to hear him say that Mr. Hitler had a phenomenal mind for facts and figures. We had long known that Mr. Hoover put the greatest importance on facts and figures and to hear him say that he had never known a man who carried more exact information in his mind than Mr. Hitler impressed us. There was a tendency for Americans to consider Mr. Hitler a fool or a crazy man with delusions of grandeur. Mr. Hoover had no such opinions and we didn't either after that day.

The former president told his companions that Hitler would go into great exhibits of passionate rage when certain subjects were raised in conversation, and with other subjects he was self-contained and careful in his statements. In short, Mr. Hoover said, the Nazi system was very evil and very powerful and more intelligent than the world knew.

The Truebloods considered Herbert Hoover a victim of his time more than a failed president, and history has proven their point. "The people in general never knew about the groundwork he was laying for national and individual financial security in the four years of his presidency," reflects Pauline. "He made no attempt to popularize his dreams for the future and consequently he was a victim of the period in which he lived."

Once established on the Stanford campus, the Truebloods held Quaker meetings for worship in their home. Although the former president rarely attended, Mrs. Hoover attended regularly. A dream of Pauline's was to build a Friends Meetinghouse near the Stanford campus, and she eagerly solicited Mrs. Hoover's support. The former first lady suggested that Pauline write Mr. Hoover for help in securing funds, which she did. Mr. Hoover supported the project, but soon Mrs. Hoover died. "Now I truly think my Meetinghouse is doomed," wrote Pauline. The subject was never raised again.

In Mrs. Hoover, the Truebloods witnessed the spirit of a woman who was able to live through the bitter experience of the election of 1932 and support a man who suffered deeply. They knew she was a strong woman who lived above the personal affronts and the stigma of failure. When Mrs. Hoover died, Elton conducted the service in the university chapel, and she was buried in Palo Alto cemetery. Later, in 1964, her body was taken to West Branch, Iowa, to be laid to rest next to her husband. Shortly after Lou Hoover's death, the former president moved to New York City to live in the Waldorf Towers. The beautiful home the Hoovers occupied on the Stanford campus was given to the university as a gift to be used as the president's home.

THE PREDICAMENT OF MODERN MAN

Unless the spiritual problem is solved, civilization will fail...

"The terrible danger of our time consists in the fact that ours is *a cut-flower civilization*. Beautiful as cut flowers may be, and much as we may use our ingenuity to keep them looking fresh for a while, they will eventually die, and they die because they are severed from their sustaining roots. We are trying to maintain the dignity of the individual apart from the deep faith that every man is made in God's image and is therefore precious in God's eyes."

With words such as these, found in chapter 3 of *The Predicament of Modern Man*, Elton Trueblood changed his life. With courage and enthusiasm he helped the American people in their search for hope as they sought to rebuild a civilization at the end of the most destructive war ever fought. He wrote this small, pocket-sized book of 105 pages after the model of books by C. S. Lewis. "What size of book will the ordinary, busy, yet thoughtful person pick up and read?" Elton asked himself. He concluded that it would have to be large enough to win respect and small enough to be read—perhaps in one sitting. Another important consideration was the cost, which he wanted to limit to one dollar. By producing this size of book, he was able to do so.

The Predicament of Modern Man was released in 1944 and had the enthusiastic support of Reinhold Niebuhr, who called it "an able and profound analysis of the spiritual situation of our time." Norman Vincent Peale wrote, "A powerful book. One hundred and five pocket sized pages of common sense. Convincingly shows that only the gospel can save our decaying society."

The *Reader's Digest* quickly picked up on the popularity of this little book and reprinted it in condensed form. "This brought correspondence so heavy that it took some time before I finally was able to respond to every letter,"[6] wrote Elton. Although he was already a popular speaker on the lecture circuit, the success of *The Predicament* really launched his career as a sought-after national religious figure. He had always been gifted at stating profound truths in the language of common men and women, but now he had proven that he could compact such truths in a way that was not only understandable but readable as well.

The first four chapters of *The Predicament* set forth the problem, beginning with "The Sickness of Civilization." To start, Elton used the words of Albert Schweitzer as an epigraph, "We are living today under the sign of the collapse of civilization. The situation has not been produced by the war; the latter is only a manifestation of it." This practice of using an epigraph to begin each chapter was one he started with *The Logic of Belief* and has continued throughout his writing career. In this first chapter Elton writes about the most urgent problem of the day being spiritual, stating clearly,

Unless the spiritual problem is solved, civilization will fail; indeed, we already have a foretaste of that failure in many parts of the world. Man's sinful nature is such that he will use instruments of power for evil ends unless there is something to instruct him in their beneficent uses. Without the conscious and intelligent buttressing of what has been demonstrated as precious, human society goes down.[7]

This theme of focusing on the need for "conscious and intelligent buttressing of what has been demonstrated as precious" is one that Elton has spoken on throughout his life. He is fond of quoting Alfred North Whitehead's famous line, "Advance or decline are the only choices available to mankind." The point being that *if* we are not advancing, then we are declining. With emphasis Elton points out, " There is no such thing as a 'holding operation'!" He has warned audiences and congregations for forty-five years that we cannot just take our civilization for granted. It took work to build it, and it takes work to keep it.

In the second section of *The Predicament*, Elton writes about "the failure of power culture." Early in his argument, one of the most insightful paragraphs is this:

What is so amazing in our day is not rejection of Western Civilization in *practice*, for that has always occurred, but the rejection of Western Civilization in *theory*. So long as the theory remains intact there is always hope of regeneration, since some men will be disturbed by their hypocrisy. But when the theory goes, too, there is no hope; there is nothing to give man a bad conscience. It is bad enough to fail to live up to humane standards, but it is far worse to glory in that failure.[8]

In outlining the creed of "power culture," Elton sets forth three points:

1. The accent on *sheer power*, where the fundamental human relation is that of master and slave, and all science is used to make "the strong man's arm longer and his feet swifter."
2. The concept of *leadership*, where human equality is categorically denied. It renounces three fundamental Christian teachings: First, the notion of human equality; second, the belief in the oneness of the human family; and third, the centrality of humility. "Christ's words 'call no man master' are arrant nonsense to the one who accepts the leader principle as valid."[9]
3. The principle of *authority*. For "power culture" adherents, the ideal organization is that in which individuals live in unquestioning obedience and glory in doing so. This is a direct denunciation of two highly prized elements of Western civilization: *experimentation*, which takes as its text "Try all things; hold fast that which is good," and *individualism*, which believes each person is a separate object of infinite worth because he or she is a child of God.

In his third chapter, Elton writes about "the impotence of ethics." "We are now trying the utterly precarious experiment of attempting to maintain our culture by loyalty to the Christian ethic without a corresponding faith in the Christian religion that produced it."[10] In other words, we have become a "cut-flower civilization." In conclusion, Elton summarizes his argument:

The only experience we know that is revolutionary enough both to support the downcast nation and to chasten the victorious nation is the sense of existing under the eternal Providence of the Living God. In this, as Lincoln discovered in the tragic days of the Civil War, we find a level of experience which does the seemingly impossible of making us firm in the right, "as God gives us to see the right" but also humble because we are conscious that "the Almighty has his own purposes!" It is religion and religion alone that does this for men. For this reason we can never have a real civilization without it.[11]

As Elton proceeds to develop his argument he moves into the fourth chapter by writing about "the insufficiency of individual religion." Here he sets forth a theme that is a Trueblood trademark—"You cannot be a Christian alone!" He takes on the prevailing attitude of believing in Christianity but not churchianity that, in Elton's words, leads to a "vague religiosity."

The person who says so proudly that he has his own religion and consequently has no need for the church is committing what has been well called "the angelic fallacy." If we were angels, we might not need artificial help, but, being men, we normally do need it. And, whether we need it or not, others need it and we have some responsibility to them.[12]

Finally, the fifth and final chapter focuses on "the necessity of a redemptive society." In the epigraph, Lord Tweedsmuir succinctly states what is to be Elton's theme: "There have been high civilizations in the past which have not been Christian, but in the world as we know it I believe that civilization must have a Christian basis and must ultimately rest on the Christian Church." For Elton Trueblood, however, it is not just that civilization needs the Church, "but the church itself needs something to revive it. What do we do when even the salt has lost its savor?"

To this question the author responds by writing about a "redemptive fellowship" that takes seriously Paul's words about being "members one of another." He proposes a society that is not bound by denominational labels and that is truly committed. Using Hitler's words from *Mein Kampf* about membership, Elton turns these words to the Christian Church and suggests that we form cells made up of men and women "who are as single-minded in their devotion to the redemptive task as the early Nazi party members were to the task of National Socialism."[13] Showing hints of his developing thought and ideas that would be further expressed in many books to come, Elton wrote,

The kind of organized movement that the need of the hour suggests does not at present exist. Certainly the existent church cannot function in this way because *Christianity has long ceased to be scrupulous in membership.* Some may be members because they are greatly concerned over the redemption of our civilization, but they are surrounded by millions who are members because they were born that way or because membership helps their social standing. Since the devoted and effective group cannot be *found,* it must be *made.*[14]

The Predicament of Modern Man is both timely and timeless. It is timely in that Elton spoke to the needs of the world at the end of World War II, using contemporary examples to make his point. The book is timeless, however, because the points he made are relevant to the human condition regardless of the particular moment in history in which we happen to live. The danger Elton Trueblood foretold over forty years ago has, in many ways, become a reality. We are, indeed a cut-flower civilization.

SABBATICAL AT NORTHWESTERN AND HARVARD

Oh, not at all, not at all. Any man who thinks of himself as an elder or better would not be an elder or better.

With *The Predicament* due to be released in August 1944, Elton spent the summer on sabbatical from Stanford, teaching at the Garret Biblical Institute on the Northwestern University campus in Evanston, Illinois. "The summer brought me in touch with colleagues not known before," writes Elton, "The most interesting of whom was Professor Nels Ferre."[15]

In the autumn he had every intention of resting. The Truebloods rented an old home in Newtown, Connecticut, so that Elton and Pauline could be close enough to New York City for occasional visits, yet far enough away to avoid its busyness and the accompanying strains. Just as they became settled at Newtown, a call came from his old mentor at Harvard, Willard Sperry, inviting Elton to teach the course Philosophy of Religion for the fall term. He accepted the invitation, deciding that he could teach in Cambridge during the week and have weekends free in Newtown. He would leave Newtown on Sunday afternoon, travel to New Haven, and board the train for Boston. He would stay in Cambridge until Thursday afternoon, when he would return to Newtown. "At Cambridge I occupied a suite in Lowell House," Elton writes, "where I was very comfortable, and taught a class of about fifty men, many of whom were mature students."[16]

The most lasting memory of this third experience at Harvard, in the fall of 1944 (the first being his days as a student in the divinity school from 1924 to 1926 and the second being his interim work as dean of the chapel in the summer of 1935), was the opportunity to meet, for the first time, Alfred North Whitehead. Whitehead had emigrated from England after retiring as a professor at the University of London. While a student, Elton felt there was very little chance of ever meeting the great man personally, and now as a professor at Harvard in 1944, he learned that Whitehead was ill, thus seeming to make a meeting a most remote possibility.

One afternoon the telephone rang in his apartment at Lowell House, and Elton immediately knew that the voice on the other end of the line was Whitehead's. The old professor invited Elton to a dinner along with others in the Harvard Society of Junior Fellows. Of course, he jumped at the chance to go!

The events of that evening have long been an important part of Elton Trueblood's oral tradition. He loves to recount the details to anyone who asks. He had the chance to sit at Whitehead's right hand, and in the midst of their conversation he said, "Professor Whitehead, I suppose the real purpose of this gathering is so that those of us who are younger might have the beneficent influence of those who are our elders and betters." To this, Professor Whitehead responded in a style that was peculiarly his own: "Oh, not at all, not at all. Any man who thinks of himself as an elder or better would not be an elder or better." He spoke aphoristically all of the time.

Elton considered this meeting with Whitehead one of the most fortunate occasions of his life. Whitehead's aphoristic style of writing and speaking made him a most quotable person, and Elton has quoted from him extensively. What he learned from Whitehead that night was that the style of a person's writing could, indeed, also be the style of his or her speech.

The most meaningful Whitehead aphorism in the life and thought of Elton Trueblood is the one concerning education. "Moral education," Whitehead said in 1929, "is impossible apart from the habitual vision of greatness." This has served as an epigraph in Elton's writing and as a theme throughout many of his lectures. "All along, he [Whitehead] had seen deliberate mediocrity as the enemy of civilization," Elton writes, "but he had never expressed his convictions so well before. Unless education has moral content, he was convinced, it is little more than 'scraps of information.' Always the purpose of the teacher must be to 'shed details in favor of principle.'"[17] One direct result of this famous Whitehead aphorism was that it led Elton to a famous one of his own: "Deliberate mediocrity is a heresy and a sin." In a volume on "the quotable Dr. Trueblood," this would rank at the top of the list.

Alfred North Whitehead was a model for Elton in both writing and speaking, but his greatest lesson from Whitehead came in observing the old professor working with young people. "He saw that he didn't have much strength," Elton said at the 1988 Yokefellow conference, "and so the question was, 'How to use it?' He put what energy he had left into young people." This idea has affected Elton's life tremendously. So much so that in the autumn years of his own life, when most his age are retired and enjoying the company of their own contemporaries, Elton continues to seek out promising young people whom he can help to think and write. Although this is certainly a Whiteheadian model, it is also Socratic. Socrates states his concern about giving his time to the young in the *Theaetetus*, another important classic on the Trueblood shelf.

The sabbatical at Harvard came to an end with the beginning of the winter term at Stanford. Elton returned to California not nearly as rested as he had hoped, but certainly reinvigorated for his tasks ahead. Immediately he began a new writing project of a completely different character than what he had ever done. Dr. Samuel Johnson had been a favorite of his ever since he was first introduced to Johnson by Willard Sperry during his student days at Harvard. Now he wanted to edit the prayers of the great Englishman, with the intention of making these available anew to students and other who would be helped by them.

The publication of *Dr. Johnson's Prayers* went through several stages. Elton did the original work at the end of the war in 1945, and since ordinary publication was difficult, he accepted the offer of a private publisher, James Ladd Dilkin of Stanford, who found it possible to bring out a beautiful edition with printing by Taylor and Taylor of San Francisco. Only 350 copies were printed in this way. The paradox was that an excellent edition was possible at the war's end, but an ordinary edition was not! Finally in 1947, Harper & Brothers was able to produce a fine edition of its own, all hand set in Weiss type. The Student Christian Press of London brought out its edition in late 1947, and the Yokefellow Press reprinted it in 1981, with Dr. Johnson's portrait on the cover. In 1987, Templegate Publishers reprinted it again, this time in "daily reading" form, though employing the same text.

To hear Elton Trueblood read from this collection of prayers is a spiritually moving experience. In his slow and deliberate style, I have witnessed his ability to bring audiences to tears, especially when reading Dr. Johnson's *Last Prayer*. The written style of this prayer has been a style Elton has sought to emulate in his own prayer life.

> Almighty and most merciful Father, I am now, as to human eyes it seems, about to commemorate, for the last time, the death of thy Son Jesus Christ our Saviour and Redeemer. Grant, O Lord, that my whole hope and confidence may be in his merits, and his mercy; enforce and accept my imperfect repentance; make this commemoration available to the confirmation of my faith, the establishment of my hope, and the enlargement of my charity; and make the death of thy Son Jesus Christ effectual to my redemption. Have mercy upon me, and pardon the multitude of my offences. Bless my friends; have mercy upon all men. Support me, by the grace of thy Holy Spirit, in the days of weakness, and at the hour of death; and receive me, at my death, to everlasting happiness, for the sake of Jesus Christ. Amen.

LASTING CONNECTIONS

I know that it is easy to neglect friendships. . . . To be encouraging at the outset of a relationship is a necessary beginning, but cultivation and nurture is what keeps a sustained relationship.

Elton Trueblood's final year at Stanford University was a rich one. As a member of the board of the Church Peace Union, he went as an official representative to the founding conference of the United Nations in San Francisco. It was during this conference that he had his first and only opportunity to hear, in person, President Franklin Roosevelt. The speaking style of Roosevelt was infectious to all who heard him, and Elton was no exception. Also at this conference he heard General Jan Smuts of South Africa. He was already familiar with the philosophical works of Smuts, but had never heard him speak. Later in his life Elton would visit General Smuts's home in South Africa.

The idea for the book, *Foundations for Reconstruction*, first came to Elton as he sat in the San Francisco conference. "It occurred to me that world reconstruction . . . is impossible apart from a moral basis," he wrote, "and that in this regard the Decalogue is as pertinent as ever." The author reinterpreted the commandments in positive form, that is, if theft is evil, then ownership is good; or, if adultery is wrong, then fidelity is right. Following the pattern he had set with *The Predicament of Modern Man*, he wrote a thin volume of 109 pages, thus making it understandable and readable for the general public. It was released in 1946.

The chapters of this book, as with all of his others, were first delivered through the spoken word. In this case, they were ten sermons given first in the university church at Stanford. Coupled with the release of this volume, Elton wrote the Ten Commandments in verse for the children of his university colleagues. To this day children in Sunday school programs around the world are learning the Ten Commandments by memorizing the following verses that he wrote:

> Above all else love God alone;
>   bow down to neither wood nor stone.
> God's name refuse to take in vain;
>   the Sabbath rest with care maintain.
> Respect your parents all your days;
>   hold sacred human life always.
> Be loyal to your chosen mate;
>   Steal nothing, neither small nor great.
> Keep to the truth in word and deed,
>   and rid your mind of selfish greed.[18]

Elton wrote about his observations from the San Francisco conference in his June 7, 1945, editorial in the *Friend*:

> What has struck us first and foremost has been the deep seriousness of these men. They are concerned men and they are men of principle. One cannot listen intimately to Stassen and Vandenburg and not believe this. They are determined to use whatever powers and opportunities they have to try to make a system of world security in which the recurrent destruction of what we value most will come to an end. We get the impression that they are willing to use their energies this way, not only now, but as long as they may live. The are sensitive people on whom the tragedy of modern man has made a deep impression and they are convinced that we must find a way out if civilization is to survive. Many believe, with General Smuts, that this is our last chance.
>
> Along with this goes a keen realization that no document men can devise is ever a complete guarantee of peace. They know that the best laid plans often fail and that this plan may fail, even if it secures the adherence of the major nations. What they expect of it is not a panacea, but rather a kind of machinery which will facilitate and augment the will to peace if the will to peace exists. . . . The most hopeful single thing about the Conference is not any particular decision, but the mood in which the whole has been conceived and executed.

Throughout the war years Elton and Pauline worked tirelessly to help many of the Japanese of California who were placed in internment camps. Because their housemaid, Miyuki, was Japanese, there was a special bond between the Truebloods and this group of U.S. citizens who were being so unfairly treated. The greatest success that Elton had in aiding some of these victims came after a marriage ceremony in the Stanford chapel. Elton had performed the wedding ceremony of the daughter of the general who was in charge of the relocation of the Japanese. At the reception following the ceremony, and feeling in a festive mood, the general told Elton that if there was anything that he could do for him, to just let him know. Not being one to let any grass to grow under his feet, Elton responded, "There is something you can do for me. You can let the Takano girls out of prison. I will take full responsibility for them." Being a man of his word, the general complied with Elton's request.

A letter from a Masago Shibuya, who was being held in the Santa Anita Assembly Center in Arcadia, California, tells of his hope of release and Elton's concern for his welfare:

> Thank you for your very kind letter of August 20th, I am deeply apprecia-
> tive for anything which you may be able to uncover for me on your trip East.
> Yes, it does seem that, at present, a job is easier than study to leave camp for;
> perhaps the job which might be found could be part-time and I could study on
> the side in my spare hours. At any rate, I am quite determined that I should
> like to leave.
>
> Professor Mary Williams, emeritus of Rutgers, is also trying to help me
> find an appointment, as well as Professor Hayakawa of Illinois Institute of
> Technology and Reverend Akamatsu of New York. With the help of these per-
> sons I do hope that something will turn up—at least I shall not give up hope.
>
> A bit of gossip on the sidelines if I may: Santa Clara County residents here
> at Santa Anita have been given their orders for permanent relocation—our
> destination is the Heart Mountain Relocation Center at Cody, Wyoming. So
> the majority of the Stanford crowd will go there for the duration unless we are
> able to find appointments on the outside. You may remember Kazuyuki Taka-
> hashi, '40, he is going to Manzanar to work in the Guayule station there if army
> permit is available before we must leave.
>
> My sincere thanks to you, Dr. Trueblood, Father and Mother send their
> very best wishes.

To this day Rose and Miyuki Takano stay in close touch with the True-
bloods, who look upon them as a part of their family. It is an important "lasting connection."

While at Stanford, Elton became close to Clare Booth and Henry Luce when her only daughter was killed in an automobile accident near Palo Alto. Elton conducted her memorial service. Years later he rekindled the Luce friendship when he and Henry Luce attended a dinner in the White House hosted by President Lyndon Johnson. It was Mrs. Luce who first introduced Elton to Republican politics by taking him to the Republican National Convention of 1944 in Chicago.

The connection between Hans Roth and Elton began at Woodbrooke when he was there as a fellow in 1939. When Elton first met him, Hans had just been released from Dachau concentration camp. Soon they became friends, and Elton promised to help him if he could get to America. When he did reach this country, and eventually California, Elton and Pauline loaned him money to get started in the photography business in Palo Alto and arranged for him to stay in their garden apartment on the Stanford campus. His big break as a photographer came when he was allowed to photograph President Ray Lyman Wilbur. Soon he was a great success and was able to pay back all of the money that Elton invested in him.

This practice of not only offering encouraging words to people but also financial help has been a practice that Elton has followed for years. He recently loaned a generous sum to a former prisoner who wanted to get started in the car repair business. "I suppose people think I am an easy touch," he has said. "But if I can help, in a small way financially, to change someone's life for the better, then the risk is worth it. There is always the chance that I will never see the money I loan again, but it is a chance I gladly take and one I fully recognize before I do it."

I once asked Elton about how he was able to maintain his connections with people over the years, including those he had not seen for decades. The specific occasion that prompted this inquiry was a letter from a woman who had been a member of Woonsocket Friends Meeting, Elton's first pastorate, serving there from 1922 to 1924. It was over sixty-five years later! He told me that his work in building relationships was deliberate. "I know that it is easy to neglect friendships made in one place, if one moves away. And even if one doesn't move, friendships are something that take continuous cultivation and nurture. To be encouraging at the outset of a relationship is a necessary beginning, but cultivation, and nurture, is what keeps a sustained relationship." His chief means of keeping the connections alive is the "short letter" or postcard. He sits at his desk and writes literally dozens of these to persons all over the country. He knows that fellowship, like a good fire, needs constant attention.

His ideas concerning a marriage relationship are no different. Early in our acquaintance he told me, "James, don't ever quit courting your wife." It is a truly beautiful idea and if taken seriously could enhance or save the marriages of many who have forgotten the joys of courtship.

Elton once told me the story of speaking at a church and following the service standing at the back door with the pastor greeting people. As a young couple approached, Elton asked them, "How long have you been married?" Jokingly, the young man said, "Oh, about two years. I finally got tired of running, and she caught me!" Elton didn't laugh. What he did do was escort the young man over to a corner and told him to never say that again, for it is not at all funny, and it is terribly embarrassing to his wife. I am sure it is a lesson that the young man has never forgotten.

Another lasting connection from the Stanford years is the one with Obert C. Tanner. Dr. Tanner had been Elton's associate in the philosophy department at Stanford who went on to a successful tenure as a professor at the University of Utah. He was a Mormon who had become interested in the philosophy of religion. Today he is a well-known Salt Lake City businessman and philanthropist.

The most lasting connection from the Stanford years, however, is not to be found in the numerous people whose lives Elton touched or whose lives touched his. The most important lasting connection is with an idea whose seed was first planted in his mind during these memorable years on the West Coast. It found expression in the chapel cabinet, which he formed while chaplain. Here was the first unit in the world of what was later to be called the Yokefellowship. They began the use of a common discipline and strengthened Elton's belief that the development of small spiritual cell groups can, indeed, redeem society and change the world. At one time, every dormitory on the Stanford campus had an active "prayer cell" of students. It would be in another place, on a different college campus, however, that this idea would finally find full expression.

1945-1955

THE CHOICE OF EARLHAM

A college is a pumping station on the pipeline of civilization.

As with most major decisions of life, the decision to leave Stanford University was not easy. "For more than nine years I have been Chaplain and professor of Philosophy of Religion at Stanford University," Elton wrote in his diary dated July 31, 1945. "Two months ago I resigned, my resignation to take effect in December of the present year."

As Elton thought about his future plans, he noted in his diary under the heading "A New Life:"

> I want to be free to do whatever seems right. Having served as an academic missionary for this long I am ready for some other service. What should it be? Finally my mind is pretty clear. I want a position from which I can make the largest attack on the entrenched evils of our culture which I can do anything about. The one which I can attack best is that connected with our current failure to include religion in our education. This amounts to disloyalty to our heritage. I want to write and speak in such a way as to influence public opinion on this important point. What is at stake is not our education merely, but our total pattern of existence.
>
> I must live in such a way that I have both the contact with others which stimulates and the freedom from paralyzing demands which is necessary if I am to write anything important. The one extreme would be a college presidency. This would limit freedom. The other extreme is the life of the free-lance writer. This would, possibly, be somewhat sterile for lack of human contact in the right way. Perhaps the middle ground is plain, old-fashioned college teaching, with good classes and practically no administrative duties. Such a post might become for me a national pulpit. This would be particularly true if we could do some pioneering in one place that would influence others to follow.

Elton Trueblood had gone to Stanford at the age of thirty-five, and was preparing to leave at the age of forty-five. In this time two more children were born into the Trueblood family; World War II had come and gone, leaving a changed world; five books had been written (*The Knowledge of God, The Trustworthiness of Religious Experience, The Logic of Belief, The Predica-*

ment of Modern Man, and *Dr. Johnson's Prayers*); and with the release of *The Predicament,* the chaplain from Stanford had become one of the most sought after speakers and writers in the United States. As noted earlier, Elton was never wholly a sectarian Quaker. The Stanford experience, however, broadened his ministerial base of operation tremendously. Prior to Stanford, his journals and notebooks were filled with writing ideas for and about Quakers; now he was working on ideas for publication that would enhance the religious life of the entire Christian movement. And so the question may be asked, why would Elton Trueblood consider moving to a college such as Earlham, which was at that time a small, midwestern, sectarian Quaker school?

First of all, Elton was in demand all over the country as a lecturer. In the 1930s and 1940s there was still no adequate air travel, and with the major universities and intellectual centers east of the Mississippi River, he wanted to find a location that would be accessible to major points in the East. Richmond, Indiana, at that time was an excellent railroad center. "Pennsylvania Station was a busy and important place, with a good restaurant and trains going regularly in five directions," reflects Elton. "Each day there were famous trains, such as the Spirit of St. Louis and the Penn-Texas, carrying large numbers of passengers both east and west."[1] He could board a train in Richmond in the evening, have a quiet dinner, and arrive well rested the next morning in any major city of the East. Thus the choice of Earlham meant an excellent location for travel.

Second, Dr. Ray Lyman Wilbur had left the office of president at Stanford and had become chancellor. Under the new president (as is only natural) there were new policies and directions. Elton had a very close relationship with Dr. Wilbur, and with his departure from the presidency, Stanford was different. The chaplain, who had been recruited by Dr. Wilbur, felt a void. Years later when Ray Lyman Wilbur died, Elton was asked to return to Stanford to conduct the memorial service. This he did out of a tremendous sense of gratitude.

Third, the two older Trueblood boys, Martin and Arnold, were enrolled in the Quaker boarding school Westtown, in Philadelphia. Richmond, Indiana, would be two-thirds closer to them than California. What was from Philadelphia a four-day long and tiring trip by train across the country, would be only an overnight excursion to and from Richmond.

The fourth reason for choosing Earlham was the excitement being generated on campus because of the appointment of a new president, Thomas E. Jones. Early in Earlham's discussion with Elton, they wanted him to consider the presidency. After much thought, however, and with Elton making it clear that he did not want to give up his writing and teaching for administration, the college turned to Tom Jones. It was Dr. Jones who followed up on the contact with Elton, having the insight to know that if he could get him to come to Earlham as a professor, the small midwestern school would take a major step in becoming nationally known and respected as a place of real scholarship. Dr. Jones had been president of Fisk University in Nashville, Tennessee, and like Elton, was ready to return to his midwestern roots, having been reared in Indiana.

The fifth reason for choosing Earlham was the opportunity that President Jones and the Earlham College board of trustees were offering Elton to pursue his writings as well as freeing him to travel as a leader among Friends. In his autobiography, Tom Jones recalled a conversation he had with Paul Furnas, his vice-president in charge of business.

I suggested the possibility of engaging D. Elton Trueblood, Quaker author and professor of Leland Stanford University, to head our Department of Philosophy. He would have charge of convocations and would work with Dr. William E. Berry in the Department of Religion. To do this we would have to pay him less than half what he was then getting at Stanford, and we would have to give him time to write and do off-campus lecturing. Although we would be paying him approximately twice what the highest paid Earlham professor was then getting, if the faculty approved, I said, I had promises from half a dozen donors that would cover the salary Trueblood asked. After a period of surprise and incredulity, the faculty unanimously agreed to the arrangement.[2]

A minute from the Earlham College board meeting of August 18, 1945, explains the conditions of their offer:

The President of the College with the express approval of the Officers Committee has again tendered Elton Trueblood appointment as a professor of philosophy at Earlham with the rank and salary of a full professor and approximately one-half of a normal teaching load with a view to freeing Elton Trueblood to use the remainder of his time, with Earlham as a base, as a spiritual and intellectual leader in the Society of Friends. Elton Trueblood has taken this offer under advisement. The Committee recommends that the Board authorize the President to communicate once more with Elton Trueblood telling him that the Board as a whole has specifically approved the offer of the committee and that the members of the Board are both collectively and individually desirous that he should accept this offer and pledge him their support in the important task to which they are inviting him.

As Pauline Trueblood reflected on the move to Earlham, she offered her own reasons,

We wanted to contribute our full share toward making our world a Christian world and, at the same time, we wanted to give our children the best possible homelife for their best development. We didn't want to save the world and lose our children. We realized that position meant very little to us. We did not need the prestige of a university in order to achieve the ends we sought. We came to the conclusion that we wanted to be a part of a small community where our children could live wholesome, simple lives among people of their own kind. Our background is the Middle-Western Quaker one and we decided to make sure our children belonged to it as consciously as we do. We wanted to contribute something to that element in American life, making sure that it should not die out through our neglect. We found that our thoughts were matched by the desire of many Friends to have us back in the Quaker fold. We had come to want the fellowship of like-minded people and to feel the strength that comes from joint concern and joint action. And so we decided to come to Earlham College and settle down as permanently as it is possible for a family to do.

Elton has said, "A college is a pumping station on the pipeline of civilization." The major reason for choosing Earlham was his belief that a small college was a better "pumping station" and much more likely to produce the men and women needed to renew the spiritual condition of our civilization than a large university. This reason was expressed in written form and submitted to the *Reader's Digest* for publication ten years after his arrival on the Earlham campus. The title of the popular article was "Why I Chose a Small College," and it was printed in the September 1956 edition of the magazine. In part, it read as follows:

Some years ago, walking across the campus of a small college with its president, I noted that he called by name almost every student we met. "You must have a memory for names like Jim Farley," I said.

"It's not a memory feat," he replied. "At one time or another most of these students and I have sat down and talked over all sorts of things: their careers, their love affairs, their parents, what's worthwhile in life and what isn't. I know their names because I know *them*."

Now on the Earlham campus, calling by name so many students who in uninhibited, off-hour discussions I have come to know, I understand what he meant. And like many professors in similar schools I feel I have a stake in the future of each of these young people far greater than the information I may be able to impart in the classroom.

Whenever a friend of mine, a professor of geology in a small college, is offered a more lucrative job elsewhere, he has a stock reply: "I decided a long time ago to continue to invest what I've got where I am. Here I may help produce a few above-average geologists. But I know I can help produce more than a few above-average persons. That is what we are most in need of: in science, industry, government, professions, the home. That is why money couldn't lure me from this job."

It is this concern of the small college for the individual which led me, ten years ago, to decide to leave the security and prestige of a great university and to spend the rest of my life in a smaller school. Since many people believed then that the days of the small, independent, liberal-arts college were numbered, I was frequently obliged to explain why I was "throwing myself away."

Today I rarely hear such questions. More often I hear expressions of regret from faculty members in huge tax-supported institutions that they too have not, as one of them recently said, "made the break." For during the last ten years the small college, instead of dying, has undergone a remarkable rebirth. We know now what ten years ago had to be largely surmised: that the smallness and modesty of the small college, far from implying mediocrity, more often represent a pattern of life which produces a high order of excellence. . . .

What is there in the pattern of small-college life that produces such results and holds such promise for our future? From my experience at Earlham and my contacts with many colleges throughout the nation, these are the answers I have found.

First is the affectionate, abiding concern for the individual which I have mentioned.... The second fact which gives promise to the pattern of small-college life and works to the great advantage of the student is this: every student has the opportunity to find and engage in those activities which will develop his maximum capacities.... The third and to me most important advantage of the small college is its concern, rooted in religion, for character development. I know that in many large universities there are strong religious courses, active religious programs, and beautiful places of worship. But in institutions which number their students by the thousands the great majority are reached only occasionally by these influences. I chose a small college because I wanted to be part of a life where this character-developing influence is pervasive, where it is shared by all the students and promoted not only by professors of Bible and religion but quite as much by men in chemistry, biology and psychology....

It is the growing recognition of these advantages of the small institution and the promise it holds for our future which accounts for the fact that, instead of diminishing as some had predicted, small colleges are actually getting stronger every day.

The Truebloods left Palo Alto on Saturday morning, December 16, 1945. Two and a half months earlier the Japanese had surrendered (September 7, 1945), thus ending World War II. A new chapter in the history of the world was to begin, and a new chapter in the personal history of the Truebloods was also beginning. It was to be a seven-day trip across the country from California to Indiana. Although Elton's duties did not begin at Earlham until the fall of 1946, he had accepted an interim position to teach at Wabash College in Crawfordsville, Indiana for the winter term. In her diary, Pauline wrote about leaving Palo Alto: "On Friday numerous people came in the afternoon and at night to give us a fond farewell.... In the last weeks many people made it a point to express their affection and appreciation and good will. It will warm our hearts all the rest of our lives."

In the car for the trip east were Elton and Pauline, Sam and Elizabeth, and Rose Takano, the sister of Miyuki Takano, the housekeeper for the Truebloods while at Stanford. Rose was a student at Earlham, and the Truebloods were taking her back to school for the winter quarter. Pauline wrote,

> As we drove away from Palo Alto we indoctrinated the children in good behavior by suggesting a competition for the most polite behavior. We knew that seven days of constant riding in a car will not be wholly peaceful.... As we started off with Rose, Sam made the first score for behavior by saying he wanted Rose to have the most comfortable seat giving her the place by the window. Later, when manners were slipping, Elton suggested a prize to the winner.... Sam remarked, very politely, "I think Rose will be the winner," thereby making another score for him.

Whether or not Sam won the competition the diary does not say. We are assured, however, that the Truebloods made it to Indiana safely, and that it was cold compared to the weather in California. After leaving Rose at Earlham, they traveled on to Crawfordsville, moving into a house at 107 Vernon Court.

In the spring, Elton sailed for Europe under the care of the Friends Ambulance Unit, and Pauline and the children settled into their new home on the Earlham campus. In her diary, Pauline wrote about the decision to settle in the house at 228 College Avenue and how well it met their needs as a family.

Let me explain how I feel about this house. It is not as I would have felt in earlier years. I am born of a line of architects and builders and it is my nature, too, to want to build and perfect. I have dreamed of many houses. Last year I made plans for the house we would build after leaving California, wherever we might go. Then we came to Earlham and I walked around the campus thinking of my house. At the same time building became more and more restricted and materials impossible to get. If it had been easy to build I suppose I would have built although I must confess I could find no site which pleased me. I did not want just a house; I wanted an environment and a view. Realizing that I could not get the right setting for my house and that the building would be a continual compromise between what is possible now and my ideal, I began to think of alternative satisfactions which can be found in a home.

Some of the immediate considerations were that we had already had two years without a home of our own and our family had been divided and wandering long enough. [The Truebloods had sold their home on Delores Avenue in Palo Alto two years before their departure and had been renting a home on Lincoln Street.] If we could not build immediately it would put too much of a strain on us for temporary living is not possible too long. One must be able to see the end, if it is to be a good thing. We had chosen to take a sabbatical year of change and another year to make up our minds and carry out our decision. Another year with a house growing under our vision would have been a worthwhile year, but we could not see the possibility of building in less than two years. Our children needed a home, and a new house meant very little to them. Our older boys would soon be away. Martin was twenty-one and would be at home just one more precious year. If we waited another year for a home it would never seem so much his home.

Then, too, Tom and Esther Jones were planning to build a new President's house on the campus. That meant that the big, old, colonial house called the *Presidencia* would be vacant and available for us. We liked this old house from the first. It has character and space and it joins the campus. The location is the best one for us as we are easily available, and at the same time the children are within walking distance of their school without having to cross the National Road. We are on quiet College Avenue with good neighbors all along the street. We have beautiful, old trees about the house. We have a large lawn and garden. The house is wonderfully cool in summer with its thick, brick walls and eleven foot ceilings. The attic has a lookout with windows on all sides which keeps the attic ventilated and cools the second floor sleeping rooms.

The Trueblood home at 228 College Avenue, Richmond,
Indiana, later to become the first Yokefellow House

The house has space to waste and no one building a house in these days could
be so lavish with space. Our family with children of such various ages and a
writing father needs space. I need space too. It keeps me sane. All of these considerations made me more than satisfied to give up all thought of ever building here and to say "this is our home." I know I shall never regret it.

Elton went to Europe with the ambulance unit out of a desire to be
among the German people who were trying to recover from the devastating effects of the war. The most important contact to be made on this trip
was not to be found *in* Germany, but on the ship *to* Germany. There Elton
first met Landrum Bolling, later to become professor of political science,
and the president of Earlham, followed by a time as president of the Lilly
Endowment and of the Council of Foundations in Washington, D.C. Dr.
Bolling recently resigned from the directorship of the Ecumenical Institute for Theological Studies in Tantur, just south of Jerusalem, and now
lives in Washington, D.C. Here, on shipboard, Elton told of the exciting
new work at Earlham College. By the end of the journey, Landrum
Bolling, who was at the time a foreign news correspondent and affiliated
with Beloit College, was determined to visit Earlham. He did and later
accepted an invitation to join the faculty.

Soon after Elton arrived in Indiana, he made the acquaintance of Eli
Lilly, the man who had built a pharmaceutical empire in the city of Indianapolis and who was an avid reader of Elton's books. "Until February of
1946," Elton writes, "Eli Lilly was almost unknown to me. I knew something of the famous pharmaceutical firm which bears the name, but little
of the philanthropy and nothing of the man himself."[3] Elton and Eli
Lilly first met at the Columbia Club in Indianapolis, where Elton spoke at

a dinner sponsored by Wabash College. In his speech, he mentioned that he would be going to Germany in the summer under the direction of the Friends Ambulance Unit. At the conclusion of the dinner, Eli Lilly approached him and asked if he could send, via Elton, several thousands of dollars worth of vitamins to help the German people supplement their poor diets. Elton said that he would take as many bottles of the pills as his luggage could hold; thus began a friendship that lasted until Mr. Lilly's death in 1977.

One important consequence of this initial contact with Eli Lilly was the immediate connection with Earlham. "After beginning my teaching duties at Earlham in the autumn of 1946, the time came for visits to Eli Lilly, along with President Thomas E. Jones, seeking funds for the erection of new buildings."[4] Not only did Eli Lilly generously support the construction projects at Earlham, but through his generosity came gifts to initiate the Yokefellow movement, the building of the Yokefellow Institute, and the start-up funds for the Yokefellow Prison Ministry.

Through the years Elton has delighted in telling people about the "Lilly lunch." On occasion he would travel to Indianapolis for lunch with Mr. Lilly, and each time the pharmaceutical philanthropist would only order "pie à la mode." Since Mr. Lilly could not afford the calories in both a full lunch and the "pie à la mode," he made the deliberate choice to eat only what he enjoyed the most. In reflecting on the Earlham/Lilly connection, Elton has joked about what he believes should become "the golden text" for the school: "Consider the lilies . . ." (Matt. 6:28, KJV).

"As we began the autumn semester at Earlham in September of 1946," Elton writes, "there was a pervading sense of intellectual excitement. With the war over, nearly all of the men and women students knew *why* they had come to college. The fact that many had endured hardships during war years gave an added character to the entire academic undertaking. *In all of my years of teaching I have never, at any other time, known so many students who were receptive to learning.*"[5]

I have often heard Elton say that eighteen-year-olds should not go directly to college but should go to work for a few years first. Then, after being in the world for a time, with the burden of making a living, they can return to their educational pursuits, ready to be serious about the learning task. "College is too often wasted on young people," he has said. His experience as a teacher makes his argument convincing and especially his work with the more mature students at Earlham immediately following World War II.

In his first year at Earlham, Elton taught a new course called General Philosophy, which was based on the course that Alfred North Whitehead taught at Harvard. It became the most popular course offered, and in the first session 106 students enrolled. At that time Earlham had only 700 students, and so in this one course alone he had attracted one-seventh of the student body! Later he wrote,

I tried not only to make each lecture an exciting occasion, but also to arrange a personal contact with every member of the class. This was made possible by using the hour immediately following each lecture to take six or seven selected students to the coffee shop for further discussion. Each student wrote an essay each week. In order to secure an outside view, I invited a Yale philosopher to visit Earlham, at the end of the semester, as the examiner. I knew, of course, that this scholar was testing me as well as my students because we were, in fact, on the same side of the table.[6]

This idea of being examined by someone from "the outside" has been a part of Elton's thinking for years, especially in connection with his thoughts on the topic "The Redemption of the College." In an address before a National Colloquium on Christian Education in 1976 in Williamsburg, Virginia, he outlined a fourfold plan of action he believes is necessary to redeem the Christian College:

1. *We must accept our uniqueness.* "A Christian college is an institution of higher learning in which the Christian revelation provides the major premise for the entire intellectual operation. . . ."
2. *We must accept, unapologetically, the principle of requirement.* "Permissiveness is a disease which has infected contemporary education. . . ."
3. *We must be sincerely devoted to excellence.* "We are not in the entertainment business! We can maintain graduation by achievement and not merely by accumulation of credits in easy subjects. We can require study in both logic and ethics if we think that they are necessary for the accomplishment of our magnificent purpose. *We can employ outside examiners, thus avoiding the danger involved when the teacher is the sole judge of his own product. This may be difficult to introduce in the state institution, but the Christian college has the freedom to innovate for the sake of excellence."*
4. *We must reinstate the vision of wholeness.* "As Christian educators we affirm the necessity of a number of values, and believe that they can be nourished together, better than in separation."[7]

The vision for the Christian college that Elton outlined in 1976 was the vision he brought with him from Stanford when he settled at Earlham in 1946. In the forty-two-year span of his tenure at Earlham, the school has grown numerically to where the student enrollment for the fall of 1988 was 1,160 compared to 700 in 1946. The school has also matured academically, becoming an institution that is known nationally for its emphasis on community values and academic excellence. In October 1980, the famous journalist and radio personality Lowell Thomas wrote Elton and said, "When young people come to me for advice about where they might get the best college education, I invariably mention a few like Kenyon in Ohio, Carlton in Minnesota, and Earlham in Indiana." Few would have given Earlham such a strong recommendation in 1946, including Elton.

When the Truebloods left Stanford for Earlham, they departed regret-
ting the fact that they were unable to build a Meetinghouse for the
Quakers of the Palo Alto area. With the death of Mrs. Herbert Hoover, the
dream of a Meetinghouse died as well, since the project was dependent
upon her financial and moral support. Although a Meetinghouse was not
essential for the Stanford campus, since the university already had a beautiful chapel to serve as the spiritual hub of the school, it would have been
nice for the Quakers. Earlham, however, had *no* Meetinghouse for use as
a spiritual hub, and this fact did not escape Elton and Pauline.

Almost immediately upon arrival at Earlham, the dream of a Meetinghouse on the campus occupied a place in the hearts of the Truebloods.
"As soon as I began my Earlham residence, in the late summer of 1946,"
writes Elton, "I began to discuss with President Thomas E. Jones and others the prospect of a building devoted to the encouragement of the spiritual life."[8] Actually, the dream of a Meetinghouse on the campus had
begun with Joseph John Gurney, the famous English Quaker and spiritual
founder of Earlham. A sum of money had been given to Earlham from the
Gurney estate, for the purpose of building a Meetinghouse. Due to the
heavy financial burdens in other areas of college life, however, this money
was diverted for other things. Now, a century later, Elton was reviving
the dream.

In 1949, a number of things came together to make the idea of a
Meetinghouse take on life. First of all, a letter from Mrs. Arthur Edding-
ton of the Wymondham Friends Meeting in England told of the need to
disperse the furnishings from their Meetinghouse, which was being laid
down (closed). She offered to Elton some of the 250-year-old benches and
other furnishings that could be used in a new Meetinghouse at Earlham.
This was a special gift to Earlham because the Wymondham Meetinghouse located near Norwich, England, had been attended by Joseph John
Gurney.

Second, Elton was contacted about a gift of cherry wood offered by a
local Richmond resident, Rose Dougan. Ms. Dougan had had a cherry
tree cut down and wanted to give the wood to Earlham. Elton graciously
accepted the gift and gave it to a local craftsman for the building of a large
cherry conference and seminar table. Elton already envisioned it being
used in the new Meetinghouse.

Shortly thereafter, Elton traveled to Memphis, Tennessee, to talk to
Charles B. Stout about the Meetinghouse dream. Eventually the Stout
family donated $110,000 toward construction, and the dream was soon to
become a reality. A Meetinghouse cabinet was formed, and an architect
was secured.

Under the skilled direction of Earl Prignitz, Friends minister and carpenter, the Earlham community was organized into groups of volunteers,
with even Elton and President Tom Jones working on construction. On
April 27, 1952, the Stout Meetinghouse was dedicated, and Earlham Col-

lege finally had an official center for the purpose of worship and religious education, which could serve as a "spiritual hub" for the entire campus.

THE IDEA OF A REDEMPTIVE FELLOWSHIP

The redemptive society we need is an order within the church universal, devoted to the recovery and fulfillment of radical Christianity.

On a morning in June 1987, Elton entered the office of Yokefellows International with a bold pronouncement. "The greatest period in the history of my thought occurred exactly forty years ago this month. Without the burst of intellectual energy and insight which occurred at that time, it is doubtful that we would be sitting today in the office of an organization called Yokefellows International." Curious to discover what had occurred forty years ago, I asked him to share what was so special about that time.

For sixteen days in June 1947, Elton wrote in an office in Carpenter Hall on the Earlham campus, producing a book to be titled *Alternative to Futility*. His thoughts concerning the idea of a redemptive fellowship had a start in the last chapter of *The Predicament of Modern Man*. To fully grasp the revolutionary idea he was proposing, however, an entire volume was needed. In June 1947, what had been simmering for three years was finally brought to a boil.

Alternative to Futility was a response to the need to write more than *criticism* of our situation as outlined in *The Predicament*. It was Elton's attempt to formulate an understandable *solution*. Recognizing the importance of diagnosis, he stated, "Our main emphasis *now* must be placed on prescription and cure. We have discarded the blasphemy of optimism; we are wholly humble about our condition; but there must be some path of recovery and renewal."[9]

In search of the recovery and renewal of human purpose that was so desperately needed in these early years after World War II, Elton Trueblood turned to the example of Jesus Christ and his followers:

Once there were a few unlettered men in an obscure province, and their movement was obviously a failure; for their Leader had been executed! Yet something so remarkable happened that, within a generation, these men and others like them were beginning to make a difference in the entire Hellenic-Roman world. They brought to a civilization suffering from a sense of futility a genuine lift and, finally, when the Roman power fell into decay, they provided the main structure of faith upon which civilization could be rebuilt.

If we ask how this most remarkable of the miracles of history was performed, we are amazed at the simplicity of the method. The world needed a saving faith and the formula was that such a faith comes by a particular kind of fellowship. Jesus was deeply concerned for the continuation of his redemptive work after the close of his earthly existence, and his chosen method was *the formation of a redemptive society*."[10]

The fellowship Elton envisioned was different from the average church. Although he acknowledged that the church began as a redemptive fellowship, in the span of two thousand years it had evolved into something quite different. It had gained respectability! What he sought to clarify was just how such a fellowship "fit" into the mission of the church. "The essential experiment we need to make in our day," he wrote, "is an experiment in radical Christianity. *The redemptive society we need is an order within the Church Universal, devoted to the recovery and fulfillment of radical Christianity.*"[11]

And what are the marks of such a fellowship? Elton suggested the necessity of five: *commitment, witness, fellowship, vocation,* and *discipline*. His definition of *commitment* embodied not mere intellectual acceptance of Jesus as the Christ but acceptance by a full act of the will. It is the "acted out" belief that God really is, and that he is like Jesus Christ. "Here, then, is the first plank in our platform. We seek groups of genuinely committed men and women . . . who are willing to follow one major clue wherever it may lead."[12]

The second mark is *witness*. Taking his understanding of witness from the Sermon on the Mount, Elton described how the redemptive fellowship is to be the "salt of the earth" and "Light of the world." He took to task the number of persons who claim the name Christian, yet who are unwilling to "stick their necks out" and instead keep their light "under a bushel."

Third, the redemptive fellowship involves a deeper understanding of the term *koinonia* than is generally understood or practiced in the contemporary church. Returning to Scripture, for example, Elton told about how "the heart of the idea of membership as experienced by the early Christian fellowship . . . was that of being members one of another. They, like other groups in which there has been a serious attempt to practice radical Christianity, found that membership in the Body of Christ causes men and women to temper their own wishes by the wishes and needs of their fellow members."[13] As Elton surveyed the contemporary church scene and balanced his findings with the great need for a fellowship of concerned people who truly love one another, he found the church lacking.

Fourth, if the fellowship that Elton envisioned is to be truly redemptive, it must take seriously the idea of *vocation*. Here he distinguished between what is a *profession* and what is a *vocation*. "This is a magnificent idea," he wrote.

It means that all true members must be fountains, not cisterns. It means that each member must be willing to think of himself as engaged in the ministry, by a divine imperative . . . we must think of all recruits as entering a new estate, beyond clergy and beyond laity. In the new order there are no clergymen and no laymen, but all are engaged in the same divine vocation, which means putting the claims of the Kingdom of God first, no matter what profession one may follow. *The formula is that vocation has priority over profession.*[14]

Elton Trueblood has given the major part of his life's thinking to the ideas that can be labeled under the broad heading "church renewal." In *Alternative to Futility*, he expanded his belief about the ministry of every Christian, which he began to formulate in his chapter "The Abolition of the Laity" in *The Essence of Spiritual Religion*. If you claim the name *Christian*, he asserted, you must also be a "minister." For that time, this was a radically new understanding. Though Martin Luther had stressed "the priesthood of all believers," and many others, including Henry Hodgkin had written about *Lay Religion*, Elton was able to write about this central truth of the Christian faith in a fresh way that captured the attention of church leaders. Coming from a Quaker background, which already stressed the belief that all are ministers, he was able to speak and write with a sense of authenticity.

The fifth criterion for membership in the redemptive fellowship is the acceptance of *discipline*. This is another of Elton's central themes throughout his ministry. As he analyzed the distinctions of many "faithful and courageous minorities," such as the Mormons, the Seventh-Day Adventists, or the local "Inter-Varsity Fellowship," he mentioned that there is one factor that all have in common: *the acceptance of discipline*. Although many minority movements within the religious circle make mistakes in their forms of dogmatism, they do unite around a sturdy, positive force, namely *discipline*. What Elton became painfully aware of was the lack of discipline in matters of faith within Protestantism and how this lack of discipline would lead to a lack of commitment. He suggested a "minimum" discipline as a starting point for any group of concerned people who would like to begin the redemptive task:

1. *Worship.* Regular and unargued sharing in the public worship of God is expected of all who would truly be members of a redemptive society. The minimum attendance is once a week, but may well be more.

2. *Solitude.* Each person who seeks to proceed from nominal to real membership in the church of Jesus Christ must agree to spend some part of each day alone, in private prayer or other devotional exercises. These may include the devout reading of classic prayers, the use of devotional literature, silent meditation, and the reading of the Holy Scriptures. In the reading of the Scriptures it is strongly advised that a definite plan be followed and that the practice of rereading the same passage for many consecutive days be tried, until the deeper meanings become plain. Most Bible reading is too quickly accomplished. Frequently it will be desirable for a genuine fellowship group to decide together on an order of reading and expect its members to follow this order. Such acceptance of group guidance is often a valuable antidote to our conventional individualism.

3. *Silence.* Each person who wishes to be creatively Christian must learn the discipline of silence. He must learn to get his body still, and he must learn to get his mind still. Apart from this the deeper messages of the still small voice will not be heard. In countless churches, services of worship begin with the words, "The Lord is in His holy temple; let all the earth keep silence before Him," and then, instead of obeying these sacred words, the congregation immediately does something

noisy. We say, "Be still and know," and then proceed to talk. It is not likely that we can cultivate the art of listening apart from silence. One danger is that we tend to become restless and make the silence brief. It is important to recognize that "a moment of silence" is almost worthless. Long experience indicates that an hour is required for the emergence of the best which this method makes possible.

4. *Humanity*. The concerned Christian must be identified with the sufferings of his fellow men and active in the lifting of burdens wherever found. The rule is that every day must include some outgoing activity, that is not for ourselves alone. It is easy to make this sound sentimental, but it need not be. [John] Woolman's concern for the relief of oppression was not sentimental and ours need not be. This service must go beyond conventional philanthropy to various deeds of social action, in many of which each person can act alone. The extension of real friendship to a representative of another race, the lending of a hand to an overworked young mother—these are not grand or colorful acts, but they are the stuff of which Christian behavior is made. One of the chief concrete ways in which social concern can be expressed daily is in care for the reputations of others. This involves refusal to participate in slander and malicious gossip, which are such a temptation to otherwise good people. One of the most disciplined of another generation put it memorably when he said, "O how good it is, and how it tendeth to peace, to be silent about other men, and not to believe at random all that is said, nor eagerly to report what we have heard."

5. *Austerity*. The tradition for simple living is more than a tradition. It has a double justification in that the rejection of luxury serves, on the one hand, to release the mind from worldly interests, and, on the other hand, to release income for the service of God and man. Many poor groups of concerned Christians are able to give foreign or domestic relief in amounts which shame more wealthy congregations, largely because they live in such simplicity that they do not require all of their earnings for their private and family use. *Austerity and charity go together*. The reason why the Seventh-Day Adventists can give regularly a tenth of their incomes and thus provide phenomenal amounts for missionary work is not that Adventists are rich, for they are not, but rather that they discipline themselves by frugal living. It is not required of us that we reinstitute a plain garb or return to horses and buggies, but it is required of us that we learn to regulate our personal finances in such a way that planned and intelligent giving is possible. The present practice, in many churches, of placing the gathered offering on the communion table is not just a tricky device. It touches the reality of the situation. All true religion is concerned with money, because money makes a difference in human life.[15]

Elton summarizes his vision for a new world in the last paragraph of *Alternative to Futility*:

We need not despise any effort, no matter how secular, which aims at world reconstruction, but we are very sure concerning what the primary and central need is. We need a new sense of life's meaning to end our mood of futility, and this comes only by a saving faith. The faith, in turn, is nurtured by a special kind of fellowship in which Christ himself is the central member. It is our holy privilege to help to nourish such fellowships. If enough persons do the same, we shall have a new world.[16]

The message of hope, and the practical outline Elton spelled out in *Alternative to Futility*, captured the mind and hearts of great blocks of people within Christianity. Here was the antidote for which so many had been searching since *The Predicament* was written three years earlier. It was an immediate best-seller, and continued to help build the reputation of a man who was becoming known as one of the most articulate speakers on the condition of contemporary society in the nation. Not only could he analyze the problems, but by studying and interpreting the history of the Christian movement, he was now able to clarify a possible solution. He was, himself, an encouraging sign of hope in a world of despair.

Upon its release, *Alternative to Futility* found a particularly attentive audience in a group of people who were seeking to form a new kind of church. Speaking at Massanetta Springs, Virginia, Elton noticed a small group of people near the front of the meeting hall, each clutching a copy of *Alternative to Futility*. At the conclusion of his message, the seven people all came up to him and told him that they were the Church of the Saviour, which was being organized in Washington, D.C. Principal among them was Gordon Cosby, the pastor. This was the beginning of a most important relationship for both Elton and the Church of the Saviour, since the committed fellowship that Gordon Cosby was beginning provided Elton a powerful example of a model of what the church could be, and Elton was influential in helping the church become known as a center for creative ministry. Later, Elton wrote the foreword to Elizabeth O'Connor's story of the Church of the Saviour in a book entitled *Call to Commitment*.

COMMON VENTURES AND MAJOR PLANS

Make no small plans. They have no power to move the hearts of men.

At 10:00 A.M., Friday, January 30, 1948, Pauline Trueblood noted in her diary: "Off for Texas!" The Trueblood family had made arrangements to stay for one and a half months in the Heart of the Hills Inn near Kerrville, Texas. This would give them a more moderate climate than Indiana in the winter and would provide Elton uninterrupted time to study and write.

The trip from Indiana to Texas turned out to be an adventure in itself. The Truebloods had hoped to be free of the ice and snow as they drove south, but, instead, it became more treacherous. "As we proceeded we learned that all trucks had been called off the highway," wrote Pauline. "Next we learned that the roads into Tennessee were closed. This was quite upsetting to our theory that we would go directly south below the snow line and then turn west. The farther west we went the worse the roads became. Finally we learned we were heading into the worst winter weather in the memory of southern people. We *would* get in on the unusual."

They finally made it to Texas safely and quickly became settled in their new quarters. The pattern that Elton developed was to write all day and then in the evening he would share what he had written with all who cared to hear while seated around the big fireplace in the main room of the inn. It was a most effective way to write, since one can quickly judge by expressions and questions whether what has been written is clear and understandable to the general public.

Elton's focus in his writing was centered in what he called the four "common ventures of life"— *marriage, birth, work, death*. Although he originally gave these major chapters in his book as the first Willson Lectures at Southwestern University in Georgetown, Texas, and was thus able to express them at their beginning through the "spoken word," he discovered that by sharing them to a group as the "written word," he was able to "fine tune" them even more.

Elton's main concern in writing *The Common Ventures of Life* is succinctly stated in the last paragraph of his opening chapter, entitled "The Recovery of Wholeness."

The differences in human life depend, for the most part, not on what men *do*, but upon the meaning and purpose of their acts. All are *born*, all *die*, all *love their loved ones*, nearly all *marry* and nearly all *work*, but the *significance* of these acts may vary enormously. The same physical act may be in one situation vulgar and in another holy. The same work may be elevating or degrading. The major act is not, "What act do I perform?" but, "In what frame do I put it?" Wisdom about life consists in taking the inevitable ventures which are the very stuff of common existence, and glorifying them.[17]

On February 21, Pauline recorded in her diary that "Elton finished his book on marriage, birth, work and death." He was without a title for this volume for some time after completing the initial writing. Elton has struggled with titles throughout his writing career, and he will be the first to say that they never came easy. The search for a title for this work was especially frustrating.

In the spring of this year following the Trueblood's return to Indiana, their son Arnold became seriously ill. He was diagnosed with acute pneumonia and was admitted to the Christ Hospital of Cincinnati, Ohio, a one and a half hour drive from Richmond. Each day his health would continue to decline, and the doctors were unable to reverse his worsening condition. At the near desperate point, Elton and Pauline received a call from William B. Bell, then president of the American Cyanamic Company, in New York, who had heard about the condition of their son. He told them about a new antibiotic that had just been developed that had had positive results in testing against the virus attacking Arnold. Anxious for any sign of hope, Elton told Mr. Bell to send the new product immediately. The doctor in Cincinnati administered the new drug, and Arnold responded positively. Soon he was fully recovered, thanks to a new medicine later named aureomycin.

During one of the many trips to Cincinnati from Richmond in the spring of 1948, Elton finally fastened on a title for his new book. He had been struggling to find the right words to describe what *marriage, birth, work,* and *death* actually were in the human situation. At a small restaurant in Millville, Ohio, he hit upon the combination of words for which he had been searching. What suddenly occurred to him, as he sipped on a cola, was that these were *common ventures* of humanity. Thus the title became fixed, and he could now call his publisher with the news.

The summer of 1948 was again given to travel across the Atlantic. Elton delivered the Robert Barclay Tercentenary Lecture at Edinburgh, Scotland, as a part of the London Yearly Meeting of Friends. Since 1939, he had been researching the life and thought of Barclay, and although he had not yet had time to produce a major volume on his favorite Quaker subject, he was able to share, in lecture form, what he had discovered about this most important of Quaker theologians. Focusing his attention in this particular lecture on Barclay's thought, Elton sought to make the point that early Friends did not look upon themselves as one denomination among others, and they certainly did not consider themselves Protestant or as a part of Protestantism. He developed this idea by showing how Robert Barclay, because of his "particular training," was able to clarify this point. "By education he was as well acquainted with Catholic as well as with Protestant doctrine, and it is essential to an understanding of his career to realize that he reacted *equally* against *both*." Elton continued, "He considered it his vocation to carry on a running fight against both sides in the Reformation dispute *and to lead Christian men into a new day in which both Catholicism and Protestantism would be superseded*."[18]

Elton considered the work of Robert Barclay essential in helping the people called Quakers survive as a religious movement. The concluding paragraph of this important lecture stated his reasons.

The vocation of Barclay was important, not only in his own life, but in the developing Society of Friends. It was his appeal to the learned world and not some treatise for sectarian consumption that came to be looked upon as the best exposition of what Quakers believed. This had the effect of saving Quakerism from many abuses and uncritical assumptions. Because he was writing for the thoughtful people of the world, many of whom were savagely critical, Barclay had to be extremely judicious in his statements. This led to balanced judgments as against fanatical *clich'es*. This factor, more than most others, served to help Quakerism within the main stream of Christian history and Christian thought, and helped to resist the temptation to become a form of esoteric mysticism, with a neglect of historical Christianity. Eventually Quakerism *did* become a sect, in spite of Barclay's efforts to the contrary, but because of his central thought, Friends have ever since been restive under the sectarian status and the basis of a new conception has been provided for later generations.[19]

After delivering this Tercentenary Lecture, Elton traveled to the Isle of Iona to see the important reconstruction and renewal work that was being conducted by Lord George MacLeod. It was here, in 1948, that Elton first met Lord MacLeod. They began a friendship that was very important to the founding of the subsequent Yokefellow movement. Elton has said, "If it were not for Iona, I doubt there would have been a Yokefellow movement." Here again was another important piece to the developing renewal concern that Elton translated into the Yokefellow work.

"Long before I first saw Iona," Elton has written, "I was aware of its significance in Christian history. I was aware that the beautiful island of the Inner Hebrides, off the west coast of Scotland, represented an important step in the penetration of North Britain by the gospel of Christ. I admired Saint Columba (521–597) and felt sure that his method of evangelism could be given contemporary application, fourteen hundred years later. I naturally wanted to see, with my own eyes, where the famous saint landed in an open boat and where the Cathedral of the Isles had been reconstructed in the twentieth century. I wanted to share in the powerful fellowship which had been started in our time by George MacLeod, and to adopt, if I could, some of the spiritual discipline for which he is justly famous."[20]

Iona represented for Elton the model of a base/field concept of ministry from which Christian missionaries penetrated the world with the gospel of Jesus Christ and then returned to "the base" for renewal and revitalization. He was already thinking about the tremendous value of such a concept in America, where retreat homes could be built in which Christians could gather for mutual sharing and spiritual enrichment and from which they could go into the world to witness. Although the church was fulfilling some of this need, Elton believed that a more intense kind of spiritual revitalization was needed and that for contemporary Christians the retreat house idea was the answer. Also, the retreat house would break down the denominational barriers that keep Christians separated. For Elton, strength comes from cross-fertilization.

The similar interests and concerns for Christian ministry of Elton Trueblood and Lord George MacLeod were a binding force. Each represented similar ministries in their respective homelands. The concern for the "ministry of common life" was the most important common denominator that each articulated with powerful enthusiasm.

Following the spiritually invigorating experience of Iona, Elton traveled to Amsterdam to participate in the formation of the World Council of Churches. Since he had been named chair of the Friends World Committee in the summer of 1947, he acted as the official representative for the Society of Friends. Each morning this founding group would worship after the manner of one of the religious groups represented at the conference. Elton was in charge of one of these times and led those gathered in an experience of worship in the tradition of Friends. All present were moved by the Quaker pattern and inspired by the idea of waiting in silence in a spirit of holy expectancy. For many, it was the first time they had ever experienced the simple, Quaker style of worship.

It was in Amsterdam that Elton became acquainted with John and Don Baillie, the famous brothers from the University of Edinburgh. Elton had long admired the scholarly work of both brothers. It was John Baillie's little volume entitled *A Diary of Private Prayer*, published one year following their initial meeting, that has become such an important part of the Trueblood library. In John Baillie, like Rendel Harris before, Elton discovered another model of a man who combined the "clear head" with the "warm heart," and he was immediately attracted to him.

Elton returned home from Europe to encounter another busy fall on the Earlham campus. The year 1948 had been a hectic one, with the assumption of the duties that accompany chairing the Friends World Committee, the writing of *The Common Ventures of Life*, the difficult struggle of having a child critically ill in a hospital seventy miles from home, and the joy of seeing that child revive again. In addition, there was the delivery of the Robert Barclay Tercentenary Lecture at London Yearly Meeting of Friends in Edinburgh, Scotland, and the subsequent trip to the Isle of Iona, the meeting at Amsterdam for the founding of the World Council of Churches, as well as the continuous speaking engagements and teaching responsibilities at Earlham. It was, indeed, a full year.

In November of that year, Elton and Pauline traveled to Flint, Michigan, for an engagement at the Central Methodist Church. As they traveled north from Indianapolis, Elton told Pauline about a saying he had seen over the mantle of a fireplace in a home in England. It read, "Make no small plans. They have no power to move the hearts of men." "These words express the way in which Elton has lived his life," reflected Pauline. When they had returned home from their weekend in Michigan, they put these words on a board, and placed them behind the fireplace of their College Avenue home. It would become the Trueblood family motto.

THE LIFE WE PRIZE

The life we claim to follow, though we have never wholly done so, and which we are about to have, though we have never wholly had it.

Throughout 1949, Elton continued to speak around the country and teach his courses at Earlham. He also began to gather information for a new and major literary project, which he would write in the autumn of 1950 in a Quaker guest house near Oxford, England. Two major events in the life and thought of Elton Trueblood preceded the writing of this book.

In May 1949, Elton traveled from Richmond to Cleveland, Ohio, where he was to speak at the First Baptist Church. He has written,

I traveled by Pullman train from Dayton so as to have a good night's rest and if possible to be alert on Sunday morning. After completing my sleep and a quiet breakfast in the Terminal Building, I boarded the Rapid Transit for Cleveland Heights.

Already under the influence of Frank Laubach, I had begun the practice of reading every morning from the New Testament, whatever my location might be.
Instead of skipping about in the Scripture, I had adopted the discipline of going
straight through a book, reading slowly about eleven verses a day if the topic
admitted of such a division, and noting, in the margin, the place and date of
reading. . . .

My reading that morning was Matthew 11:25-30. Though I had of course read
the passage on many former occasions, it struck me with unique force. It was
almost as if I had never before read the words "Take my yoke upon you." Suddenly,
I saw that this is Christ's clearest call to commitment. I realized that the yoke meta-
phor involves what we most require if the vitality of the Christian faith is to be
recovered. . . . Within a minute or so, as an entire complex of thinking came
together, I had a different sermon. . . . The words which came to me on the train
that morning I preached within the hour, recognizing that I was participating in
a new development.[21]

This initial insight eventually led to the placement of Elton Trueblood's
ideas concerning the redemptive society under the umbrella called the
Yokefellow movement. It occurred nine months after his first visit to the
Isle of Iona and the meeting of Lord George MacLeod.

Another very important experience in the life and thought of Elton
Trueblood occurred January 1, 1950, in Rock Island, Illinois. It was here,
at a conference sponsored by the Inter-Seminary movement, that he first
heard Anglican Bishop Stephen Neill speak on the text from Eph. 4:11-12:
"And his gifts were that some should be apostles, some prophets, some
evangelists, some pastors and teachers to equip the saints, for the work of
ministry, for building up the body of Christ. . . ."

In the seeds planted from Bishop Neill's speech, Elton began to
develop the idea of "the equipping ministry" and to make the case for
training pastors as equippers of those involved in the ministry of common life, rather than the pastors having to carry the full ministerial burden alone. This initial acquaintance with the thinking of Bishop Neill led
to subsequent meetings in his home in Nairobi, Kenya, and at Wycliffe
College, Oxford University, as well as a visit from Bishop Neill to this
country for a seminar in the guest quarters of the Trueblood's summer
home at Lake Paupac, Pennsylvania.

Elton Trueblood was in his fiftieth year when he began to write *The Life
We Prize.* He wrote it in the autumn of 1950 in Charney Manor, a Quaker
guest house just fourteen miles from Oxford, England. This delightful
house is said to be the oldest inhabited house in England, having endured
for more than seven hundred years. *The Life We Prize* was to become his
only book on moral philosophy and would produce one of his most
famous aphorisms: "A man has made at least a start on discovering the
meaning of human life when he plants shade trees under which he knows
full well he will never sit."

As with the previous Trueblood books, there was the struggle to find

The Trueblood family, 1954

the correct title. While speaking at the Hampton Institute in Virginia, the president of that institution, President Wright, jokingly suggested that Elton might call it "The Life We Claim to Follow, Though We Have Never Wholly Done So, And Which We Are About to Have, Though We Have Never Wholly Had It." They both agreed that it was a bit long! But how to capture the essence of the suggestion? It became *The Life We Prize*.

Following this major work on moral philosophy, Elton produced a book on the ministry of common life, entitled *Your Other Vocation*. This was released in 1952 and became a classic in the genre of literature concerned with the ministry of the laity. Here he was able to build on what he began in *The Essence of Spiritual Religion* in the chapter "The Abolition of the Laity" and continued in the last chapter of *The Predicament of Modern Man* and *The Alternative to Futility*.

In 1953, Elton and Pauline wrote a little volume entitled *The Recovery of Family Life*. As can be witnessed by reading her well-written journals and diaries, Pauline was an excellent writer in her own right. This combined effort focused on five areas: "The Withering Away of the Family," "The Idea of the Family," "The Vocation of Married Women," "Responsible Fatherhood," and "The Sources of Family Strength." It was received by the reading public with critical acclaim and was the Religious Book Club Selection for November 1953.

A big event in the lives of the Truebloods and the Earlham community in the spring of 1953 was a conference, "The Ministry of Laywomen," held April 18–19. The major speaker for the conference was Catherine Marshall, who had just written the best-selling book *A Man Called Peter*. The conference was the beginning of a close relationship between the Truebloods and Mrs. Marshall, who would afterwards confide in Pauline about various personal matters.

In a letter dated September 14, 1953, Mrs. Marshall wrote about her upcoming trip to Hollywood and her sense of anxiety as she contem-plated the task of working on the screenplay of *A Man Called Peter*. Her stated hope was that it would glorify God. At the time of its release, *A Man Called Peter* became an immediate box office hit, and was responsible for changing the lives of thousands.

A pattern of ministry that Elton established with his move to Earlham was to teach in the fall, lecture around the country in the winter and spring, and write in the summer. A good example of the lecturing "around the country" portion is seen in the three months of February through April 1954.

January	30–31	Huntington, WV
February	1	Springfield, OH
	3	Connersville, IN
	4	Springfield, IL
	5	Dayton, OH
	6	Chattanooga, TN
	7–11	Rock Hill, SC
	13–18	Presbyterian Church near University of Florida, Gainesville, FL
	21	Bristol, VA
	22	King's College, Raleigh, NC
	23	Bartlesville, OK
	26	Memphis, TN
	27–28	Memphis and Oxford, MS
March	1–4	University of Mississippi, Oxford, MS
	9–11	Fayetteville, AR
	14–17	Mobile, AL
	18	Staunton, VA
	19–20	University of North Carolina, Chapel Hill, NC
	21	Duke University, Durham, NC
	22	Martinsburg, VA
	23	Danville, VA
	24	Haddonfield, NJ
	27	Buck Hill Falls, PA
April	4	Collins, NY
	5	Buffalo, NY
	6	Toronto, Ontario
	7	Grand Rapids, MI
	8	Mt. Vernon, NY
	9	Oak Park, IL
	10–11	Laymen's Conference, Earlham College
	15	Goshen, IN
	16	Urbana, IL
	20–21	Louisville, KY

23   Spiceland, IN
24   Westfield, NJ
26   Pendle Hill, PA
27   New Jersey College for Women,
     New Brunswick, NJ
28   Englewood, NJ
29   Columbia University, New York, NY
30   Montclair, NJ

What the reader may be surprised to learn is that this type of speaking schedule was fairly typical for Elton, even to age eighty-five.

By the winter of 1953–1954, the Truebloods were feeling somewhat restless about their situation at Earlham. In many ways they had outgrown the little midwestern college, but in other ways it provided just the right atmosphere and base for their continued writing, speaking, and teaching. It was fast becoming a nationally known institution for its quality of life and academic excellence, but still they felt questions needed to be raised about the future. Pauline had spoken to President Tom Jones about her restlessness, and he responded by drawing up a plan for Elton and Pauline's ministry that would build "solidly on [their] devotion and effort in the last eight years." He wrote Pauline on January 19, 1954: "The outreach and continuity of your service would be incomparably greater, in my mind, according to this plan than if you break ties by going to New York or some other place and begin with no such foundation back of you."

Less than two months later the announcement was made that Elton had accepted the position of chief religious information officer for the United States Information Agency. Although the Truebloods had decided to leave Earlham for this public service, it was not considered a resignation, only a "leave of absence." Thus, a compromise was worked out. It was good for the Truebloods to be away from Earlham for awhile, and it was good for Earlham to have one of their own in such a strategic position in Washington. In April 1954, the Truebloods took up residence in the nation's capital.

1954–1956

THE U.S. INFORMATION AGENCY

It is a matter of undergirding our whole set of convictions, the fundamental beliefs and values which we share with the missions of men and women in the free world.

Elton Trueblood was contacted about becoming the chief of religious policy for the U.S. Information Agency in January 1954. On March 9, the Richmond, Indiana, paper reported the decision to accept the position: "Dr. Trueblood To Start Full-Time Federal Religious Duties in April."

> Formal announcement was made over the weekend in Washington of the appointment of Dr. D. Elton Trueblood to the newly created post of Chief of Religious Policy for the U.S. Information Agency (USIA) which conducts overseas broadcasts and other programs.
>
> Dr. Trueblood was sworn into office in ceremonies Saturday morning at the USIA headquarters on Pennsylvania Avenue in Washington. The USIA formerly was the "Voice of America."
>
> He remained in Washington until Saturday afternoon when he left by plane for Fayetteville, Arkansas, where he is scheduled to begin a series of lectures at the University of Arkansas on March 9.
>
> The appointment was for an indefinite period, during which Dr. Trueblood will be on leave of absence from Earlham College, where he is professor of philosophy and religion....
>
> Theodore C. Streibert, director of the agency, said, "Dr. Trueblood's great talents and outstanding reputation as a teacher, author, administrator and speaker will be a valuable asset to our information program abroad...."

The March 15, 1954, issue of *Time* magazine referred to Elton as a "truth salesman" who would provide the "three P's" for the nation: a philosophy, a program, and a passion. They wrote that Elton Trueblood would be in charge of "one of the busiest, farthest-flung and best-known religious enterprises in the world." When asked to comment for *Time* on the new position, Elton said, "It's very exciting. The job seems to take in everything I've ever known and learned. It's really an enlargement under government auspices of what I've already been doing." *Time* expanded on what Elton had been doing:

What he has been doing is to conduct one of the most effective ministries to laymen, churched and unchurched, in the U.S. In 1944 Iowa-born Dr. Trueblood, then chaplain and professor of philosophy and religion at Stanford University, decided to begin writing and working for all literate people instead of merely other writers and scholars. He wrote a successful book called *The Predicament of Modern Man.* But he was still unsatisfied. "We knew what the Nazis believed," he says. "All we had to do was read *Mein Kampf.* We knew what the Russians believed; we could read Lenin and Stalin. But where was the Western way stated? Only in snippets, here and there."

Trueblood went to England, "to get a better perspective on the West," wrote *The Life We Prize,* which he considers the most important of his 13 books. Since 1946 he has been professor of philosophy at Quaker-run Earlham College in Indiana and a leading light in the Society of Friends.

"There is more good life to the square inch here than any place else in the world," says Trueblood. But "we need the Three P's the Communists have: a philosophy, a program and a passion.... We must learn to wage peace as boldly as we wage war.... We are noted for salesmanship but we sell the wrong things.... We have kept silent about our spiritual possessions, which really have the power to kindle human minds."

In midlife, Elton had made a major career move. From professor in a small, midwestern school to a department head of a major governmental agency in Washington, D.C., was no minor jump. In the words of his wife, Pauline, "I have been alive for forty-six years and I have learned how to live in the midst of change. Our family has been noted for making decisions for the future and then carrying them out very soon afterward. Such living has great rewards and it develops character...."

Not all were pleased with Elton's appointment. A right-wing newspaper from Texas labeled Elton a liberal with Communist sympathies. It was a different time, for sure, when the term *Communist* was bantered about quite freely. I'm sure that Elton found such criticism amusing, since he has often said. "If you are attacked on the extreme right and the extreme left, then you know that you must be doing all right!"

The work in Washington was exciting, especially since this was a new appointment for the USIA, following on the executive decision that President Eisenhower had made to speak out more forcefully about the nation's moral and spiritual heritage. As one source reported, Elton "was determined to demonstrate to the world the strength of the spiritual ideals and values that the United States had to offer and the great tradition of its spiritual heritage. With the support of President Dwight Eisenhower, he developed an exhibition, 'The Church of America,' showing by picture and word the richness and vitality of America's spiritual life." Elton's appointment reflected "much more than a matter of an occasional religious broadcast or news story." Theodore Streibert [Director of the USIA] said, "It is a matter of undergirding our whole set of convictions, the fundamental beliefs and values which we share with the missions of men and women in the free world."

To coincide with his new work at the USIA, and to share in written form much of what was being broadcast over the Voice of America, Elton wrote a book entitled *Declaration of Freedom*. Reflecting on his purpose for writing it, he said,

We have in the Western World the most thrilling set of ideas the world has ever known, if only we were awake enough to see it and brave enough to demonstrate it in every aspect of our daily life.

Instead, we have become a little apologetic, and let the Communists take the offensive in attempting to convince the world they are the idealists and we are the materialists. . . . It is we who have the permanent revolution, and the Biblical concept of the Supreme value of the individual, his rights, freedoms and responsibilities, as imperfectly but nevertheless partly evolved by the West, its foundation.[1]

Milton S. Eisenhower, the President's brother and then president of Pennsylvania State University, wrote,

The great struggle of our time turns on moral issues. In his *Declaration of Freedom*, Dr. Trueblood has brought those issues into sharp focus. His brilliant analysis of today's ideological conflict and his constructive approach to the basic problem of our time should be required reading for all thoughtful citizens. Dr. Trueblood has made an important contribution to international understanding.

Ralph McGill, editor of the *Atlanta Constitution* newspaper, praised Elton as "one of the clearest thinkers in America in the field of ethics and religion." Concerning the new book, he wrote, "*Declaration of Freedom* contains the answer to many of the more perplexing problems of our time, and a philosophy which will be helpful to every person who reads it."

The reviews from the *Chicago Sunday Tribune*, the *Christian Advocate*, and *Commonweal* were all excellent, as were countless others. The book became an important addition to literary America, which was yearning for a response to the perceived Communist threat on the way of life that was so strong at this time in our nation's history. In the debating style that he had mastered since high school, Elton "took on" the Communists and provided for the common men and women a logical defense of Western values, which had been so venomously attacked.

While at the USIA, Elton continued his interest and concern for the "lay ministry" and church renewal. In April 1955 he consented to an interview in *Cosmopolitan* magazine entitled "America's New Religious Vitality." Here in a "question/response" format he was able to clarify for the common reader some of the exciting things happening in American religion at mid-century:

Q. Dr. Trueblood, we have heard a great deal about what religion can do for people, but almost nothing about what people can do for religion. Certainly, there are many people who wish to do more for their church, but who do not know how to begin. To find this out it might be best to ask you first to explain the basic idea behind this deepening sense of religious responsibility, commonly called "lay participation."

A. I'd be glad to try. The basic idea is that no man can be truly religious as a mere observer or spectator. You cannot understand the depths of the religious life unless you are on the inside, working at the job, helping to pull the load. You cannot know what the love of God means unless you are tying to bring the love of God to more people. Therefore, participation is intrinsic to the very idea.

Q. What, in your opinion, Dr. Trueblood, is the reason for this trend?

A. The chief reason is that so many people in the western world are becoming skeptical of a merely materialistic society. They find that it doesn't work. You do not get the good life simply by earning more money, buying more gadgets, having more material resources. People have found that something deeper is required. And this realization has left the way open for a deeper conviction.

Q. How widespread has this idea of lay participation become? Is it apparent, in all denominations?

A. It is extremely widespread, though oddly enough it has not been widely publicized in newspapers and magazines. We find it in all the major denominations and across all faiths. It is very strong, for example, among the Roman Catholics in the Christopher movement. It is strong in some of the lay movements of the Jewish people and in all the major Protestant denominations, especially the Episcopal, the Methodist, the Congregational, the Presbyterian, and the Lutheran.

Q. Is this an American phenomenon or is it happening in churches all over the world?

A. It is happening in churches all over the world. We find it in England in what is called the Christian Frontier Movement. We find it in Switzerland in the Institute at Bosse, which is devoted wholly to the training of laymen in theology. And we find it in many parts of Canada. But it is in the United States that it is having the most striking evidence of power.

Q. Dr. Trueblood, is there a spiritual rule of thumb by which lay people can check themselves to find out if they are effective members of their church?

A. There is no simple rule, but here are some suggestions. We might ask ourselves these questions: First, is my religion a matter of genuine commitment—a total dedication of my life? Second, do I really act as an evangelist for the faith that I profess both in my deeds and my words? Third, have I found a fellowship of those who share life with one another to which I give myself? Fourth, have I accepted a voluntary discipline, so that my life goes beyond empty freedom, and is directed toward noble channels?

Shortly after their arrival in the nation's capital, Pauline had a massive stroke, which was caused by a cancerous tumor on her brain. On November 11, 1954, her medical chart read, "Unable to speak—right side completely paralyzed—some movement in leg." It was a tremendous blow to the Trueblood family, for although Pauline had been frail for much of her life, the stroke and accompanying paralysis was very difficult to cope with and accept. Elton and his children would have to begin to prepare for a life without a wife and mother.

THE DEATH OF PAULINE

Meet my death with silence
Round and firm . . .

In his autobiography, Elton wrote about his wife's last year:

In the Spring [of 1954] we had our last big house party, with Martin and his family home from his second naval duty. Pauline was able to enjoy her four children, two daughters-in-law, and four grandchildren in a really happy gathering, extending over several days of spring vacation. . . .

As I recall those difficult months, I am deeply grateful that Pauline, weak as she was in her last year, was able to participate in two public experiences which gave her a sense of fulfillment. The first was her address at New Haven before the National Assembly of the Congregational Churches, and the second was her attendance at Evanston, in August of 1954, as a delegate to the Assembly of the World Council of Churches. . . . Already the brain tumor must have been growing, but we did not of course know about it then.[2]

Following her time at Evanston, Pauline traveled to what the True-bloods had named Pen Point, in the Pocono Mountains of Pennsylvania.

Pauline, just prior to her death in 1955

This was a cottage on Lake Paupac that they had built as a family retreat. Here she stayed alone with her thirteen-year-old daughter, Elizabeth, for ten days, just after the completion of the building of the house.

In the winter days following her devastating stroke, the hard decision was made to move Pauline to a nursing home. Each day she weakened until she passed away on February 7, 1955. She was fifty-three years old. In preparation for her passing, Pauline had written a poem for Elton entitled "Advices To My Husband."

> Meet my death with silence
> Round and firm.
> Give the news out bravely
> Handclasp warm.
>
> Lay away the physical
> In a niche.
> Let not my poem end as
> A distich.
>
> Gather then in worship
> With our friends.
> May the silence yield rich
> Dividends.
>
> Live thy life so joyous
> None could guess
> There were any sorrows
> Between us.
>
> Memories be with thee
> Through the years
> Of our mortal passion.
> Save thy tears,
>
> Until they drop like jewels
> On my hair;
> A diademic symbol,
> Heaven-wed pair.

Burial was private. The family took Pauline's ashes and placed them in a natural stone wall at Pen Point, Lake Paupac. One month later, on March 6, a memorial service was held in the Stout Meetinghouse on the Earlham campus. "The service was a triumphal occasion," writes Elton, "ending, as all stood, with the singing by the concert choir of Handel's Hallelujah Chorus. Many people spoke spontaneously of her life and faith, one of the most moving being that of President Thomas E. Jones."[3]

Reflecting on their life together, Elton listed in his diary what he called, "Scenes in life with Pauline:"

Penn Dining Room	Oct.	1919
First Date	Oct. 12	1919

Bob Sled Ridge	Dec. 12	1919
First Visit to Union	June 21	1920
Pauline's Return to Penn	Sept.	1920
Giving of Society Pin	Autumn	1920
Report of 1st football success	Autumn	1920
Long visit to Union	Summer	1921
Visit after Extemp Contest	Winter	1922
Evening by the River	June	1922
Meeting at Earlham	July	1923
Parting at Grinnell	April	1924
Wedding in Rhode Island	Aug.	1924
New life in Roxbury	Sept.	1924
Christmas at Hospital	Dec.	1924
Departure for Iowa	Feb.	1925
Our first-born	July	1925
Decision to leave Cambridge	Winter	1927
Arnold born	Jan. 2	1930
Union Springs & Catskills	Aug.	1933
Doctor of Philosophy	June	1934
Return to Philadelphia	Sept.	1935
Letter from Pres. Wilbur	Dec.	1935
Entrance into California (at the Nevada line)	June	1936
Sammy born	Dec. 4	1938
Leaving for England	Dec. 16	1938
Meeting at Southampton	April	1939
Edinburgh	April	1939
Swarthmore Lecture	May	1939
Return from Cape May	July	1940
Naming Elizabeth	April 30	1941
Return from East	April	1942
San Francisco Airport	June 14	1942
Left California	Dec. 15	1945
Moved to College Ave. (in Richmond, Ind.)	July	1946
Dedicated Meetinghouse	April	1952
Died, near Washington, D.C.	Feb. 7	1955

Pauline Trueblood was Elton's greatest fan and most ardent supporter. Although she was ill throughout much of her earthly life, she was able to provide Elton with the strong home base so important to a public person who is traveling all of the time and who needed the security of knowing stability in the most important aspect of his life, the family. Though death in Pauline's case was a triumphant freeing from the painful shackles of her physical body after the stroke, the loss to Elton and the children was great, and they now had to learn to live without her.

THE EISENHOWER CONNECTION
AND MARRIAGE TO VIRGINIA

If Elton wants to get married here, of course it's all right. I accept his "spiritual baptism" as real.

With Elton's work as chief religious information officer of the USIA, he found himself involved, more than ever, in the mixture of religious faith and politics. On May 23, 1954, he accepted an invitation to speak at the National Presbyterian Church, where he had the opportunity to speak before President and Mrs. Eisenhower. This was the second chief executive of the United States before whom he had spoken, having spoken before President Hoover some years earlier.

Elton's sermon topic on that particular morning was "Too Late?" using 1 Kings 21:1–20 as his Scripture lesson. His primary focus was on the Supreme Court's decision to ban segregated public schools. The headline above the Associated Press article in an Indianapolis paper read, "Lauded In Pulpit—As Ike and Mamie Hear Richmond Man Preach About Segregation." The story went on to recount how President and Mrs. Eisenhower heard the Supreme Court's antisegregation decision described as "logic to its fruition." Elton said that the salvation of the world "lies in a positive ideology, the dignity of the individual man. If the people can see and accept the Supreme Court decision we will be moving into one of the greatest phases of history."

Concluding this important message, Elton emphasized that in the Western world "it is not too late to move in the right direction. The door is not closed if we can have a revival of the Christian spirit. . . . We'll not be combined in the long run by what we hate, but by what we love. The only way out is to take a positive ideology so clear it gives us an affirmative answer by which we may live. Where do we find it? Only in the dignity of the individual man."

His relationship with President Eisenhower was one of mutual respect. Elton had the opportunity to visit Mr. Eisenhower in the Oval Office where the president openly discussed his religious background. He was born into a modest family, with spiritual roots in the Brethren in Christ Church. Although he did not continue his membership with the Brethren (he joined the National Presbyterian Church in Washington), he was never ashamed of his background and seemed to find the simplicity of the church of his childhood a real source of strength.

One of the spiritual traits of the Brethren tradition is humility, which President Eisenhower's mother exemplified. Elton has often told a story about the president's mother that provides a beautiful example of this trait and that Elton verified with Milton Eisenhower, the president's brother, who at the time was president of Johns Hopkins University. He tells it in this way:

The elder Mrs. Eisenhower was traveling by train during the period of the war when her gifted son was supreme commander of the Allied forces. On the train she sat next to another woman passenger who had no idea of the older woman's identity and took advantage of the opportunity to talk endlessly about her son, telling proudly how he had been made a corporal. Finally, a bit ashamed of dominating the conversation so long, the stranger said to Mrs. Eisenhower, "Tell me about your son." The entire reply of the humble lady was, "He's in the army too."[4]

Following his two terms as president, Mr. Eisenhower retired to Gettysburg, where Elton visited with him again. The fact that it was President Eisenhower who added the phrase "under God" to the salute to the flag and that he lived at Gettysburg, near the spot where President Lincoln had inserted the phrase "under God" into his Gettysburg Address, was not lost on Elton. As a Lincoln scholar, it was Elton who first guessed that Lincoln got "under God" from the address to King James that precedes the Authorized Version of the Holy Bible. "Though Eisenhower did not have the same gift of eloquence that Lincoln demonstrated," Elton writes, "he understood what it means to say 'under God.' We cannot know all that Lincoln meant when, on November 19, 1863, he made the fortunate interpolation of the now familiar phrase; but we do know that he was seeking to express a nonidolatrous patriotism. Fortunately, this is what the thirty-fourth President likewise sought. We remember him with gratitude."[5]

Elton Trueblood married Virginia Zuttermeister on August 5, 1956, three months before President Eisenhower was re-elected to a second term. With Pauline's death in February of 1955, Elton had lost a wonderful wife and helper, and he was experiencing the pain of loneliness and separation. With the entrance of Virginia into his life, a new chapter was unfolding; one in which Elton was rediscovering the joy of falling in love.

Virginia was the widow of Marion Zuttermeister, and the mother of Henry and Dindy. She was the daughter of Simeon Hodgin, the well-respected chief engineer for the city of Richmond, Indiana and Estelle Goddard. She had a similar background to Elton's, with both of their ancestors stemming from the Quakers of North Carolina. Since the death of her husband she had worked as a secretary at Earlham. At the time of her marriage to Elton, she was assistant to Dr. Ronald Bridges of the USIA in Washington.

Elton first met Virginia on the train riding from Cincinnati to Richmond. She informed Elton that she possessed secretarial skills, and loved to type. He hired her to type his manuscript, *The Life We Prize,* in December of 1950. Of course, neither suspected at the time that their chance meeting on a train would change their lives so, that six years later they would be husband and wife.

Virginia was a dignified and cultured woman, holding a bachelor's degree from Miami University, in Oxford, Ohio. She possessed an ability to remember names, dates and places that would often amaze those in her presence. She was a "lady" in the most respected sense of the word, and all who had the opportunity to meet her and know her, never forgot her kind and gentle ways. She was well matched to become Mrs. D. Elton Trueblood.

The wedding took place in the Washington Cathedral. In preparation for the wedding, Virginia went to the cathedral office to make arrangements, and in the course of talking to the secretary to the dean of the cathedral, the secretary interrupted and said to Virginia, "Mrs. Zuttermeister, it is all right if you want to get married here, but Dr. Trueblood cannot. I know that Quakers do not practice water baptism, and therefore Dr. Trueblood does not meet the requirements for the use of our cathedral." Stunned and disappointed, Virginia did not know what to say. Fortunately, the dean of the cathedral overheard the conversation and intervened, saying, "Aw shucks! If Elton wants to get married here, of course it's all right. I accept his 'spiritual' baptism as real."

Seven and a half months before his marriage to Virginia, and ten months following the death of Pauline, Elton resigned from his position as chief of religious information of the USIA. Commenting on his resignation, Elton said,

> My philosophy is that a citizen ought to give his services for the benefit of his government when he can, and I therefore accepted the U.S. Information Agency assignment. During my time in Washington I have been on leave from Earlham College, where the administration has been generous in waiting for my return, which I cannot, in fairness, longer delay. I go back, not only grateful for the opportunity and cooperation accorded me, but appreciative of, and impressed with the aims and work of the Information Agency. . . . "

Elton returned to Earlham in the midst of writing *Philosophy of Religion* and ready to resume his duties in the religion and philosophy department. He had left Indiana for Washington with Pauline and was now returning without her comforting presence. Once again, Elton's understanding of the inequality of life was being played out. More had happened in the Trueblood family in two years than had happened in many years before. The return to Earlham would provide a helpful and needed source of stability.

1956–1966

EARLHAM REVISITED

Now he could focus, once again, on his first love: teaching.

The beautiful, tree-lined entryway leading to the new Earlham Hall was a welcome sight to one who had been a part of the people-congested and automobile-filled hustle and bustle of Washington, D.C. As in his move from Palo Alto, Elton was returning to his roots in the Midwest and to his vision for revitalization by way of the small college. His work in the nation's capital had been rewarding, and it was an important chapter in his life. But now, with the advantage of a two-year perspective from five hundred miles away, the Earlham campus seemed most inviting. Although he had been at Earlham at least once each month during his "leave of absence," it did not "feel" the same as when he had lived there. Now he could focus, once again, on his first love: *teaching*.

Elton returned to Richmond during a time of relative tranquility. It was a decade before the campus upheavals of the sixties, and so the strains between the "town and gown" had not yet developed. After his marriage to Virginia, they decided that it would be good to live away from the Earlham campus, and so they settled at 2114 Reeveston Road in the eastern part of the city. Elton explains his reason: "With the College Avenue house sold back to Earlham and slated to be used as the Yokefellow Institute, we decided to purchase a house on the east side of Richmond and thus to be identified with the city rather than merely with the college. We occupied the house for nearly ten years. . . ."[1]

His book *Philosophy of Religion* was the major writing project with which Elton was involved during this time. It was to be his fifteenth book. This was his effort to "carry on and to update" what he had done previously in *The Logic of Belief.* According to Elton, "It was my most ambitious effort up to that time."[2] After thirty-three years, this book is still a standard text for colleges and seminaries around the country. In the preface to this 318-page work, Elton writes that "all through my adult life this book has been in preparation, so that nearly everything I have done has contributed to the thinking."[3]

Elton with Earlham students laying a brick walk in
front of Teague Library, 1957

In commenting about this work, Will Herberg wrote, "*Philosophy of Religion* is a brilliant effort at synthesizing the conflicting trends in contemporary Christian thought ... lucid, systematic, balanced, persuasive, well thought out ... a mature statement of intellectual conviction and a stimulating guide to creative religious inquiry." Harry Emerson Fosdick added his praise: "An eminently able statement of the solid intellectual bases of Christian faith. In these days, when the dogmatic belittling of reason afflicts so much of our current theology, this book is a godsend." Perhaps the most important comment on the book came from Alexander Purdy, Elton's beloved teacher at Hartford Seminary. Purdy wrote this

The professor with his students in Teague Library
at Earlham

Elton talking with a student in the tumble of the old
Earlham Hall and in front of the new Earlham Hall

about his former student's work: "Elton Trueblood belongs to the great
central line of classical interpretation of religion who maintain the rights
and obligations of reason against all attackers."

Back at Earlham, Elton continued his pattern of teaching half time
and writing and lecturing the other half. In 1958 he delivered 105
speeches in England and the United States. In this country, he was in
Louisville, Pittsburgh, Miami, Norfolk, New York, Chicago, St. Paul and
Minneapolis, San Francisco, Oakland, Plainview, and Amarillo (Texas),
and all over Indiana. In April he sailed from Montreal for Great Britain,
where he was invited to speak, once again, before the London Yearly
Meeting of Friends. Before reaching London, he spoke in Edinburgh and
Glasgow, Scotland, and Canterbury, England. At the end of May, Elton
departed Liverpool for New York on the ship *Brittannia.*

"The voyage from Liverpool to New York on the Britannia in 1958 was
made memorable to me by new friendships," he wrote. "It will not be a surprise to my readers to be told that my first act, after embarkation, was
an examination of the passenger list, in order to see whether there were
persons on board from whom I might learn."[4]

The two people on board who most interested Elton were Paul Tillich,
the famous systematic theologian, and Edith Hamilton, the noted classical scholar. Although he enjoyed the company of Tillich, it was with Edith
Hamilton that he spent the bulk of his time. Elton was fifty-seven years
old, and Mrs. Hamilton was ninety. She had just received, on her nineti-
eth birthday, the honor of being named an honorary citizen of Athens,
Greece, being given the gift of a key to the city.

Elton's most beloved story about Edith Hamilton was one she shared
with him and Virginia when they visited her in her house in Washington,

D.C., in 1961, rekindling the friendship Elton began in 1958. Surrounded by proof copy of her introduction to the Bollingen Series on the *Dialogues of Plato,* she told the Truebloods about her father's concern for her education. "Her father, sensing the danger of mediocrity, and believing that school might hold them back from the development of which they were capable, never allowed his daughters to go to school. Accordingly, he taught them himself, with primary stress upon the Latin language."[5] At seven years old, Edith was told by her father that she must master Caesar's *Gallic Wars* in only six weeks. She did. When Elton responded to this story by saying that she must have been smarter than other girls, Mrs. Hamilton said, "On the contrary, I was more stupid than others. In fact, I was so stupid that I didn't know but what I had to do it."[6]

Now that he was back on the Earlham campus, Elton was more and more active in the administration of the Yokefellow movement, of which he served as president. The idea of a redemptive fellowship and the various outgrowths of such an idea were gathering strength around the country and, indeed, the world. Individual lives were changing, and churches were being revitalized. It was an exciting time for Elton and for the Christian movement.

THE YOKEFELLOW MOVEMENT

As I came into middle age . . . I saw, at the same time, both the futility of empty freedom and the fruitlessness of single effort.

In the epigraph preceding his "Yokefellow" chapter in his autobiography, *While It Is Day,* Elton quoted the words of one of his favorite writers, William Temple: "The supreme wonder of the history of the Christian Church is that always in the moments when it has seemed most dead, out of its own body there has sprung up new life."

The Yokefellow movement represented the kind of new life of which William Temple had written. At this midpoint in the twentieth century, in countless churches across the United States and Canada, small groups were forming that were established as a result of the Yokefellow idea and, more specifically, the inspiration of Elton Trueblood. "As I came into middle age, two separate dangers were simultaneously impressed upon my mind," he wrote.

I saw, at the same time, both the futility of empty freedom and the fruitlessness of single effort. Affirmatively stated, the latter led to the idea of the small fellowship, while the former led to the idea of voluntary discipline; in conjunction they led to the recognition that hope lies in the creation of an order. Now, for a quarter of a century, much of my thought and energy have been employed in both the dream and its embodiment in one particular order, the Order of the Yoke.[7]

By 1949, Elton had had the experience of reading the "yoke passage" (Matt. 11:28–30) with a burst of new insight. Out of this seed of an experience, the Yokefellow movement developed. It arose at midcentury as an almost spontaneous yet widespread response to the recovery of the idea that the ministry of Jesus Christ need not be limited to a special class or special profession but is equally open to *all* sincere followers of the Lord. Elton was helping the Christian movement recover the doctrine set forth by Martin Luther concerning the priesthood of every believer.

The Yokefellow movement has always been interdenominational. Although small yoke fellowships were being founded in particular congregations, these groups were never wholly sectarian. Each Yokefellow group took seriously the four pillars on which they were founded: *commitment* to Jesus Christ, *fellowship* with one another, *ministry* to the world, and a *discipline* to follow. The *discipline* was printed on "yoke cards," which Yokefellow members carried in their purses or wallets. There are seven disciplines:

1. The discipline of *prayer.* To pray every day, preferably at the beginning of the day.
2. The discipline of *scripture.* To read reverently and thoughtfully, every day, a portion of Scripture, following a deliberate plan. [Elton organized a plan whereby a person could read the Gospels and the Book of Acts in small "bite-size" portions in one year.]
3. The discipline of *worship.* To share, at least once each week, in the public worship of God.
4. The discipline of *money.* To give a definite portion of one's annual income to the promotion of Christ's cause.
5. The discipline of *time.* To use any time as a special gift, not to be wasted, striving to make by daily work, whatever it may be, a Christian vocation.
6. The discipline of *service.* To try, every day, to lift some human burden.
7. The discipline of *study.* To develop mental powers by careful reading and study.

Although the Yokefellow organization can be traced to a beginning in 1952 when Elton organized a small fellowship of supporters, it was not until after he returned from his service at the USIA in Washington that things truly began to develop. Harold Duling, the first director of the Lilly Endowment in Indianapolis, attended some of the original lay conferences at Earlham College. He felt that if more financial undergirding could be given to the Yokefellow idea, it could really begin to expand around the country and world. "When he learned that I expected to return to full college duties in 1956, he felt that the time had come to lay greater stress on the Yokefellow idea."[8] It had not occurred to Elton to seek foundation support for the infant Yokefellow movement, and so when Mr. Duling wrote to him in late 1955 suggesting the possibility of a "matching fund" gift from the endowment, he was surprised. "We accepted the offer with gratitude," Elton later wrote, "and had no difficulty in raising funds of our own to match the grant dollar for dollar."[9]

In April 1954, the first annual Yokefellow conference was held at Stout Memorial Meetinghouse on the Earlham campus. Gordon Cosby, the founding pastor of the Church of the Saviour in Washington, D.C., spoke on the topic "A New Kind of Church for Our Day." Dr. H. V. Scott, a physician from Fort Wayne, Indiana, and the first chair of the board of Yokefellows International, spoke on the topic "Why I am a Yokefellow." Elton led a discussion on "practical opportunities for the ministry of disciplined men and women in common life" and then delivered the Sunday morning message, "The Power and the Glory." Since the beginning of this annual spring gathering on the Earlham campus, Yokefellows have been privileged to have as speakers some of the most important figures in the Christian movement, including Malcolm Muggeridge, Keith Miller, Tony Campolo, Richard Foster, Mary Cosby, Richard Halverson, Bruce Larson, D. James Kennedy, Charles Colson and many others.

Growing out of the seedbed of the Yokefellow idea came the dream of a retreat house where lay men and women could come for spiritual renewal. What was clear to Elton and many others in the mid-1950s was that churches could not meet all of the spiritual needs of their congregants. With the use of a retreat center where people could come and eat and worship together for two or three days, a new spiritual vitality could emerge within individuals that would be played out in a renewed spirit in their local congregation. What was needed was a *place* where people could come and capture the vision of renewal that the Yokefellow movement represented.

The first such retreat house was at 228 College Avenue in Richmond, Indiana. This was Elton and Pauline's former home before they moved to Washington, D.C. For a number of years this house, which could sleep ten comfortably, served as the center of Yokefellow activity. Samuel Emerick, then a Methodist pastor from Bluffton, Indiana, was invited to serve as director, and under his creative leadership the Yokefellow House, which became the Yokefellow Institute, was remarkably effective in serving the purpose of spiritual renewal. By 1964 the movement had outgrown this house, and a larger, modernized structure was built on Earlham's back campus.

Elton's vision of renewal continued to expand, and soon Yokefellow centers were being built or converted from existing structures in various locations around the country. Today there is the Tri-State Yokefellow Center, founded by Robert and Naomi Pickering after they converted a huge barn on their farm into a beautiful retreat center near Defiance, Ohio. Their son, Duane, is the executive director. Near Chicago there is the Acorn Yokefellow Center, which is a converted hunting lodge made possible by the dream and financial support of Homer and Alice Dickson of Yorkville, Illinois. On the West Coast in Burlingame, California, Cecil Osborne heads a very active Yokefellow Center, and at Rising Sun, Maryland, under the creative leadership of Hal and Cher Owens, the most recent Yokefellow Center has been established. Converting a huge old house, Hal and Cher have given their lives to the dream Elton implanted within them many years ago.

Over time, many centers have begun, and many have been discontinued, the victims of changing times and waning dedication. The remarkable way in which Elton could speak in a particular community, instill his dream and enthusiasm, and then leave for his next engagement, has never ceased to amaze me. He has the uncanny ability to make people feel *needed* and to help them realize that if the spiritual revitalization of the Church and our society is to take place, then you are going to have to help get it started. Regardless of the size of the group to which he would be speaking, each one present could sense that he was speaking directly to him or her. His penetrating books, articles, teaching, and speaking were changing lives, and in the desire of people to want to repay the man who had done so much for them, they joined the ranks of the Yokefellow movement with spirited enthusiasm.

In the summer of 1955, Elton was asked to speak before a conference of prison chaplains meeting in the old Supreme Court room of the Capitol in Washington. "I spoke on the power of the small group of people who have a common discipline and who share both their problems and their faith with one another," wrote Elton. "Though it had never occurred to me that such groups could be nurtured in prison communities, two of the chaplains present saw the possibilities and soon, working independently of each other, established Yokefellow Groups in the federal penitentiaries both at McNeil Island, near Tacoma, Washington, and at Lewisburg, Pennsylvania."[10] Out of this experience the Yokefellow Prison Ministry began. Today, under the guidance of John Mostoller of Williamsport, Pennsylvania, this Yokefellow program has established small fellowship groups in hundreds of jails and prisons around the country.

Because Elton first spoke to these prison chaplains in 1955, he has had the opportunity to speak in many prisons and jails. Often he has received small gifts from prisoners whose lives have been changed because of his encouragement, and one of these gifts has been given a permanent place in his study at Teague Library, Earlham College. Atop the table on the northwest side of his study sits a picture of Abraham Lincoln holding a small boy. In the bottom right hand corner of the picture are the words, "To Elton Trueblood, with warm regards, A. Lincoln." Every visitor to Teague Library is asked to go over and look at the picture. Each time Elton asks, "How do you explain that?" Upon reading it many will ask, "Did you really know Abraham Lincoln?" With a smile Elton will inquire, "Do you really believe

I am 130 years old?!" After he has had his fun, he explains that the picture and forged signature were a gift from a prisoner who was serving time for *forgery*. Elton's encouragement of him had meant so much that he wanted to repay him. But how? Knowing of Elton's love for Lincoln, he came up with the idea of the autographed picture. The signature is a perfect copy.

The most recent Yokefellow venture has been what is called the academy. It is really the educational arm of the Yokefellow movement. What Elton learned in the development of his concern for the ministry of every Christian was that if you believe in it, then it is important to be serious about training for ministry. Most Christians accept the idea of the universal ministry but do not know how to begin training congregations *for* ministry. The Yokefellow Academy, which has become the D. Elton Trueblood Academy for Applied Christianity, was established to help congregations develop lay educational programs.

Since its inception in 1974, until 1987, the academy operated out of the small, white garage behind 228 College Avenue in Richmond. It organized a five-year study program that was put together so that it could be easily adapted to local congregational settings. Based upon a similar outline developed by Elton in his book *Your Other Vocation,* the five-year program is divided into nine months of study in each of five areas: (1) Old Testament, (2) New Testament, (3) the basic Christian classics, (4) an intellectual understanding of the faith (philosophy and theology), and (5) the history of Christian thought. Along with these programs for Christian groups, the academy offers individuals an opportunity for study by correspondence in a program called "Ministers of Common Life." In twelve months' time the student studies the Bible, the Christian classics, Socratic logic, and vocal and written expression.

In 1987, the academy, on a three-year trial basis, became a part of the Earlham School of Religion and was given a planning grant from the Lilly Endowment to study how an academy devoted to lay education and a seminary devoted to the training of persons for professional ministry could work together in programming. This new and exciting concept is still being studied.

Over the nearly forty years of its life, the Yokefellow movement has gone through many periods of change. Because there has never been a centralized controlling office, each entity that has grown out of the Yokefellow idea is autonomous, with the responsibility to succeed programatically and financially left up to its own board of directors. The giant presence of Elton Trueblood is the major source of inspiration, and each year he will write three of the *Quarterly Yoke Letters* to the faithful constituency, and I as director of the academy write the fourth one. He continues as president of Yokefellows International and will always be the guiding light of the individual and church renewal programs that justify the existence of the movement.

TEAGUE LIBRARY

Now I am deeply grateful to Edward Gallahue that God has put it into his heart to build this lovely place. . . .

"Sitting today, December 22, 1958, in my new library, with the sun streaming in through the south window, I am very happy," Elton wrote in his diary. "I realize that life is always beginning anew. Certainly it is beginning for me. No wonder that the Bible starts, 'In the beginning.'"

The quiet serenity of Teague Library, overlooking the beautiful front campus of Earlham, is a place of peace, tranquillity, and exquisite beauty. It was built thirty years ago on the northeast corner of the Earlham College campus as a study for Elton. The man who so generously contributed the needed finances to build Elton's library was Edward F. Gallahue, who, at the time, was the president of the American States Insurance Company of Indianapolis. He built it in honor of his mother, representing the Teague family, and because he wanted, in some substantial way, to repay Elton for the valued spiritual insights he had received from his books, particularly *The Logic of Belief.* It is to be used by Elton for as long as he lives, and then it will be given to Earlham College as a place for contemporary Christian authors to write and study.

Completely paneled with beautiful walnut wood, Teague Library is most conducive to serious writing and reading. Upon entering the front door, one becomes aware of the ticking of the clock that sits on the mantle over the fireplace. The Seth Thomas clock was the first purchase Elton's parents made after they were married. It is over one hundred years old but still keeps perfect time. In the southeast corner sits the George Washington–style desk, behind which Elton has sat and worked for thirty years. To the left of the desk is one of the built-in bookcases, this one housing all of the volumes he has written, in most of their editions, as well as many of the books he has helped others to write or to which he has written the foreword. It is a formidable display, indeed, of one man's influence on the world of twentieth-century Christian publishing.

In the companion bookshelves on the other side of the fireplace are all of the personal copies of Elton's devotional classics. Here you will find *The Confessions of St. Augustine, The Imitation of Christ* by Thomas à Kempis, *The Practice of the Presence of God* by Brother Lawrence, and John Woolman's *Journal,* to name a few. Ever since his professor at Harvard, Willard Sperry, encouraged him to "soak yourself in the great models," Elton has had a special place in his life for the classics of literature, especially the religious classics. For Elton Trueblood, as for Malcolm Muggeridge, they are his "third testament."

Directly across from the fireplace are five sections of built-in bookshelves, in front of which sits a table for students who are writing. To

understand Elton's main interests in life, a person need only study the
books in his library. The first of the five sections is devoted wholly to
books about Quakers. Robert Barclay, George Fox, William Penn, Thomas
Kelly, and Rufus Jones are all familiar names in this section. On the shelf
in front of the other volumes rests the prized "Baskerville edition" of
Robert Barclay's *Apology*.

Next to the Quaker section are shelves devoted to philosophy and
logic, theology, biography and autobiography, and reference works.
Elton is particularly proud of the Harvard five-foot shelf of classics,
which occupies the last two shelves in the reference section. All of these
2,000-plus volumes attest to Elton's important idea concerning the choosing of one's companions. "The written word," he is fond of saying,
"has liberated us from the confines of time. If I want to have Plato or
Samuel Johnson or Blaise Pascal as my companions, I can do so." And so
he does.

In a special section of shelves, almost directly across the room from
the front door, are the collected works of two of his favorite authors and
thinkers—Samuel Johnson and Abraham Lincoln. To appreciate Elton's
indebtedness to both of these men, we need only hear the many times he
quotes one or the other. When we traveled together in England in 1982,
we sat down for breakfast with Clare and Ethel Trueblood, Elton's brother
and sister-in-law, and while discussing the upcoming events of the day,
Clare said to his brother, "Elton, the longer we stay in London, the more
you resemble Samuel Johnson!" Elton has often said that the first person
he wants to meet in heaven is "Dr. Johnson."

On that first day in his new library, Elton was especially inspired to
focus his thoughts in his diary on new beginnings.

> Man is a creature who has a remarkable time sense with a keen conscious-
> ness of the difference between "occur," "recur," and "endure." Often men fall
> into a pattern, but it is not necessary to continue the same pattern all the rest
> of one's life. Life *can* be new.
>
> Part of the glory of the life of Dr. Samuel Johnson inhered in his ability
> to emphasize the crucial points of stock taking, particularly those symbolized
> by birthdays and new years. Each was always a chance to do better. The deep
> wisdom of the best men shows that old dogs can learn new tricks, that it is
> never too late to learn and that it is the nature of human nature to change.
> We are perhaps the most malleable stuff of all experience because our
> behavior can be altered, not merely by external pressures, but also by inner
> purposes.
>
> As I sit in my new study today I am doing the very first writing in it. Perhaps
> I shall be able to do a great deal more during a period of twenty or thirty years,
> but this today is unique in one sense.
>
> My thought is full of thanksgiving because my life, though it has not been
> easy, has been such that my major powers could be used. I am grateful that I
> was led to Harvard and to Johns Hopkins, always with circumstances of

intellectual stimulation. Now I am deeply grateful to Edward Gallahue that God has put it into his heart to build this lovely place.

Elton indicated in his diary that he hoped to say no to more speaking invitations so that he could stay home and enjoy his new study. This, of course, was difficult for him to do since he so loved to interact with people who were excited about his writings and messages of spiritual revitalization. As he considered his work, he wrote about how he is humbled by his responsibilities, and how his many opportunities make him feel very happy. For support in his ministry, he wrote, "I have the constant help of two good women, one living and one dead, and the unlimited affection of my children." Concerning his beloved Earlham, he said that it "has turned out to be a really great place of learning and teaching. No other connection would suit me as well."

On December 12, 1958, Elton was fifty-eight years old. As he sat in his new study ten days after his birthday, he noted, "Now that I am 58 years old I must arrange to use a little less energy daily. To this end I expect to take a short nap each afternoon and to arrange my life so that this is possible. . . . In my last chapter I want to be as tender as my father and consistently kind. May God help me do this!"

The last notation in his diary for December 22, 1958, is especially interesting since I have rarely heard Elton make mention of his father. Perhaps this is due to the fact that his father passed away over fifty years ago, while his mother lived to be 101, living until 1969. From all that we know about his mother, Effie, and her very strong, driven personality, it seems as though Elton is more a product of his mother's side of the family. At this "new beginning," however, or in the modern vernacular, "transition" time, Elton felt close to his father and appreciative of his tender and loving ways.

As much as he loves to be with people, the quiet times in his beautiful Teague Library are very precious to Elton. Here he can write and reflect on life as all good philosophers need to do. He can dream big dreams and think great thoughts. At this particular time in his life he was preoccupied with those major dreams that would, he felt, change the Society of Friends. It was the dream of a Quaker seminary for the purpose of educating Friends' ministers. Although Quakers have always been concerned with education at the undergraduate level, they had not, up to this time, felt the need for a seminary. With the pastoral system in the Society of Friends nearly one hundred years old in the last half of the 1950s, it was clear that it was here to stay. Thus the need for a school of religion was now apparent.

Sitting in his library on that first day, December 22, 1958, Elton wrote, "The Yokefellow Movement has, for five years, been growing in power and is now firmly established. The next big task is that of our School of Religion, which may turn out to be the greatest chance of all."

FOUNDING A SEMINARY

His base of operation was Earlham and the Society of Friends.

The Goddard Auditorium was full to overflowing, and Elton was becoming concerned. As the chair of the convocation committee, he had arranged for Martin Luther King, Jr., to speak on the Earlham campus. Dr. King was late, having spoken in South Bend earlier in the day. Evidently, the trip from South Bend to Richmond was taking longer than expected. A strict disciplinarian regarding time, Elton considered it a moral matter that time could be wasted by the student body waiting for Dr. King, rather than working on their studies. Elton has always felt that if you are five minutes late starting, that is not just five minutes. The actual waste is five times the number of people who are waiting! And so when the hour came for the convocation to begin, Elton stood and began to introduce Martin Luther King, Jr., even though he was not yet present. It was indeed, an act of faith. As Elton's luck would have it, Dr. King appeared at the back of the auditorium, and he was quickly ushered to the front just as Elton concluded his introductory remarks!

Elton Trueblood used his considerable gifts in logic and speech to further the cause of civil rights throughout this country. In his sermon before President Eisenhower at the National Presbyterian Church in 1956, he had lauded the Supreme Court's desegregation decision, and he had also used his position as a religious leader to help Christians understand the inconsistency between segregation and a Christian commitment based upon the love of Jesus Christ. At least in one church in the South where he was asked to speak, his conscience would not allow him to deliver his message until the black people who had come to hear him were invited to come down from the balcony and join other worshipers in an integrated congregation. Since the church didn't want to offend Elton Trueblood, those in the balcony were invited to join the rest of the congregation.

On more than one occasion Elton wrote to Richard Nixon, then vice-president, a Quaker and friend, urging him to follow in the line of his religious tradition and take a strong moral stand on the civil rights issue. In a letter to Stanley E. McCaffrey, executive assistant to the vice-president, Elton noted that "the Vice-President is in a strong position on Civil Rights, and it would do no harm to link this up with the Quaker background, which includes the underground railroad and the opposition to slavery." Later, on December 19, 1963, Elton wrote Mr. Nixon in Los Angeles, urging him to "help the Republican Party to take a position on the negro question, which is our most urgent one, that is in line with our Quaker heritage and that of Abraham Lincoln." Elton felt that the Republican party could win "in 1964 as Lincoln won in 1864, but only on similar grounds."

Following his time at Earlham, Martin Luther King, Jr., wrote Elton a letter of gratitude, dated May 18, 1959. In this letter, Dr. King expressed his appreciation for the enthusiastic response he received while at Earlham, and for Elton's conscientious work in making arrangements for his visit. In conclusion, he invited Elton to visit him the next time he was in Montgomery.

Elton was never able to accept Dr. King's kind invitation to visit him in Montgomery. In 1978, however, ten years after the assassination of the civil rights leader, he did share in the program of the Southern Baptist Convention in Atlanta with his widow, Coretta Scott King.

The late fifties and early sixties was an exciting time on the Earlham campus, as it was for all of America. There was a restlessness beginning to develop within the hearts and minds of many students, and the issue of civil rights was the focal point of concern. Because Earlham is a Quaker school and the Society of Friends has a long tradition of working for the equality of all people, it was only natural that the faculty and student body would find itself on the forefront of this struggle.

Also at work during this time was the concern for a new school of religion. As much as Elton was sought after as a lecturer and religious leader in the world at large, his base of operation was Earlham and the Society of Friends. He was a Christian first and a Quaker second, which is as it should be for all who claim allegiance to Christ as well as loyalty to a particular denomination or sect.

At this time in the history of the Quaker movement, Elton was concerned about the numerical decline and spiritual inertia that had become evident in so many Quaker Meetings and churches. He was convinced that the Society of Friends had a message to share with other Christians and the world at large, but because of a lack of well-trained leadership, the Quakers were not able to effectively share their concerns.

In his book about the beginning of the Earlham School of Religion, Wilmer A. Cooper wrote about the interest some at Earlham had expressed, namely President Tom Jones and Elton Trueblood, about the need for a Quaker seminary: "Although Earlham College had no special priority in the developing concern for a new and vital ministry among Friends, there did emerge at Earlham at the close of the 1950s a few key Friends who felt the time had come to do something about it."[11] Wilmer Cooper joined the Earlham staff in April 1959 to study the possibility of establishing a school of religion at Earlham, and six months later, following much discussion, the school was established.

Elton's deep concern for his beloved Society of Friends was forcefully stated in his first "Plain Speech" column, which he had agreed to write monthly for *Quaker Life* magazine:

There is no doubt that a great deal of what passes for Quakerism today is highly discouraging. There are a few bright spots, but the general picture is far from satisfactory. . . . All that we have left in many neighborhoods is a little congregation, dutifully droning through three gospel songs, listening patiently to a sermon and a benediction. This is not Quakerism; it is simply Protestantism at the end of the line.[12]

The Earlham School of Religion came into existence to change this sorry picture. It was decided that the new school should be situated on the northeast corner of the campus, with Elton's former home, now the Yokefellow Institute, to become the eventual classroom building. This was made possible when the Yokefellow movement built the new retreat cen-ter on the back campus in 1964–1965.

Today, Elton's dream for a Quaker seminary is a fully established real-ity. A new classroom building has been built, and in his honor a classroom in this new facility bears his name. It is a fitting tribute to a man who has given so much to Quaker education over the years and who has never let rest a concern for a better educated group of Quaker leaders, who will, in turn, infect the world with a hoped-for spiritual vitality.

THE COMPANY OF THE COMMITTED

. . . the Bible in one hand and The Company of the Committed in the other.

The years 1960 and 1961 were a time of renewed emphasis upon famil-iar Trueblood themes. At Bethel College in Kansas as the Menno Simons Lectures; at McMurray College in Abilene, Texas, as the Willson Lectures, and at New Orleans Baptist Seminary as the Wayne Lectures, Elton gave messages such as "The Necessity of Commitment," "The Call to Enlist-ment," "The Vocation of Witness," "The Strategy of Penetration," and "The Criterion of Validity." In the fall of 1961, these lectures were pub-lished in book form as *The Company of the Committed,* and it has been Elton's best-selling book.

It is always difficult to speculate on the reasons why a book ignites with the reading public and becomes a best-seller. But it would not be too speculative to suggest that the type of church outlined in *The Company of the Committed* is the kind of congregational model that gives new meaning to the work of the pastor and provides a purpose in ministry for all Chris-tians regardless of profession. With his ability to shed new light on Scrip-ture and his talent for putting theological truth in the language of the ordinary person, as well as limiting his books to around 125 readable pages, Elton produced a classic.

Personally I shall never forget the first time I read *The Company of the Committed* and how it excited my passion for ministry. At that time I was a pastor in rural Ohio and a first-year student at the Earlham School of Reli-gion. I was in Washington, D.C., attending a conference quite unrelated to the reading material I had brought with me. I began reading the book in the evening and did not put it down until I had finished it well after mid-night. Today, sixteen years later, I still love to slowly peruse my well-worn and heavily marked copy. At the back of my copy I made my own index, with such topics, as "a third way," "solitude once a month," "the universal ministry of Christ," and "a true church building" listed for reference.

Oliver Hogue, a ministerial colleague in West Virginia once told me that he used to preach with "the Bible in one hand and *The Company of the Committed* in the other." And this type of remark is not uncommon among pastors throughout this country who found new meaning in their ministry and ideas for spiritual vitality. The religious mood of America was ready for a more committed understanding of the ministry of the Church, and Elton's book captured this mood.

The Company of the Committed has become Elton's favorite book title, but he did not settle on it until after great struggle. It was not until he had discarded ninety-nine other titles that he was able to affirm the selection of *The Company of the Committed*.

With the release of this latest work, Elton was treated to a special luncheon at the Twenty-One Club in New York City, commemorating twenty-five years of publishing with Harper & Brothers and Harper & Row. In his remarks from the head table, Cass Canfield, then president of the house of Harper, praised Elton's accomplishments and then jokingly said, "Dear friends, please understand that the house of Harper is in no way philanthropic in picking up the luncheon tabs for everyone here." Then, pointing at Elton, he said, "This man has made money for us!" It was a grand occasion where Elton was made to feel, again, "that it was good to be associated with a firm for which I had unqualified respect."[13]

Shortly after completing *The Company of the Committed*, Elton began a writing project of a wholly different character. For many years he had been teaching the course General Philosophy, and for some time he had wanted to write a book by the same title. "What I wanted to produce," wrote Elton, "was a thorough and scholarly book which could become an instrument for study on the part of people working alone, as well as involved in classes. . . . It was not my purpose to cover again the arguments presented in *The Philosophy of Religion*, but to deal instead with the broader field of inquiry, which underlies all scientific, aesthetic, and moral reflection."[14]

Elton considered this work "the most arduous task of my academic career," and as he walked the "Philosophers Way" above Heidelberg, Germany, in April 1961, he stopped and wrote the first paragraph of a book that would keep him writing and editing until it was published in 1963. The choice of his opening epigraph for this volume came from the writings of one of Elton's favorite literary models, Blaise Pascal: "Man is obviously made to think. It is his whole dignity and his whole merit; and his whole duty is to think as he ought."

In June 1963 Elton received one of his fourteen honorary doctorates, this one a Doctor in Divinity from Kenyon College in Ohio. In presenting the degree, the president of Kenyon spoke of Elton as "interpreter," citing the definition of "interpreter" given by the sixteenth-century lexicographer

Thomas Cooper as "a stickler between two at variance." He went on to say, "This describes your professional calling, for you have sought to mediate between the world of religion and the world of the university. At Haverford, Harvard, Stanford and, most recently, Earlham, you have successfully avoided the strait jacket of professional isolation, and have consistently interpreted the achievements of philosophy to the layman."

When this degree was awarded, Elton was in his sixty-third year. He had just completed his largest and "most arduous" book, and he was beginning work on *The Humor of Christ.* The "interpreter" continued his calling through the rhythm of life to which he had become accustomed — writing, speaking around the country, and teaching at Earlham.

In October 1963, Elton stopped to visit an old friend while he was in New York City, the former president, Herbert Hoover. In a letter to Herbert Hoover, Jr., Elton told of his visit, "When my wife and I were in New York on October 19, we visited your esteemed father. Even though he did not seem very strong, the improvement in his condition which has occurred since I was with you in June is really remarkable. He says he hopes that the time is short, for he feels that his work is done. . . . I expect to be in this country until next October when I go to Japan."

The former President lived for another year, dying on the morning of October 21, 1964. At the time of his death, Elton and Virginia Trueblood were on the ship *President Adams,* traveling up the Saigon River in Vietnam, on a trip around the world.

FUNERAL FOR A PRESIDENT

You do not make promises lightly, but once made you keep them.

Dr. Elton Trueblood
SS President Adams

THIS CABLE SENT AT REQUEST MR. ALLAN HOOVER TO SECRETARY GENERAL STAFF HEADQUARTER FIRST ARMY GOVERNORS ISLAND NEW YORK TO INQUIRE IF YOU CAN RETURN TO UNITED STATES TO CONDUCT SERVICES FOR FORMER PRESIDENT HOOVER WHO DIED THIS MORNING. SERVICE WILL BE AT WEST BRANCH IOWA SUNDAY OCTOBER 25TH AT 2:40 P.M. THE FAMILY EAGER TO LEARN IF YOU CAN RETURN IN TIME TO CONDUCT SERVICES AND WOULD APPRECIATE CABLE. ADVISE APL SAIGON BEING REQUESTED. SET UP PRELIMINARY AIR RESERVATIONS. SUBJECT YOUR ACCEPTANCE ON ARRIVAL SAIGON AND WILL HELP IN ANY OTHER MANNER POSSIBLE.

Scribbled under the message on this telegram is Elton's response, "Will fly to U.S. Thurs., Oct. 22." The willingness of Elton to travel 12,000 miles from Saigon to West Branch, Iowa, is one of the best illustrations of how important it is for Elton to keep promises once made. I have heard him say, "You do not make promises lightly, but once made you keep them." Elton had promised the Hoover family that he would conduct the funeral

At the graveside of President Herbert Hoover,
1964

service for President Hoover. The fact that he was on the other side of the
world when the president died did not change the promise, it just made
it more difficult to keep. But keep it he did, arriving in Iowa on Saturday,
October 24. The burial service was to be on Sunday afternoon, October 25.

The crowd gathered that day in West Branch was estimated to number
near 75,000. Only 365 persons had been sent special invitations by telegram,
President Landrum Bolling of Earlham being one. In a letter sent to friends
following the service, he describes the arrival of the funeral procession:

> The funeral procession itself arrived right on time. There were several police
> escorts, cars and a convoy of perhaps 25 large black cadillacs. After they
> stopped and the casket was unloaded, the band came to attention and played
> "Ruffles and Flourishes" as the funeral party moved from the circular driveway
> inside the park up the slope to the final resting place. A color guard of three,
> a soldier, sailor and a marine, preceded Elton Trueblood who walked just
> ahead of the casket borne by military pallbearers. There were the two sons,
> Allan and Herbert Hoover, Jr., their wives and children plus other long-time
> friends and close associates of the former President. A few others I noted in
> the party who had flown from Washington included Lowell Thomas and Barry
> Goldwater. . . .
>
> The entire funeral service lasted about twenty minutes. There was a brief
> period of silent prayer after which Elton Trueblood read from the Scriptures
> and delivered the sermon which he closed with prayer. Afterwards there was
> the ceremony in which the military pallbearers carefully folded the flag which
> had lain atop the casket. It was then presented to Herbert Hoover, Jr. After this
> we slowly filed away.
>
> As members of the family funeral party were getting into their cars to drive
> away, Elton Trueblood came looking for us and insisted that his brother and
> sister-in-law and Frances (Landrum Bolling's wife) and I should ride back to
> the Cedar Rapids Airport with them. The Hoovers had asked Elton and his
> wife to fly with them back to Southern California immediately on their special
> plane, the famous *Columbine,* provided for this occasion by the Air Force. We

had a good visit with Elton and Virginia as we sped along the Interstate Highway, all the entrances to which had been closed off as we passed by.

At the Cedar Rapids Airport we saw Goldwater climb into his Boeing 707 campaign plane and take off to resume his hectic electioneering schedule. With the Truebloods, we stood within the circle of four Air Force planes which had flown from Washington and visited with the Hoover family until they climbed aboard.

The funeral message which Elton shared on this occasion was later published in the 1964 volume of *Representative American Speeches* and widely distributed in other forms. He stressed the Christian understanding of death, which is one of "rejoicing instead of pagan sorrow." In part, he said, "This is not a time for tears. . . . The story is a great one and it is a good one. It is essentially a story that is triumphant . . . and our mood today should be rejoicing."

Elton spoke of the former president's life as being lived in six major chapters: (1) boy in Iowa and Oregon, (2) student at Stanford, (3) engineer in various countries, (4) director of relief, (5) Statesman, and (6) Elder.

The six chapters are now over, and in one sense the volume is complete, but there is another sense in which it is still going on. Herbert Hoover will be remembered as long as the American dream is cherished because he is, to such a great extent, the last of the famous pioneers. He represents the westward trek; he represents dignified simplicity; he represents to a remarkable degree the unity of a faith which expresses itself in compassionate service to mankind. He has worked hard; he has been very brave; he has endured. How appropriate that what is mortal of him should finally rest, after all his struggles and his victories, in his native soil, midway in the western trek and near the middle of North America. He never wavered from the living faith in Jesus Christ which was indigenous to his heritage and in which he lived and served and died.[15]

Many letters of gratitude for Elton's effort to return for the Hoover graveside service were received. A note from Mark Hatfield, then governor of Oregon, was typical: "Although it was a sad day for all Americans upon learning of the death of President Hoover, I am pleased that Dr. Trueblood was able to return to conduct the Memorial Service for this great President." The little Yokefellow office was flooded with requests for Elton's remarks, and Bob Pitman, loyal secretary, worked hard to keep up with them.

Elton and Virginia returned to the Far East following the service, picking up their round-the-world tour in Malaysia. A cable to Herbert Hoover, Jr., was sent by Elton telling him of their safe arrival. In response, the eldest of the Hoover sons wrote:

It was with great pleasure—and much relief—that I received your note from Kuala Lampur telling me of your safe arrival. Of the many things that happened at the time of Dad's death, your journey with Mrs. Trueblood from the other side of the world to be with us in West Branch was to us the most touching and devoted incident of all.

The simple services at the graveside, and your wonderful tribute to Dad, were in the finest tradition of everything that we have come to know and respect. On behalf of all our family I want you to know how very, very grateful we are to you both.

The tour, which had been made possible because of a distinguished-teacher award Elton had received from Leland Doan, former president of the Dow Chemical Company, had been interrupted by this momentous occasion but was not in any way harmed. The trip could continue, and the promise to conduct the funeral of President Hoover had been kept.

CLOSING A CHAPTER

His style was sometimes harsh, and he could be very demanding, but only because he cared for his students and sought to bring out their best.

In 1964 *The Humor of Christ* was published, and in 1965 *The Lord's Prayers.* "The book on Christ's humor was the outgrowth of an experience in our home on the Guilford College campus," Elton has written. "Our eldest son, then about four, began to laugh while the Scripture was being read. It was something of a revelation to see that a little child would appreciate humor of which sober adults were totally unaware."[16] The passage that so humored Martin Trueblood was from the seventh chapter of Matthew's Gospel. "He laughed because he saw how preposterous it would be for a man to be so deeply concerned about a speck in another person's eye, that he was unconscious of the fact his own eye had a beam in it."[17]

This volume has been another one of Elton's best-sellers and remains in print with Harper & Row, now twenty-five years after its first printing. One of the delightful stories associated with this book was recently shared with me by Clayton Carlson, publisher at Harper & Row, San Francisco, and surrounds the celebrated "conversion" of Larry Flynt, the publisher of *Hustler* magazine. You may remember that it was Ruth Carter Stapleton, the evangelist and sister of President Jimmy Carter, who was instrumental in what was believed to be at the time the Christian conversion of Larry Flynt. After his "experience," Mr. Flynt had plans to make *Hustler* a Christian magazine. How "Christian" we do not know.

Flynt began to read Christian books, one of which was Elton's *The Humor of Christ.* Believing in the importance of what Elton had written and wanting to reproduce some of this book in his magazine in order to reach a wider audience, he called Mr. Carlson at Harper & Row. Mr. Carlson, in turn, told Mr. Flynt that he would have to check with the author before granting permission. It was an awkward position for the publisher to have to call his author and explain the request. It was Virginia who answered the telephone, and then Elton picked up the extension. "Imagine the embarrassment I felt," recalled Clayton Carlson, "Trying to explain to Elton Trueblood what kind of magazine *Hustler* is, especially knowing that Virginia is on the line!" In the end it was decided not to allow portions of the book to be published in *Hustler*, but Clayton Carlson has never forgotten Elton's remark as he struggled over the decision. His main question was, "What would Christ do?"

The Lord's Prayers came as a result of a series of addresses Elton had promised to deliver at St. Paul's Church in Richmond, Virginia. He explains the circumstances surrounding his time there in his preface.

Most of us admit that our days are radically unequal. On some days we accomplish more or understand more than we understand or accomplish in entire months, under less favorable circumstances. There are dull days, when we see very little, but there are also some which Rufus Jones loved to call days of high visibility. Such a day came to me in March, 1964, when I was worshipping with the noonday congregation of St. Paul's Church, in Richmond, Virginia.

Having promised to give a series of talks for the week, a set of addresses had been prepared, but suddenly, on Monday noon, an entirely different series came to me. I realized, more keenly than ever before, how inept it is to speak of the Lord's Prayer, since we were all aware of more than one in the Gospels, and also since the "Our Father" was primarily intended for the followers rather than for the Leader. The possibility of the plural appealed to me strongly and I decided to announce a series on the Lord's Prayers.

The series was given to the St. Paul's weekday congregation and the experience of giving the separate talks was, to me, a minor revelation. Soon I saw that the theme had a universal application and therefore ought not to be limited to a single company. Consequently, I determined to put my meditations on this important theme into book form.[18]

In writing about this volume in his autobiography, Elton has said, "Like others, I feel now, as I have always felt, genuine difficulties in accepting the efficacy of prayer, but the difficulties begin to vanish in the light of Christ's own reported experience."[19]

In the last year of his full-time professorship at Earlham, it was fitting that Elton concentrate his writing on a topic dear to his heart—he wrote *The People Called Quakers*. Although many books about the Quakers had been written, few were easily readable, and most were unavailable in contemporary form to the general reading public. With Elton's positive reputation with the reading world at large, he wrote a volume about the Society of Friends, noting in the preface that it is "more philosophical than historical because it is an effort to depict a people who represent one experiment in radical Christianity, with emphasis on their ways of thinking."[20] He told the story of Quakerism as "a practical alternative for contemporary men and women. Far from being historically interesting and no more, it is a live option."[21]

Next, Elton concentrated his writing time on a sequel to *The Company of the Committed*. Riding the crest of the "church renewal" wave, Elton wrote *The Incendiary Fellowship* in which he applied his gift of writing to produce a hymn entitled "Baptism by Fire." Usually sung to the Welsh tune *Hyfrydol,* the words are particularly powerful:

> Thou, whose purpose is to kindle:
> Now ignite us with Thy fire;
> While the earth awaits Thy burning
> With Thy passion us inspire.
>
> Overcome our sinful calmness,
> Rouse us with redemptive shame;
> Baptize with Thy fiery Spirit,
> Crown our lives with tongues of flame.
>
> Thou, who in Thy holy Gospel,
> Wills that man should truly live:
> Make us sense our share of failure,
> Our tranquility forgive.
> Teach us courage as we struggle
> In all liberating strife!
> Lift the smallness of our vision,
> By Thine own abundant life.
>
> Thou, who still a sword delivers,
> Rather than a placid peace:
> With Thy sharpened word disturb us,
> From complacency, release!
> Save us now from satisfaction,
> When we privately are free,
> Yet are undisturbed in spirit,
> By our brother's misery.

The title for this work originated in the words of Christ from Luke 12:49, "I came to cast fire upon the earth." It was Elton's attempt as the "father" of the church renewal effort to try to bring together the many different parts of the movement that had arisen since midcentury. This was his last work written before retirement from Earlham College.

Elton had been a professor at Earlham since 1946, with only his brief interlude in Washington, D.C., interrupting his continuous pattern of teaching. Even so, this was just considered a "leave of absence." In June 1966 he had been associated with Earlham for twenty years. He was concluding his Earlham chapter with the tremendous satisfaction of a professor who had had the opportunity to share the gift of knowledge with students that were hungering for enlightenment.

Earlham College has a rich history and tradition and is over 140 years old, yet it is hard to imagine any other one person who has influenced the reputation of the school more than Elton Trueblood. Those who studied under Elton learned to love and respect him. His style was sometimes harsh, and he could be very demanding, but only because he cared for his students and sought to bring out their best.

At sixty-five years of age, Elton was beginning to hit his stride. Where most professionals at this time in their lives are thinking about a more relaxed life, Elton was becoming stronger and his life busier. He has written ten books since retirement and has had four more published that were edited by others but were from his collected material. At the retirement dinner in his honor, President Bolling suggested that he maintain his important relationship with Earlham by being named "professor-at-large." This he likes, for it keeps an important connection for Elton and for the school. One of the favorite jokes Elton loves to tell groups or individuals who ask him about his title is that he prefers "at-large" to "emeritus." The usual response is "why?" "Because," says Elton, sharing his knowledge of the Latin language, "*E* means you're out, and *meritus* means you deserve to be!"

1966–1972

PROFESSOR-AT-LARGE

Hurry up and become 65 as fast as you can, it is a liberating experience.

Throughout the summer of 1966, Elton kept busy speaking, and he also did some relaxing at Pen Point, Lake Paupac, Pennsylvania. He had decided to be away from Earlham when the fall semester began so that his successor in the philosophy department would have ample freedom to conduct classes without feeling his presence. To this end, Virginia and Elton made plans to live in England for several months. The choice of England was deliberate, since Elton wanted to complete his work on the Quaker theologian Robert Barclay, which he had begun in 1939 while a fellow at Woodbrooke College in Birmingham.

It was while he was a fellow at Woodbrooke that Elton had discovered Robert Barclay's personal notebook. This was an exciting discovery and perhaps the most important scholarly find in Elton's research and writing career. The notebook was in the theologian's own handwriting, and much of it was written in code, that is, seventeenth-century shorthand. Colonel Barclay, a descendant of Robert Barclay and the owner of the prized notebook, allowed Elton the freedom to make photocopies of the pages, and he returned to America in the hope of finding someone to break the code. Soon after his return, however, the Second World War broke out, and he had to postpone his research.

In August 1948, nine years later, Elton was in Britain to deliver the Barclay Tercentenary Lecture in Edinburgh, Scotland. While there he had the opportunity to travel to Aberdeen, where Barclay had been imprisoned for his religious conviction, and to visit where he had lived. The title of Elton's lecture was "The Vocation of Robert Barclay," which was eventually to become a part of his biography. He did not feel satisfied going ahead with this project, however, until he could learn the secret code of the notebook.

The big break came in 1959. Elton received a letter from Muriel Hicks of the Friends House Library saying that a man by the name of Douglas G. Lister might be able to help. Lister was an Englishman living in Ethiopia whose hobby was deciphering seventeenth-century shorthand. "It is really a fascinating story," writes Elton in the preface to his *Robert Barclay*, "connecting Ethiopia, America, and England."[1] Immediately, Lister was able to break the mystifying code but postponed the complete translation until Elton was able to give full time to the project in 1966.

The writing of *Robert Barclay* was a tremendous joy, and he felt, throughout the writing and with the eventual publication, that he was repaying a debt to someone who had sacrificed so much to further the course of Christian truth. In many ways the role played within Quakerism by the seventeenth-century Robert Barclay is similar to the twentieth-century role of Elton Trueblood. Both were called to be careful thinkers in the writing and publishing of Christian truth and to help the world-at-large understand philosophically and theologically the importance of the Quaker message as basic Christianity. Throughout the fall and winter Elton wrote in London, and by spring the Barclay project was completed.

"After a long stay in London," Elton wrote in his diary, "we are on our way. I gave the manuscript of *Robert Barclay* to the Oxford University Press on Friday morning, May 26. Harper and Row received the duplicate MS on Friday May 19, 1967." Elton and Virginia traveled by rented car to Norwich, York, and then Edinburgh, speaking to small groups of Friends at each stop. On June 8 they went to visit George MacLeod at Iona. Then after a number of other speeches in small communities between Iona and Glasgow, Elton noted the following, on June 14: "At 4:30 visited Professor William Barclay [The twentieth century biblical scholar and no relation to Robert Barclay] and found him delightful."

Elton testified to the greatness of William Barclay in his book, *Essays in Gratitude*. "More than any other biblical scholar in our generation," he wrote, "William Barclay has shown that it is possible to be popular without being superficial and profound without being dull."[2] Although Elton's personal visit with the great Scottish Christian scholar was brief, his influence has been enduring.

One of the many things the two scholars shared in common was their dislike of "noise pollution." Since William Barclay was very hard of hearing, he wore a hearing aid. He confessed to Elton that when he wanted peace and quiet all that he had to do was disconnect the aid from his ear. As one who is not hard of hearing, yet always searching for experiences of "quiet" in a loud age, this practice greatly interested Elton.

In a recent *Quarterly Yoke Letter*, Elton wrote about the problem of noise pollution, pointing out the fact that we have eyelids we can close when we do not want to see something, but we have no similar natural device that we can use over our ears! In his later years, as quiet has become more of a pursuit, he has made the important philosophical point that in our age there is a great deal of emphasis on "freedom to"– freedom to play loud music, etc. But what is also needed is an equal emphasis upon "freedom from"– freedom from the experience of having to listen to someone else's loud music, etc.

From Glasgow, the "professor-at-large" and Virginia continued to travel south, reaching the Lake District and "Quaker country" of England by June 16. In his diary dated this day, Elton noted: "Wrote eight air letters and later sat with great peace in the Grasmere Church. Copied memorial to Wordsworth and looked affectionately at his grave. Had some real leading in the Church." After visits with Elfrida Foulds and other Quaker friends, they left for Lichfield where they visited the birthplace of Samuel Johnson and the beautiful three-spired cathedral.

When the Truebloods arrived back in London on June 27, Billy Graham was in the midst of one of his crusades, and so they went to hear him. Elton remembers, "We saw Ruth Graham who took us to Billy. It was a noble time." Four days later they were shipping the last of the possessions they acquired while in England back to Indiana, and saying their good-byes to the Cora Hotel staff, their home while in London. The Truebloods were off to Heathrow Airport, where they would board a plane for Copenhagen and then from there to Germany to join a Yokefellow tour group.

Elton and Virginia arrived back on the Earlham campus in the fall of 1967, in the midst of a capital funds drive for the School of Religion. Earlier, Elton had returned to Indiana from England to visit with the officers at the Lilly Endowment, asking them to financially support the capital campaign. They agreed to contribute $500,000. In a letter from Charles Williams, then director of religion at the Lilly Endowment, he reflected on the persuasive power of Elton and Earlham's former president, Tom Jones: "No other two men in the train of George Fox—or, for that matter, John Calvin, John Wesley or John Knox—could have extracted a half-million dollars from us so quickly, painlessly and joyously." The campaign was a success.

Elton soon discovered that it was impossible to release oneself and move into a completely different chapter of life without experiencing a lot of pressure to continue in the work to which one has been devoted for twenty years. In many positions, one can retire, receive a gold watch, and walk away because a new person will be found to fill the position made vacant. In Elton's case, however, he was so closely identified with Earlham and its new School of Religion that he could not just "walk away." Soon he was teaching some courses, helping with fund-raising, and even serving a term as acting dean when the founding dean, Wilmer Cooper, was on sabbatical.

The speaking schedule did not lessen in intensity either. For as long as I have known Elton, he has attempted to free himself from his many speaking commitments. The problem is his tremendous feeling of indebtedness to so many people, which he believes he must repay by giving speeches. Of course, he also wants to encourage people and make a difference in their lives, and his gift of speech is a vehicle for this. Each of the last ten years I have been with him he has, almost ritualistically, asked his secretary to type his engagement dates and put at the top "Last Speaking

Schedule." Each time he will say, "Now James, I know you don't believe me." I don't.

After Elton had completed his book about Robert Barclay, his literary work turned, once again, to the small-book format. In 1968 he wrote *A Place to Stand,* which was his only attempt to write a readable book in theology and the one book, in his judgment, that "may be read longer than any of my other thirty books."[3] He dedicated it to his friend Eli Lilly, who responded to the news of the dedication with this note: "Your idea of dedicating one of your books to me is just about the finest compliment that I ever had. Coming from you makes it appreciated to the Nth degree!" Elton's focus in this important volume was to share what he believed and why concerning rational Christianity, Christ, God, prayer, and the life everlasting. The title was taken from Archimedes, who said, "Give me a place to stand and I will move the earth."

The *Church Herald* wrote, "He has cut through a lot of the contemporary theological fog and given us a place to stand." *Eternity* said, "This book is of such pivotal importance that it is difficult not to overpraise it . . . what will surprise the skeptic . . . is how logical biblical Christianity can be made." And the *Lutheran Witness* stated, "Yes, its goal is accomplished. The book does offer assistance to the ordinary seeker who is attempting to be a Christian and intellectually honest."

One of Elton's favorite statements is "The Christian need not be ashamed of his belief. He can, if he wants, outthink all of the contemporary opposing philosophies." In *A Place to Stand,* Elton sought to strengthen the Christian position intellectually and to provide the average Christian believer a model of thinking that will help him respond to the tough questions of attack. In the words of the *Lutheran Witness,* the "goal is accomplished."

Elton's next book was similar in size to *A Place to Stand* and was a response to the prevailing mood in the late 1960s and early 1970s. *The New Man for Our Time* was written to help Christians develop a pattern of wholeness in their lives. The three areas that need to be held in conjunction are the life of prayer or inner devotion, the life of service or ministry to the world, and the life of thought. In short, Elton said, we are called *to pray, to serve,* and *to think,* and we are called to do this as a part of our whole life pattern. Here, again, he drew upon his relationship with his friend and teacher Rendel Harris, who taught him that in the big issues in life, we do not have to choose. His practical illustration for the need to hold these three together comes from his farm background. He told his readers that these emphases in one's life can be compared to a three-legged milking stool. If any one leg is not attached, the whole stool falls!

As one who was profoundly touched by this book, I can witness to its power. At the time I read it I was a senior at Friends University in Wichita, Kansas, and a major in sociology. Throughout these difficult years on the college campus (1967–1971) I had been developing my social concern (that is, the Vietnam war and civil rights) and my intellect—believing that knowledge is power. But not until I read this book did I fully understand how important it was to develop a life of reverence as the "third" leg of my life's stool. Elton had touched me at my weakness, and it changed my life's vocation.

Being a professor-at-large allowed Elton the freedom to accept other teaching opportunities. When an offer came from Mt. Holyoke College to be the Purington Lecturer for the winter and spring of 1970, he accepted. He wrote about his experience at South Hadley, Massachusetts, and the "high point" of the semester:

I found in 1970 that I enjoyed my teaching, and I was especially glad to round out my experience in this particular way. I now know at first hand what it is to teach in a college for men, in institutions for both sexes, and finally in a college for women. Every time I walked through Mary Lyon Gate, I felt a conscious appreciation of a really noble heritage. The high point of the semester was a service of worship in which we tried to lift the sights of all above the raging political controversy and the unfortunate student strike then in progress. To our amazement the chapel was filled to capacity. All walked out in absolute silence until the big clock struck. It was a lifting experience which those who participated in it will not easily forget.[4]

Elton's literary work during this time was devoted to a book entitled *The Future of the Christian* in which he responded to all of the speculation within various circles of thought that we are in the post–Christian age. He wrote chapters entitled "The Miracle of Survival," "The Church of the Future," "The New Strategies," "The New Evangelicalism," and "Civil Religion." The big point he made was that, given the history of world religions, Christianity is relatively young and those of us living in the latter third of the twentieth century can still be considered "early Christians"!

"Hurry up and become sixty-five as fast as you can," the retired professor repeats to individual visitors and groups alike. "It is a liberating experience." For Elton this time of newly acquired liberation did not mean, in Webster's definition of retirement, "to withdraw from action." Instead it meant to be free to serve more fully. This he has done. As professor-at-large of Earlham College, he has continued to teach, preach, and write, unaffected by our culture's arbitrary setting of age sixty-five as a time to quit being productive.

In June 1969, the *Indianapolis Star* newspaper magazine did a feature on Elton entitled "Eminence at Earlham." In this article, the author described Elton's beginnings on a farm in Iowa and all of his academic pursuits and books written. She said his schedule for 1969 "resembles an AAA tour criss-crossing the country." This particular year he spoke on more than two hundred different occasions. The writer mentioned the pioneer stock from which Elton was reared and his mother who had died one month earlier.

On Monday, May 19, 1969, Mrs. Effie C. Trueblood was buried in the

Motor Friends Church cemetery in Iowa. At the time of her death, she was 101-and-a-half years old. She was one of the last pioneers of Warren County, Iowa. In his "Plain Speech" column for *Quaker Life*, Elton had this to say concerning his mother:

> By any standard of comparison Mother was a strong person . . . though she bore five children, she was never a hospital patient until after the age of 93. At her death her living descendents numbered 43. She outlived all of her contemporaries, so that she was the last of the original settlers of the Quaker Community in Iowa, where, as part of the westward trek 96 years ago, she arrived with her parents from Ohio.

Elton was close to his mother, who was rightly proud of her number-two son. In her latter years she would knit for hours on end, while scattered about her would be copies of her famous son's many books. Elton loves to tell about the time his mother ordered new carpet for her house at age 85 and insisted on a thirty-year guarantee! She was a strong woman who bore the marks of pain and struggle on the Iowa frontier. With her passing, an important era in the life of Iowa and the Trueblood family passed along with her.

At the conclusion of the "Eminence at Earlham" article, the author mentioned a line in one of the letters sent to Elton in honor of his fifty-seventh birthday. It read, "It was a great day for humanity when Elton Trueblood was born." And then the author wrote the following, which seems to capsulize Elton's continuing ministry as a professor-at-large.

As I thought of that statement, I remembered something once learned long ago in an English class — George Elliot wrote in *The Chair Invincible:*

> 'of those who live in scorn
> of miserable aims that end with
>   self
> In thoughts sublime that pierce the
>   night like stars
> And with their mild persistence
>   urge men's minds
> To vaster issues.'

For Elton, continuing to "urge men's minds to vaster issues" is what being a professor-at-large is all about.

WORLD TRAVELER

Select absolutely necessary baggage, set aside the necessary money; then halve the former and double the latter!

Elton has always loved geography. Though he had never been out of the state of Iowa until age twenty-one, since then he has not stopped

Elton and Virginia Trueblood in Pasadena, California, 1969

traveling. He is, by nature, a most inquisitive man, and so the personal glimpses into different cultures or the joy of seeing a natural wonder is a thrilling experience for him.

He made his first round-the-world trip before retiring from Earlham in 1964, but since his retirement he has been free to travel much more. Elton has traveled in all fifty states and in forty-four different countries. The most frequently visited country has been England, and this is only natural for someone who is a Quaker with English roots.

Reflecting in his diary about travel, Elton made these observations.

On change of plans: "The amateur tourist supposes that even a long trip can be completed as planned. In this expectation he is almost sure to be wrong. Something, in a course of a long trip, will make alteration necessary. It may be a riot, a strike, a lack of a seal, a change in plane schedule, or just simple lateness. This is one reason why so many telegrams are used. The professional learns to expect the unexpected!"

On luggage: "It is a law that bags get heavier in each country. Therefore the traveler must expect to send home a series of packages. These must be progressively better tied and sealed as one advances into Asia. Even in Rome the preparation of a package is a big operation. Each new object seems slight, but soon the 40 kilos per couple is surpassed, unless there is obsessive care."

Elton and Virginia with Japanese
kindergarten students

Under "Travel wisdom," he has written, "Select the absolutely necessary baggage, set aside the necessary money; then halve the former and
double the latter!" Concerning inns, he noted: "Dr. Johnson was right that
few things contribute to human happiness more than a good inn. But the
adjective requires emphasis. There is a big difference between an inn and
a *good* inn." Finally, he wrote down three truthful, yet humorous expectations for the traveler: "Expect a big outlay for postage; expect emergencies
to arise; expect some diarrhea."

From November 1970 to February 1971, Elton and Virginia made a
slow journey around the world, traveling mostly by freighter. What the
Truebloods discovered was that when you travel by freighter you can be
more relaxed. Elton explains. "At each port-of-call there are items to be
put aboard, or items to be taken off the ship. Sometimes this requires several days lay-over, which means the passengers can see the sights."

In the early part of this journey, Elton lectured in Hong Kong. Believing that the Christian is never off duty, he was particularly attentive to
those students who, he felt, had special gifts and needed encouragement.
One such student was a man by the name of John Wong. Taking a special
interest in this young man, Elton helped him to immigrate to the United
States and enroll at William Penn College in Iowa. Today, three degrees
and three children later, John Wong is the chair of the marketing department at Iowa State University. Out of affection for his mentor, John
named his first son Elton.

If the beginning portion of the Trueblood journey paid a personal
dividend in John Wong, the later part of the journey paid a literary dividend. Elton and Virginia were staying in the International Hotel in Kam-
pala, Uganda, and were scheduled to go to Kenya to visit the Quaker
mission work at Kaimosi. A telephone call from the airline told them that
their flight had been cancelled. Because of Elton's insistence on keeping
promises (on this particular occasion, to the Quakers of Kenya), he told

Virginia that they must find another way. He called the rail station and was told that all seats "out of the country" were taken. By now he was becoming very concerned and was sensing that a revolution was about to take place in the Ugandan government. As a last resort he called the bus station and was told, "Yes, we have a bus leaving for Kenya at 9:00 A.M., but we do not take reservations. You will have to take your chances." Elton and Virginia were able to get the last two seats on the bus, but they were not together. "For the entire trip," he said, "I had to sit next to a drunken man who made sounds through a paper megaphone, and Virginia sat next to a man who stared at her the whole time. We were the only two white people on the bus." The Truebloods learned later that the reason for the flight cancellation and other travel disruptions was because of the revolution in Uganda, perpetrated by Idi Amin.

When the Truebloods finally arrived in Kenya, a number of the Africans asked them where they were going, and Elton kept repeating, "Kaimosi." What Elton soon learned was that there are three places called Kaimosi. Finally, out of desperation, he said, "Quaker." This struck a responsive chord, and for a hundred shillings the Truebloods were taken to Kaimosi—the one where the Quaker mission is located!

In the preface to his book *The Validity of the Christian Mission,* Elton wrote how the idea for such a literary project evolved.

One day as I was riding in a car near Nairobi, the decision to write was suddenly formed. As the wonder of the mission burst upon me, I saw that the idea of Mission, far from being something peripheral or incidental to the Christian faith, is actually the factor which brings the entire Christian cause into focus. Now I see that in my public career I have been approaching the unity idea of mission for a long time and from a variety of angles.[5]

In this work, launched at the end of his world tour, Elton writes in his famous five-chapter style: "The Phenomenon of Mission," "The Criticism of Mission," "The Defense of Mission," "The Field of Mission," and "The Theology of Mission." The book was published in 1972.

Elton Trueblood travels as inexpensively as anyone I know. He will often stay in the YMCA of a large foreign city rather than spend money on a luxury hotel. For him it is a matter of principle, founded on his belief in the Quaker testimony on simplicity in manner of living. A humorous episode occurred in Rome when Elton wanted to go from the airport to the YMCA. The driver didn't understand. After about five minutes of trying to explain about the YMCA, Elton finally wrote it out on a piece of paper. Immediately the driver recognized the letters and said, "You mean the *yemca.*" Elton was pronouncing each letter, while the taxi driver knew it as one word.

The Great Depression made an indelible impression upon Elton, and he still vividly remembers how difficult it was to make ends meet. Each Thursday afternoon following the Yokefellow luncheon, I would take him to the local "Milkhouse" for milk. Since this is a drive-in store, I would hand the attendant the money for the milk, pass the milk over to Elton, and when the change was given, pass it over to him as well. When the milk was $1.99, and Elton had given me two dollars, he would always have his hand out waiting for the penny in change. When I would tease him about what appeared to be his overconcern for making sure he received his penny in change, he would respond, "James, a Christian is financially careful in the little things, so that he can give to the great things." On another occasion, obviously referring to his days in the Depression, he said, "If people could have seen some of the things I did, they wouldn't be so wasteful."

Even though Elton enjoys traveling alone or with his family, he loves the opportunity to lead a tour. On these occasions he can do two of the things he enjoys most — travel and teach. Two of these opportunities stand out as highlights in his life.

The first was an event sponsored by Word Books. Along with Keith Miller and Dr. Paul Tournier, he led a group in the spring of 1974 on an "Adventure in Living" tour of Greece and Turkey.

A memorable picture was taken of Elton on the Acropolis, with the Parthenon serving as background, while the professor-at-large taught his students. The words he spoke on this occasion have been preserved. It is easy to imagine how comfortable he felt on that special spot where so many of the people about whom he has taught and spoken all of his adult life once studied and taught. In part he said,

We are keenly aware, as we gather here, of the flowering of the human spirit which occurred in this city in the fifth century before Christ. What occurred was simultaneous brilliant development in a variety of fields, including philosophy, architecture, historical writing, and drama. Many of the cultural standards of subsequent centuries were established here, with a combination of excellence rare anywhere in the world. Here Socrates was born in 469; here Pericles died in 429, after his brilliant political leadership of the government; here Herodotus originated the writing of history as we understand it; here lived Thucydides and Xenophon, who continued the work Herodotus had started; here were produced the plays of Aeschylus, Euripides, and Sophocles; and, above all, here Plato established his Academy and wrote his immortal dialogues.[6]

Elton loved this opportunity to stand and speak where his academic discipline of philosophy was born, and those who had the privilege of hearing him will never forget it. Each time I talk to someone who was with him on this tour, his or her eyes light up and they tell about what that experience meant. It was truly a life-changing event.

Another opportunity to lead a group came in 1982 when Elton and I led what he called the "Great Minds" tour to England. In June of that year, forty persons traveled with us while Elton shared his knowledge of places visited. There were special times with the late Bishop Stephen Neill of

Oxford and the ever-vivacious Malcolm Muggeridge of Robertsbridge. We dined with Lord and Lady Caradon at the House of Lords and visited the haunts of Dr. Samuel Johnson up and down Fleet Street. As we traveled to Oxford and Stratford-upon-Avon and then to Birmingham, etc., Elton would sit up front in the bus and share the history of each location.

One of the fun things that Elton encouraged the travelers on this trip to do was to write limericks. He loves a good limerick (a love that inten- sified following a visit to Limerick, Ireland, when he was in that country in 1972 to deliver the annual lecture at Ireland Yearly Meeting of Friends). One he wrote to his wife Virginia shows his fun style:

> My wife's a fabulous beauty
> And even in age she's a cutey;
> She sits in the sun
> And thinks it is fun
> To be far, far away from her duty.

As limericks were written by the tourists, they would be broadcast to the entire bus over the P.A. system. Some were very poor and received the predictable groans from the other travelers, and some were quite clever. It was a wonderful way to build camaraderie on a trip that none of us will ever forget.

Elton's world-traveling days are now over. The physical exertion such travel demands is too great for a man his age. Now he has beautiful memo- ries, and there are reminders throughout his home of the many places he has been and the wonderful people he has met along the way. In every country visited there has been a life touched and a memory made. As I write, Elton is planning to address our next Yokefellow tour group in the Philadelphia airport just prior to our departure for a two-week trip to England. Although he will not be going with us physically, his large spiri- tual presence will be felt. In this way, he is still traveling.

RATIONAL EVANGELICAL

He has traveled through the maze of complexity that always surrounds the difficult questions of faith and has come out proclaiming a profoundly simple truth: "Jesus Christ is my Lord and Savior."

As the contemporary Evangelical movement caught fire in the 1970s, Elton Trueblood was right there with it. As early as 1924, Elton under- stood the major weaknesses of liberal theology. Out of his own experience as a Friends pastor, he wrote in his diary:

> So much of our preaching from liberal pulpits is likely to get nowhere definitely. I tell them what to do and they listen carefully, but they do not

change. They need a new and vital experience of God. We must be born again. The weakness and foolishness of my theology during the last few years appals me. There has been too much emphasis on the intellectual and a failure to seek men's souls in apostolic fashion. It is no wonder that my mother feared for me. She was right. It is a wonder to me that I have been able to maintain as much fire and spirit as I have. From now on, I want to make my dominant note evangelical. I see no reason why a liberal in theology cannot also be an evangelist. At least I want to try to prove the possibility of this.

The most accurate theological term by which to describe Elton True-blood is *Rational Evangelical.* This is where, he believes, "the power is," because it is equidistant from old-fashioned liberalism and old-fashioned Fundamentalism. It combines what he has sought to make a reality in his own life of ministry: "the clear head and the warm heart." He would not have described himself as an Evangelical all of his life, even though he would always have considered himself a committed Christian.

After one year at William Penn College as a young student, Elton came home to the farm and announced to his grandmother that he believed in evolution. "Oh, Elton!" she exclaimed. "I wish thee had never gone to college." This statement by Elton's grandmother reflects the mood of anti-intellectualism that was so pervasive among Quakers in Iowa at the time—the belief that the more one knows, the less of a Christian one becomes. For her, the question of evolution and the existence of God were wrapped in the same package and to believe in the one automatically meant disbelief in the other. The question of evolution, however, is not the point to be made about Elton's belief system; the point is the influence education was having on him as he went beyond the protective confines of the Motor community.

Always questioning, Elton left William Penn for graduate school on the East. He was going through the process of struggling with the complex issues of the faith, and he was able to share this by way of the pulpit or classroom in each place he studied, taught, or preached. He could not accept a system of belief filled with holes that had not been dealt with adequately. The old phrase "You just have to have faith" was not enough for young Elton, as he sought more and more reasons why he should be a Christian committed to Jesus Christ. In his autobiography he says,

In the early days of my ministry I believed in God and undoubtedly thought of myself as a Christian, but my theology was not evangelical. Though in my spoken ministry I often mentioned Christ, I did not emphasize His uniqueness. I spoke much of His compassion, of His emphasis upon love of the brethren, and of His faith in men, demonstrated by His recruitment of such unlikely specimens of humanity as the twelve Apostles, but I tended to omit His teaching about Himself and His unique relation to the Father.[7]

Always struggling through the difficulties of his position, Elton was uncomfortable in his omission of Christ's teaching about himself.

Subtly and slowly the change in my message began to appear. The influences were of course numerous, but it may have been the writings of C. S. Lewis that first shocked me out of my unexamined liberalism. In reading Lewis I could not escape the conclusion that the popular view of Christ as being a Teacher and *only* a Teacher, has within it a self-contradiction that cannot be resolved. I saw, in short, that conventional liberalism cannot survive rigorous and rational analysis. What Lewis and a few others made me face was the hard fact that if Christ was only a Teacher, then He was a false one, since, in this teaching, He claims to be *more*. The supposition that He taught only, or even chiefly, about loving one another is simply not true. The hard fact is that if Christ was not in a unique sense "the image of the invisible God" (Colossians 1:15), as the early Christians believed, then He was certainly the arch imposter and charlatan of history.[8]

Although his "conversion" to a Christocentric faith was not as dramatic as the founder of the people called Quakers, Elton could still proclaim with George Fox that "there is *one*, even Christ Jesus, that can speak to thy condition." He had traveled through the maze of complexity that always surrounds the difficult questions of faith and had come out proclaiming a profoundly simple truth: "Jesus Christ is my Lord and Savior."

In philosophy, Elton is a personalist. "The greatest thing we know about the world," he says, "is the fact that there are persons in it." And so, where most theologians would begin to develop their theology with God and then move to the relationship of Christ, Elton began his book *A Place to Stand* by writing about Christ, saving his second chapter for God. For Elton, "the best way to know what God is like is to study the life of Christ."

In 1971 Elton wrote a chapter in his book *The Future of the Christian* entitled "The New Evangelicalism." He chose as the epigraph for this important part some words from Herbert Butterfield: "Hold to Christ, and for the rest be totally uncommitted." In brief, this is a summary of Elton's faith. Here he shows the weaknesses of the traditional liberal position and the antiquated Fundamentalist position and then proclaims his famous third way—the New Evangelicalism, that is Rational Evangelicalism. The marks of this "new" position are three:

1. "In the first place, we see around us a new emphasis among evangelicals, upon the necessity of being *rational*." Here he cites the new interest in the writing of C. S. Lewis. Although he would not state it in print, it is obvious that another reason to believe that a renewed interest in rationality was developing was the popularity of Elton Trueblood as a speaker and writer within traditional Evangelical circles.
2. "The second perceptible mark of newness, in the evangelical faith, is that many of its adherents are becoming *socially conscious*." Elton notes in this section his personal observations at a conference on evangelism and an article by Frank E. Gaebelin in the July 31,

1970, issue of *Christianity Today*. In his article, entitled, "Reflections In Retrospect," Gaebelin wrote, "I am distressed that it took me so long to realize that social concern is a vital biblical imperative." This emphasis fits well into Elton's concern for wholeness: "If a person can start with a life-changing experience of the love of Christ in his heart, and can go on to try to overcome poverty and war, without, in the process, losing the dedication which originally motivated him, the result is a really powerful combination."

3. "The third evidence of novelty among evangelical Christians is the way in which *they are ceasing to look upon themselves as an exclusive group*." Elton stresses his appreciation for an Evangelicalism that is not sectarian and that recognizes that "evangelical commitment to Christ as the Center of Certitude is not the mark of a party, or even of a group of sects, but simply the central Christian emphasis in any generation."[9]

Elton has become the spokesperson for Rational Evangelicalism. His well-respected educational background coupled with his commitment to Jesus Christ have made him a popular speaker and teacher within Evangelical circles around the world. Although still respected within the mainline Christian movement, Elton is dearly loved within the Evangelical movement.

In 1978 I was with Elton at the Southern Baptist Convention in Atlanta. Along with Ruth Graham, he was one of the speakers at the grand finale of this gathering. The crowd was estimated to be 23,000. My wife and I were seated near the back of the large convention center, and we were only able to see Elton because of the large screens placed throughout the room that broadcast his image. There was a sea of people between where we were sitting and the "speck" of a podium from where Elton was to speak.

As Elton rose to speak, the vast crowd became silent. All eyes were fixed on the man who had become the elder statesman of Rational Evangelicalism. He began with a joke about his and Ruth Graham's denominational affiliation (Quaker and Presbyterian). "Here you are, 23,000 strong, and you had to bring in two gentiles to have a program!" The convention center erupted in laughter. He then went on to say how close he felt to them spiritually and proceeded to speak on his favorite topic—Rational Evangelicalism. At the end he was given a standing ovation.

I mention this incident because it is representative of how Elton Trueblood has become so well respected within the Evangelical movement. For many years he has spoken before the national gatherings of men of the Church of God, and he has shared his faith at the Evangelical "praise gathering" held in Indianapolis. He has frequently spoken on Evangelical college campuses the world over. Those who come out of this tradition and hear him are blessed, but Elton also loves the opportunities which the New Evangelicalism have provided. He has always done his best as a speaker when the group before him is warm and attentive, both attributes that are very much a part of the Evangelical tradition. In Elton Trueblood, Evangelicalism has found a rational spokesperson, and in Evangelicalism Elton has found a "place to stand."

1972–1980

ABRAHAM LINCOLN AND AMERICAN ANGUISH

We cannot but believe that he who made the world still governs it.

In the summer of 1970, journalist Bill Moyers boarded a bus in New York City and began a journey that took him across 13,000 miles of America. He wrote about his conversations with people along the way in a book entitled *Listening to America.* His first stop on his way to "rediscover his country" was Hartford, Connecticut, and his second stop was Richmond, Indiana. His first day in Richmond was spent conversing with a number of people, primarily associated with the local American Legion. Some years before, Mr. Moyers had been treated badly by the Legion when he was serving in the Johnson administration. This time it was better.

During his next day in Richmond, the inquisitive journalist visited Elton in his study on the Earlham campus. "The name of Dr. Elton True-blood . . . was a familiar name to me," wrote Moyers. "Many years ago, in a Comparative Religion course at the University of Texas, I had been strongly influenced by *The Predicament of Modern Man,* which Dr. True-blood had written in 1944 while teaching at Stanford University."

What mostly interested Bill Moyers was the connection between Elton, the Quaker philosopher, and Richard Nixon, the Quaker president. Elton made these comments about Nixon's background:

His grandparents lived on the Muscatatuck River about a hundred miles south of here. . . . If you saw the movie *Friendly Persuasion,* the heroine in there is based on Nixon's grandmother. In that movie the southern army—Morgan's Raiders— crossed the Ohio and came up through the Quaker settlements, and my grandmother fed the soldiers in her kitchen, and Richard Nixon's grandmother did, too. . . . Nixon, you see, represents what would be called the evangelical core of Quakers . . . nearly all of the California Quakers, where Nixon's parents lived, remain in the evangelical core. I knew many of those people personally, including some of the President's relatives. They are absolutely the salt of the earth, the backbone of the Whittier community.[1]

Mr. Nixon was the second Quaker president with whom Elton had contact. The relationship extends back to the time when Elton was chief religious information officer for the USIA and Richard Nixon was vice president. It continued through the former president's time of self-imposed exile in San Clemente, California.

Elton's diary and file of correspondence shows that President Nixon and Elton had genuine respect for one another. Each time Elton was in Washington, New York, or California, he would seek an opportunity to speak with Mr. Nixon, and Mr. Nixon appreciated these times of conversation. The fact that they had similar backgrounds made their relationship more meaningful.

In the third year of his first term as president, Mr. Nixon asked Elton to speak at the White House worship service. On October 10, 1971, Elton obliged. In his introduction, President Nixon said:

Mr. Chief Justice, Members of the Cabinet, Members of the Diplomatic Corps, Members of the Congress, and all of our special guests this morning: For these worship services this is a rather unusual one. Those of you who have attended before recognize that all of them have been ecumenical in the broadest sense. We have had representatives of many of the major Protestant groups, Catholic groups, and Hebrew groups. But very seldom has the denomination of which I am a member been represented.

This morning Dr. Elton Trueblood, one of the great scholars of the Society of Friends and now Professor-at-Large of Earlham College, who is well known to many of you in this room, will bring the message. And the Secretary of Agriculture [Clifford Hardin], whose parents, just as my parents, were birthright Quakers, will read the Scripture.[2]

Before he spoke, Elton offered the following prayer:

We thank thee O Father for this day, this place, and this nation. We thank thee for the faith which united us and for the power which sustains us. We come together in simplicity, in quietness, and in humility, praying that we may know thy will and that we may have the courage to follow it. We pray especially this morning for the President of this great nation, for the members of Congress, the Supreme Court, and the Cabinet and all who make decisions in the life of this people. Help them to know that they are under thee. Help them to be instruments of thy divine will. All this we ask for the sake of Jesus Christ our Lord. Amen.[3]

His sermon was the most brief of all who participated in these White House services, a fact in which Elton takes great delight. He began by talking about Abraham Lincoln and how "one hundred and nine years ago at this time of year there was a meeting for worship in this building. It was the darkest period of the Civil War." He spoke about the agony of decision making that presidents experience and how there are "no simple answers." His Scripture text was from the parables of Christ—the parable of the seeds and the sower. His main concern was the connection between the "roots" and the "fruit" and how, if there is no depth of root, the fruit withers away. "We have tried the experiment of keeping alive wonderful things such as equality of opportunity and the dignity of the individual, but after they have been severed from their sustaining roots and in this we cannot win." The sustaining roots about which Elton was speaking are the spiritual underpinnings of our culture, a theme he has been espousing since he wrote *The Predicament of Modern Man*. In conclusion he stated one of his most enduring aphorisms: "However beautiful the flowers may be, if they are cut from their roots, they will wither and die." For a benediction, he said, "Now go in joy, sin no more, love God, serve His children. Amen."[4]

Elton was proud of the fact that "one of his own" was the president of the United States. In an article for his column "Plain Speech" in *Quaker Life* magazine, he wrote about another Quaker president:

> The American Presidency is an awesome office; to be President of the United States is to occupy the most potent position of leadership in the world. And now by a wholly unpredictable chain of events, we again have one of our own who has been elected to this great responsibility. We rejoice in the manner in which he has overcome defeat and grown perceptibly in the process.
>
> The President-elect presented frankly, in the pre-election broadcasts depicting his own story, both the hardships of his family and their depth of Quaker conviction. It is from the Quaker heritage that our new leader has drawn much of his strength of purpose. If it were not for California Yearly Meeting and Whittier College it is unthinkable that Richard Nixon would be where he now stands . . .

This position was certainly a far cry from what Elton wrote in his diary following the election of Herbert Hoover, where he openly shared his concern about Quakers being in danger now that one of their own was in the White House. He felt then that many Quakers were far too proud of this fact. Richard Nixon, however, was a friend of Elton's and he had personally counseled with this Quaker president a number of times.

On Friday, May 14, 1971, Elton and Landrum Bolling, then president of Earlham College, visited with the president in the Oval Office. Their meeting was a discussion of the options for peace in Vietnam, and because Elton was now focusing his literary efforts in writing a book about Abraham Lincoln, he was keenly aware of the criticism Mr. Nixon was experiencing as the president of a much-divided nation. As they left the Oval Office, Elton handed Mr. Nixon a copy of Lincoln's "Meditation on the Divine Will," hoping that it would be of encouragement. It reads as follows:

> We are indeed going through a great trial—a fiery trial. In the very responsible position in which I happen to be placed, being a humble instrument in the hands of our Heavenly Father, as I am, and as we all are, to work out his great purposes, I have desired that all my works and acts may be according to his will, and that it might be so, I have sought his aid, but if after endeavoring to do my best in the light which he affords me, I find my efforts fail, I must

believe that for some purpose unknown to me, He wills it otherwise. If I had had my way, this war would never have been commenced; if I had been allowed my way this war would have been ended before this, but we find it still continues; and we must believe that He permits it for some wise purpose of His own, mysterious and unknown to us; and though with our limited understandings we may not be able to comprehend it, yet we cannot but believe, that He who made the world still governs it.[5]

On August 20, 1972, Elton was invited by the president to speak before the delegates to the Republican National Convention in Miami. Elton considered this an important opportunity to penetrate the body politic with a spiritual message. At the time he was absorbed in writing his book on Abraham Lincoln's theology, and shared with the delegates how Lincoln understood his position as President to be that of "an instrument" in the hands of God. What occurred after the speech became one of the most damaging incidents of Elton's public career.

The writer Kurt Vonnegut, Jr., was in the audience. In an article for Harper's magazine entitled: *In a manner that must shame God Himself,* Vonnegut wrote about the influx of religious faith into American politics, and specifically about the delegates' worship service. Most of his article focused on Elton's understanding of Lincoln's theology, with Vonnegut arguing that the president is responsible only to the people who elect him, and criticizing Elton's suggestion that there is a higher authority to whom the president is responsible as well. The article brought a mass of negative correspondence, especially from Quakers. Many objected to Elton's claim that *all* Quakers are not pacifists, and that one does not have to espouse pacifism in order to be a Quaker.

What Elton sought throughout this very hard time in our nation's history was *rationality* and, more specifically, rationality from a Christian perspective. He shared his concern in a widely publicized article called "Watergate: A Christian View."

> There is abundant discussion from the point of view of politicians, but who has spoken as a Christian? It may be that healing will come in this way, as in no other. The Christian, if he is loyal to the New Testament vision of human life, will begin with several solid points of conviction. Among these are the following:
>
> 1. *Judgment.* While not condoning wrongdoing in any way, the Christian is keenly aware of the dangers which arise when we become judgmental. Christ warns against becoming judgmental, employing the phrase "with what judgment you judge, you will be judged" (Matthew 7:2). A paradoxical development often occurs in human experience, in that the reaction to sin is really worse than the sin itself.
>
>   In the Biblical story of the prostitute, the woman comes off better than her accusers, the suggestion being that these men may not be entirely clean themselves. "Let him who is without sin among you be the first to throw a stone at her" (John 8:7). Perhaps it is because I have not

listened adequately, but, in the furor of the past few months, I have not heard any references of this kind. Part of my sadness has arisen because the prevailing mood has been one of extreme harshness.

2. *Self-Righteousness.* It is part of the paradox of the Gospel to recognize that there is more spiritual danger in feeling righteous than in feeling sinful. The supreme illustration of this is the story of the Pharisee and the Publican, in which the Pharisee thanked God that he was not as the other man (Luke 18:11). That self-righteousness feeds upon itself has been amply demonstrated by journalists, broadcasters and members of Congress during the last few months.

The trick is to take on the look of the moral crusader who is incensed at the sin of other men. Then the crusader can be as vindictive as he likes and seem more righteous in doing so. The worst aspect of Watergate is the evidence of how widespread the Pharisaical mood is.

3. *Glee.* One of the most obvious reactions on the part of the leaders in what has many of the characteristics of a "witch hunt" is the glee with which the victims are pursued. Each new revelation of wrongdoing is reported with a virtual smacking of the lips, rather than in sorrow. This is understandable by purely pagan standards, but it is very far from the Christian way. At the heart of the inspired description of love, from the Christian standpoint is the penetrating observation, "it does not rejoice at wrong" (I Corinthians 13:6 RSV).

4. *Sin.* Underneath all of the furor is the nearly universal expression of surprise that sins have occurred. How this is possible is hard to understand, except upon the assumption of natural human goodness. It is here that the Christian position is manifestly more sophisticated than that of the known alternatives.

Elton's book on Lincoln has had an important impact on many, but it had a special influence on Republican leaders who claim Lincoln as one of their own. President Gerald Ford kept a copy of Trueblood's *Lincoln* on his desk in the Oval Office during his presidency, and in a September 1981 article for *Good Housekeeping,* entitled "My Life in the White House," Nancy Reagan wrote about finding the book in the White House library and what it meant to her. "One day I picked up a book called *Abraham Lincoln: Theologian of American Anguish,* written by Elton Trueblood," she said. "The author stresses Lincoln's idea of a special destiny for America, and as I sat reading, just down the corridor from the bedroom where Lincoln slept, I felt a shiver of recognition and agreement as I read 'Lincoln's only certainty was that God would never cease to call America to her true service, not only for her sake, but for the sake of the world.'"

After reading *Abraham Lincoln: Theologian of American Anguish,* it is easy to see why Lincoln has made such an impact on the life and writing style of Elton. All who have had the opportunity to read this slim, yet powerful little volume, can be grateful to Reinhold Niebuhr, who, many years earlier at Stanford, first put into the mind of Elton that Abraham Lincoln was the most original of American theologians. Elton never forgot Niebuhr's words, and in 1973 he paid his debt to Niebuhr, but more importantly, to Abraham Lincoln.

RELIGION AND POLITICS

What is at stake is not a set of words, but the spirit of reverence.

Elton Trueblood has tried to remain neutral in politics. It has not been easy. In his earlier years he was influenced by Franklin Delano Roosevelt, especially in speaking style, and he was a guest for dinner in the Johnson White House. Once while speaking in Atlanta, he was even a special guest in the governor's mansion when Jimmy Carter was governor of Georgia. For the most part, however, Elton has been a favorite philosopher of the Republican party. "In my boyhood in Iowa," he has shared with Republican audiences, "I heard that there was such a thing as a democrat, but I never saw one."

His love of politics is related to his love of law. In his diary, dated December 18, 1948, he writes about how he would have liked being a lawyer: "If I had not chosen my present rather complex profession I should have liked being a lawyer. The lawyer lives in the middle ground between fact and judgment. He is always concerned with delicate balances of significances. He is closer to sophistication than is the scientist and closer to actuality than is the metaphysician. His life often includes the drama of the courtroom and he owns books." Elton is especially proud of the fact that his youngest son, Sam, is a lawyer.

Jesus Christ said that his disciples are to penetrate the world with the gospel message. Elton takes this command very seriously. He believes no aspect of our lives is exempt from the message of Jesus Christ, and he sees politics as a place that needs the Christian message as much as, if not more than, anywhere else. Many years ago he was perceptive enough to see the decline of religious faith in many parts of our life together. The Supreme Court decision of 1963, ruling on Bible reading and prayer in public schools, particularly bothered him. From 1964 to the present, Elton has been an outspoken voice regarding the actions of the Supreme Court.

On at least two occasions Elton has been asked by the White House to help in the preparation of the president's annual *Thanksgiving Proclamation*. Elton believes this to be a very important part of his ministry, and he is always grateful for the opportunity to share his concern for the spiritual condition of our country. In 1983, the last proclamation he helped to prepare, Elton explained the thinking of one of his heroes, Abraham Lincoln. Through the pen of Ronald Reagan, it reads as follows:

> One hundred and twenty years ago, in the midst of a great and terrible civil conflict, President Lincoln formally proclaimed a national day of Thanksgiving to remind those "insensible to the ever watchful providence of Almighty

God" of this Nation's bounty and greatness. Several days after the dedication of the Gettysburg battlefield, the United States celebrated its first national Thanksgiving. Every year since then, our Nation has faithfully continued this tradition. The time has come once again to proclaim a day of thanksgiving, an occasion for Americans to express gratitude to their God and their country.

In his remarks at Gettysburg, President Lincoln referred to ours as a Nation "under God." We rejoice in the fact that, while we have maintained separate institutions of church and state over 200 years of freedom, we have at the same time preserved reverence for spiritual beliefs. Although we are a pluralistic society, the giving of thanks can be a true bond of unity among our people. We can unite in gratitude for our individual freedoms and individual faiths. We can be united in gratitude for our Nation's peace and prosperity when so many in this world have neither.

As was written in the first Thanksgiving Proclamation 120 years ago, "No human counsel hath devised nor hath any mortal hand worked out these great things. They are the gracious gifts of the Most High God." God has blessed America and her people, and it is appropriate we recognize this bounty.

NOW THEREFORE, I, RONALD REAGAN, President of the United States of America, in the spirit of the Pilgrims, President Lincoln, and all succeeding Presidents, do hereby proclaim Thursday, November 24, 1983, as a National Day of Thanksgiving, and I call upon Americans to affirm this day of thanks by their prayers and their gratitude for the many blessings upon this land and its people.

Because of Elton's concern for a religious influence in government he has always accepted the kind invitations of the chaplains of both the House and Senate to deliver opening prayers. The last time he did so was on the National Day of Prayer, May 3, 1984, as the guest of Senator Richard Lugar of Indiana, Senator John East of North Carolina, and Senate chaplain Dr. Richard Halverson.

After the prayer, Senator East and his wife, Priscilla, invited Elton to lunch in the Senate dining room, along with Steven R. Valentine, who at that time was the chief counsel of the Senate Judiciary Sub-Committee chaired by East. Senator and Mrs. East, as well as Valentine, are all alumni of Earlham College. During the luncheon, Senator East would introduce Elton to each of the senators who were coming into the room for lunch. Invariably, Elton would ask each of them in the professorial manner to which his students are accustomed, "Senator, were you in the Senate for my prayer this morning?" Most, of course, were not, and so he would give each a small printed copy of his prayer to be read at their leisure.

When Senator Proxmire of Wisconsin arrived, Senator East introduced Elton, and Elton asked him what was by now the standard question. The Senator from Wisconsin replied, "No," and Elton asked if he would like to read a copy. The Senator graciously said yes, took out his glasses, and began to silently read the prayer. When Elton noticed that he was reading silently, he told the Senator, "I meant out loud!" And so Senator Proxmire began again, this time vocalizing the prayer.

There is certainly humor in this situation, and Elton is one of the few persons who could get away with making a United States senator read a prayer aloud in the Senate dining room. To those of us who know Elton well, there is no doubt, however, why he did this. His point: If it is alright for you, it should be alright for millions of school children throughout this nation.

The prayer Elton spoke on that occasion is as follows:

> O Thou who hast brought our beloved nation into existence, and who hast sustained it for so many years, help us to understand thy purpose in this won-derous experiment. We are grateful that we have been enabled to endure through many dangers; we are glad to be a part of a nation that is not ashamed to pray! Teach us to value the pattern of life which combines the secular and the sacred in a fashion that is truly unique. We are confident that thy guidance will continue through all vicissitudes, so that we can pass on our heritage undiminished.
>
> Give wisdom, we pray, to our President and to the makers of our laws that they may be faithful in this holy calling. Use us, unworthy as we are, as the instruments of thy purpose, not merely for ourselves, but for all mankind. May this National Day of Prayer confirm our faith, establish our hope and enlarge our charity. Amen.

Following his time in Washington on this occasion, Elton wrote a *Quarterly Yoke Letter* telling *why* he went:

> My invitation to open the United States Senate with prayer, on May 3, 1984, was taken seriously by me. I accepted the invitation not because I think the nation's highest deliberative body cannot be reverent without my help, but because I welcomed the opportunity to make one small addition to the effort to keep our nation from sliding into official paganism.
>
> The paganism into which we are sliding is called secularism, a position which is sometimes upheld with a show of principle. The chief principle about which secularists seem to become aroused is that of separation of church and state, which they mistakenly suppose is part of our constitution. If it were part of our constitution, I could not legally open the Senate as I have done. . . .
>
> The commentators who routinely oppose school prayer are, in most instances, quick to deny that they oppose prayer as such. What they oppose, they say, over and over, is prayer which is connected, in any way, with the educational system. The poorest of all arguments against school prayer is that of people who say that they are not opposed to prayer, but want to keep it in its place. By place they usually mean the Church. They propose, thereby, a new form of segregation. Those who employ this approach do not seem to realize that they are in direct conflict with the main thrust of spiritual religion, every-where. Prophets of spiritual religion are unanimous in seeking, not segrega-tion, but penetration. They hope to penetrate the world, and schools are part of the world. Christ said to go into all the world (Mark 16:15). If He had been willing to limit prayer to synagogues, Christian Civilization would never have emerged.

Many who engage in the contemporary argument about the practice of reverence do not seem to understand how radical the cultural change which they support really is. Until the last two decades, the notion of prohibiting any expression of reverence in schools was not seriously entertained by anybody of any consequence.

The majority of editorial writers and television commentators, whom I have read or heard, have opposed school prayer; but seldom for valid reasons. Over and over they engage in the oldest of debating tricks, that of attacking some position which no one has actually upheld. Thus the editorial in the *New Yorker*, which ridicules the idea of school prayer, says, in the climactic sentence of its attack, "*God is not waiting for His invitation to drop in on the schools.*" Here is a position which no person, so far as I know, has ever supported. The problem is not what God needs, but what is sorely needed by poor befuddled persons like ourselves. We need a recovery of moral integrity: we need the humility which makes us understand our own unworthiness; we need to learn to appreciate "*Not my will but Thine be done.*" Such wisdom most people are not likely to learn unless they are taught, and they will never be taught if the present establishment is not challenged. . . .

It is sorrowful to contemplate the degree to which we have declined. Arguments about who will compose written prayers in school are singularly irrelevant and often little more than a debating point. What is at stake is not a set of words, but the spirit of reverence. What ought to concern us is the reality and not the form. Consequently, the stakes are high.

In early April 1973, Elton received a letter from Wilson O. Weldon, editor of the *Upper Room*. The opening paragraph reads as follows:

I am privileged to notify you that upon my nomination you have been unanimously approved by our committee to receive the 1974 Upper Room Citation for notable contributions to worldwide Christian Fellowship. I write to ascertain whether you will be willing to accept this award at a time and place to be arranged. We hope very much that you will accept.

Elton accepted this most gracious honor, and on March 12, 1974, a grand banquet was held at the Hilton Hotel in Indianapolis, where the citation was presented. In accepting this honor, Elton joined such Christian notables as John R. Mott, Frank Laubach, G. Bromley Oxnam, Ralph W. Sockman, and Billy Graham, all of whom have received the award in former years.

The year 1974 also saw the release of Elton's autobiography, *While It Is Day*. The title comes from John 9:4, "We must work the works of him who sent me, while it is day. . . ." These also happen to be the words Dr. Samuel Johnson had engraved on his pocket watch, a fact Elton loves to share with people when he is talking about the discipline of time. "If you saw that each time that you looked at your watch," he says, "You would not be wasteful with your hours left on this earth."

His autobiography is written *topically* rather than *chronologically* and is divided into the following subjects: *child, student, teacher, author, minister,*

Yokefellow, father, rambler. In it, as the cover of the book states, "Elton True-blood pays his toll on a road which others may have constructed but on which he has left his own, indelible 'fingerprints,' in the words of John Baillie."

Elton wanted *While It Is Day* to be his last book. "Too many people go on too long," he has often said. "They continue to write long after they have stopped having good ideas. I don't want to be one of them." He kept his promise, but several more books were produced using Elton True-blood material. A number of his lectures delivered before Quaker groups were edited by me and released through the Friends United Press in 1978 under the title *Basic Christianity*. In 1978, *A Philosopher's Way* was released by Broadman Press, edited by Elizabeth Newby. This volume was a collection of writings, such as Elton's address at the funeral of Herbert Hoover, the biographical introduction to his *Prayers of Samuel Johnson*, and a number of others. That year also saw the release of *The Encourager* by Broadman Press, which was a collection of many of Elton's *Quarterly Yoke Letters*, all of which dealt with pertinent themes. This volume was followed by *The Teacher* in 1980, another collection of speeches and writings such as Elton's speech atop the Acropolis in 1974. *The Best of Elton Trueblood: An Anthology* was edited by me in 1980 and released by Zondervan. Finally, *Essays in Gratitude* was published by Broadman in 1982. In this volume Elton wrote about people and places in his life for which he is grateful. These pieces were first published in *Quaker Life* magazine in a column Elton wrote called, "I Remember...."

Despite all of the national problems associated with 1974, Elton personally considered it "a great year." In a note to himself he wrote, "1974: a great year—Upper Room, *While It Is Day*, Greece—all seems to come to a climax!" He was healthy and busy and looking forward to 1975. In that year he would travel to a country he had always wanted to visit and speak to a group of people that were not recognized by their government—the Baptists of Russia.

VISIT TO RUSSIA

The only faith which can exist here is a faith lighting up a bright flame.

On December 30, 1974, Elton received a letter from A. Bichkov, general secretary of the All-Ukranian Council of Evangelical Christian-Baptists of the USSR. In it he invited the Truebloods to visit the Soviet Union from June 9 to 23, 1975. "During your stay in our country," the letter said, "you will be acquainted with the life of our country and that of our churches." Elton quickly accepted the invitation.

The opportunity to visit Russia is due, in large part, to the work of Robert Denny, who was the general secretary of the Baptist World Alliance. Elton's interest in going to Russia was first shared during an "unexpected"

Speaking from the pulpit of the Moscow Baptist
Church, 1975

meeting aboard an airplane, when he found himself seated next to
Mr. Denny. After learning of Elton's interest, Robert Denny did not let
it rest.

The journey to Russia was preceded by a time in England and Switzerland. The Truebloods traveled via the *Queen Elizabeth II* to England and
stayed at their favorite hotel, the Cora, from May 7 to 30. While in London
they attended the London Yearly Meeting of Friends and had the opportunity to visit with many Friends and friends from past trips. Next they
traveled to Switzerland, where Elton led a retreat at the Swiss Yokefellow
House and spoke at the World Council of Churches center in Geneva.
Here he had an important meeting with Dr. Visser 't Hooft, who was most
knowledgeable about the churches in Russia.

The Truebloods arrived in Moscow on June 9. Their tour was limited
to four cities: Moscow, Kishinev, Kiev, and Leningrad. "Since this was our
first experience in Russia," Elton wrote, "we hardly knew what to expect,
but we were reasonably sure in advance, of the high level of dedication on
the part of Russian Christians. In this we were not disappointed." The way
in which the Russian Christians would "squeeze" into the churches, and
how most would stand throughout the entire worship service, greatly
impressed Elton. He has long been concerned about the relative comfort
of American Christians when compared to others around the world, and
his Russian experience enhanced this concern. Whenever I was with Elton
for a speaking engagement after the trip to Russia, he would always tell his
host, "If there are not enough chairs, let people stand," and then he would
make reference to the "tough stock" of the Russian Christians.

In reflecting on the "most valued" aspect of the Russian Christians,
Elton noted,

> The Christian Fellowship is clearly the most valued feature of these people!
> They love one another and they address one another as Brother or Sister. Many

congregations gather five times a week, i.e., twice on Sunday and three evenings, Tuesday, Thursday, and Saturday. All of the gatherings in which we shared lasted for more than two hours, with no evidence of resistance to the long services. Some members stay in the meetinghouse all day, carrying their lunches and enjoying the fellowship which is a very important feature of their lives.

Once again Elton could not help but compare the situation in the Russian church with so many of the churches in America. This strong sense of fellowship and love for one another, and the desire to "linger" together long after the formal service is over, is so very different from the "mad dash" to the local restaurants following the Sunday morning services in this country. Of course, so much of this sense of togetherness is the direct result of the persecution the Russian churches must endure from their government.

At each place Elton spoke he had an interpreter, or, as he would lovingly call him, "the interrupter." He explains what occurred during the worship:

> Often there are two or three sermons plus many spontaneous prayers from the rank and file, including women. During prayers, there is a general buzzing sound as hundreds of people voice their private prayers in whispers. Always there is a choir of both men and women, with anthems in the Russian language. Because most of the members do not own Bibles, there is a great deal of Scripture reading.

In Leningrad, Elton and Virginia visited what is called "the academy," which is the highest educational unit of the Orthodox church. Here he spoke to the leaders of the academy who were particularly interested in the people called Quakers. Being a Robert Barclay scholar, Elton was curious about whether or not the academy library had a copy of *Barclay's Apology*, which, he knew, was hand delivered by a group of Friends to Peter the Great in 1697. "To my delight," Elton said, "I found that there are two copies, one of which is in Latin. It is highly likely that this is the very same copy given to the Czar so long ago."

Knowing of the shortage of Bibles in Russia, Elton was able to purchase two copies in the Russian language, as well as two concordances, in London prior to departure. These were not confiscated upon entering the country, and so he gave them to his Russian hosts.

This was an important trip for Elton, who had for two years during his tenure at the USIA broadcast his words over the Voice of America. Until now, however, he had not seen the places or people to whom he was speaking. The strong sense of fellowship, and the way in which the Russian Christians would endure discomfort to experience a time of Christian worship, greatly impressed him. "Moderate religion is not all characteristic of modern Russia," he wrote. "The only faith which can exist here is a faith lighting up a bright flame."

The "bright flame" Elton experienced on this journey is still glowing

in his vast array of memorable experiences. Upon his return to the
United States, Elton wrote to his Russian host,

> My wife and I reached home safely Sunday evening, June 22, full of grati-
> tude and affection. The journey from the Moscow Hotel to our home here
> occupied a little more than 20 hours. We had beautiful summer weather all
> the way.
>
> We shall long remember your great kindness in a multitude of ways. We
> were received with genuine affection and our needs were met at every turn.
> Now we shall concentrate on telling the story. We hope that our effort in going
> so far will result in one more step towards peace in our world. We are more
> than ever convinced that commitment to Christ is the key to peace, both
> among nations and in individual lives.

THE QUOTABLE DR. TRUEBLOOD

Listen to the beautiful cadence of one-syllable words!

It was the spring of 1984, and I was seated at my desk when the telephone rang. On the other end of the line a "frantic" speech writer from
the White House asked me about a quotation from Dr. Trueblood. "I can't
find it anywhere," he said, "and the president wants to use it in a speech
tonight!" I asked the caller for the gist of the quotation. "It's something
about planting trees and learning the meaning of life." Happily I was able
to assure him that the entire quotation could be found in the second
chapter of *The Life We Prize* and that it is the last sentence of the chapter.
The quotation which the president wanted to repeat is "A man has made
at least a start on discovering the meaning of human life when he plants
shade trees under which he knows full well he will never sit."

Elton is still, perhaps, the most quoted religious leader in the country.
His writing and ideas have been the driving force behind many sermons
and lectures. None of his *Quarterly Yoke Letters* are copyrighted, and he is
constantly telling people to use his ideas. Unfortunately, some have used
them verbatim. On at least one occasion a pastor literally delivered a
Trueblood sermon word for word, presenting it as if it were his own. He
probably would have gotten by with it except for one thing—Mrs. Elton
Trueblood was in the congregation, and she had typed the sermon for her
husband's book *The Yoke of Christ*. Embarrassed by what was happening,
Virginia tried to "sneak" out of the church without greeting the pastor
at the door. Unfortunately, the woman who had brought Virginia to
worship insisted that she meet her pastor. The pastor greeted her by asking, "And what is your name?" Before she could respond, her friend said,
"This is Mrs. Trueblood." Stammering, the pastor said, "Not Mrs. *Elton*
Trueblood?"

"Dear Abby" has twice printed a quotation from Elton in letters sent
by Arthur Prince, the most recent being in December 1987. It was interest-

ing to learn just how widely Abby is read. Judging from the mail and tele-phone calls that came as a result of this letter, she must have an enormous following. Elton received more correspondence because of "Dear Abby" than almost anything else he has written! The letter from Mr. Prince using the quotation and Abby's response is as follows:*

> Dear Abby: You recently wrote: "Mark Twain said, 'Man is the only animal that blushes. Or needs to.'"
> That caused me to recall these words by David E. Trueblood in his *Philoso-phy of Religion:* "It has been said that man is the only animal who laughs, the only one who weeps, the only one who prays, the only one who can invent, the only one with a written language, the only one who is proud, the only one who can make progress, the only one who guides his own destiny, the only one who is penitent and the only one who needs to be."
> Arthur H. Prince, Memphis

> Dear Mr. Prince: One wonders if perhaps Trueblood could have been con-sciously or unconsciously influenced by Twain. Trueblood, at 87, is alive and well in Indiana, but old Samuel L. Clemens cashed in his chips in 1910, so never the Twain shall meet.

In a similar letter in 1974, Abby's column attributed the quotation to "David Elton *Fine*blood." Elton wrote a response:

> Dear Abby: It will not surprise you to learn that my attention had been called to your column in which you answer a correspondent who quotes me at length. . . .
> Did you notice the amusing fact that I was given a new name? The alleged author was called "David Elton Fineblood."
> Faithfully,
> David Elton Trueblood
> Earlham College, Richmond, Indiana

Abby's response:

> Dear Mr. True(not Fine)blood: The scholar Arthur Prince who sent me your brilliant quotation did not find it very amusing, and I don't blame him. He had your name right, and so did I. How your blood became "fine" from "true" baffles me. The transformation no doubt occurred in the composing room, causing my own blood (which is "A Positive") to boil briefly when I saw the error. My apologies to both you and Arthur Prince.

As I have the opportunity to travel and speak to people around the country, I continue to be amazed at how many lives Elton has touched. Countless pastors have told about the life-changing impact he has had on their lives, whether it be through his writings or his speaking. One such pastor recently said to me, "I shall never forget Dr. Trueblood's opening

---

sentence before a convocation at my seminary. He began his remarks by saying, 'Deliberate mediocrity is a heresy and a sin!' I shall never forget those words." This is certainly one of Elton's most quotable sentences and, in capsule form, expresses his strong emphasis upon using to their fullest all of the gifts God has given us. In Elton's theology, to settle for mediocrity in our lives, when greatness is possible, is a sin.

Adorning the hallway wall of the Yokefellow Institute is a plaque presented by the late Paul Dortmund, a Yokefellow of Worthington, Ohio. On the plaque is this Trueblood quotation from the preface to his book *Confronting Christ:* "Jesus Christ can be accepted; He can be rejected; He cannot reasonably be ignored." This quotation has been a popular one for Christians around the world.

Elton's writing and speaking style, as noted earlier, has been greatly influenced by Alfred North Whitehead. Whitehead, who spoke and wrote in an aphoristic style, was a model for him. As I prepared the anthology of Elton's voluminous works, I quickly realized most of the Trueblood paragraphs can stand alone. They begin in a very strong way, and they conclude in a strong way, holding within the lines one complete thought. This is certainly a major part of his secret to writing such quotable sentences.

In March 1980, on the anniversary of Abraham Lincoln's second inaugural address, we sat together in front of the fireplace in Teague Library while he read Lincoln's entire address to me. It is short, and so it didn't take long. When he concluded, he turned back to some of the most meaningful parts and showed me one of the basic patterns in Lincoln's style, which is also a hint into the pattern of Elton's style. The particular passage he pointed to contained the words *"And the war came."* "Listen to the beautiful cadence of one-syllable words!" he told me excitedly. "That is great style."

Referring to our civilization as a cut-flower civilization was the first quotation to draw Elton into the national spotlight. Written in 1944 in his book *The Predicament of Modern Man,* it continues to be used widely today. The whole context for this phrase is as follows:

The terrible danger of our time consists in the fact that ours is a cut-flower civilization. Beautiful as cut-flowers may be, and much as we may use our ingenuity to keep them looking fresh for a while, they will eventually die, and they die because they are severed from their sustaining roots. We are trying to maintain the dignity of the individual apart from the deep faith that every man is made in God's image and is therefore precious in God's eyes.

Here are few more of Elton's most notable writings:

ON THE CENTRALITY OF COMMITMENT

When a Christian expresses sadness about the Church, it is always the sadness of a lover. He knows that there have been great periods, and, consequently, he is not willing to settle for anything less than those in his own time. But, though he is saddened by the contrast between what now is and what has been, he is saddened even more by the contrast between all periods and what Christ evidently intended. Whatever else our Lord had in mind, it is clear that He envisioned something very big. He did not propose a slight change in an existing religion! The radical nature of the proposed Church is indicated by the fact that, in one chapter of the New Testament, Christ is reported three times as saying, "Something greater is here" (Matt. 12:6, 41, 42). A small venture would not have aroused such fierce opposition, but neither would it have been worth the trouble. The Christian Movement was initiated as the most radical of all revolutions!

ON A CHRIST-CENTERED FAITH

A Christian is a person who, with all the honesty of which he is capable, becomes convinced that the fact of Jesus Christ is the most trustworthy that he knows in his entire universe of discourse. Christ thus becomes both his central postulate and the Archimedean fulcrum which, because it is really firm, enables him to operate with confidence in other areas.

ON WHOLISTIC CHRISTIANITY

The only way in which a person may achieve relative unity of life is by dedication to something outside himself, to which he gives such loyal devotion that the self is forgotten in the process. The competing parts of our lives, which cannot unite of themselves, are then united because of a unity of direction, when all parts point one way. *The ancient truth is that the health of the self comes, not by concentrating on self, but by such dedication to something outside the self, that self is thereby forgotten.*

ON THE REDEMPTIVE FELLOWSHIP

Somewhere in the world there should be a society consciously and deliberately devoted to the task of seeing how love can be made real and demonstrating love in practice. Unfortunately, there is really only one candidate for this task. If God, as we believe, is truly revealed in the life of Christ, the most important thing to Him is the creation of centers of loving fellowship, which in turn infect the world. Whether the world can be redeemed in this way we do not know, but it is at least clear that there is no other way.

ON THE CHRISTIAN HOME

We cannot change the whole world at once; we cannot alter greatly a political party or a labor union, or even a local church; each of these is too much for us. But, in the little island, which we call home, we can set the conditions to a remarkable degree. This is where each is able to make a radical difference. This is how the world can be changed.

ON THE UNIVERSAL MINISTRY

Early Christianity won against great odds, not primarily because it had a few brilliant leaders, but far more because the idea of a nonminis-tering Christian seems to have been rejected unanimously. *The mood was not so much anti-clerical as antilay.* Insofar as we are trying to abolish the laity, we are, in essence, trying to recapture the mood of first-century Christianity.

ON THE CHRISTIAN MISSION

Concern for our fellow men does not mean leaving them to their own unaided devices, when a modest but courageous witness on our part could make a difference in their lives. The chief reason for the necessity of witness is the simple fact that thoughtful men are found to share what they truly prize. If the gospel is true, our responsibility is to help to make it prevail. There is no place in Christianity for mere well-wishers. The task of contemporary Christians is to get out of the balcony and onto the witness stand.

ON THE IMPORTANCE OF HUMOR

It is true that our common lives are helped by both genuine religion and genuine humor. In the teaching of Christ the two forms are con-joined.

ON THE CHURCH OF THE FUTURE

The worst nightmare is not the disappearance of Christianity, but its continued existence on a low level. This is what may occur, for a while, unless a more demanding rationality emerges in the Church of Christ. The story of Christian history includes, we must admit, frequent decline, as well as advance. Because there is no known insurance against loss of devotion, this may occur even to the contemporary bands, but the good news is that, when old Christian societies die, others can arise to accept the responsibility of attack upon the world. This is how the Church of Christ operates.

June 1979 found the Truebloods back in London. Scribbled in Elton's handwriting on Cora Hotel stationery and dated June 6, 1979, are these reflections on "last things":

> I have in all likelihood had my last ride on a London bus. This evening I shall dine, with Virginia the expert on London Stations, at Euston. The Strand will still be a scene of traffic after I see it no more.
> I wonder how John and Agnes Trueblood felt as they left London Dock for America in 1682. I am sure they never saw London again. Departure then must have seemed terribly final.

But memory is wonderful. I shall remember the bells of St. Pancras in the tower, which copies the Tower of the Winds in Athens ... the Cora Hotel Breakfasts, the lazy days, the gardens of Friends House, the restaurants of London. My Harris Tweed jacket will be a frequent reminder of Regent Street...."

At age seventy-nine, Elton was thinking more and more of "last things." He was still speaking throughout the country, and he continued to do some writing. Now, however, he was entering an important period of remembrance and gratitude.

1980–

YEARS OF REMEMBRANCE AND GRATITUDE

We lack in British Quakerism a grand old man. . . . Elton is a Friend on whom the title does sit.

When Elton Trueblood became an octogenarian on December 12, 1980, his human pilgrimage was eight decades old. He not only had entered a new decade of life, but he had also entered a period of pronounced remembrance and gratitude. He was still strong, both physically and mentally, and he would continue to do some speaking and traveling, but he had crossed an important mark on the human timeline that would make him more cognizant of the fact that he had so little time left.

To celebrate his new status as an octogenarian, a birthday celebration was held in his honor at the Yokefellow Institute on the Earlham campus. All four of his children returned to Earlham for the event, and a huge "family" table was arranged in the center of the dining room. Surrounding this table were forty other guests, primarily Elton's associates in the Yokefellow movement. It was to this movement that Elton had decided in 1977 to give his primary energy. He resigned from the Catalyst board of Word Books, the William Penn College board, the Malone College board, as well as the Church Peace Union. His reason? To "concentrate on the Order of the Yoke for all the rest of [my] time."

Following the birthday dinner, the Trueblood party moved to the round "Yoke Room," and there, around a blazing fire, a leather-bound book of two hundred congratulatory letters was presented to him. Although Elton takes great pride in being able to find out about surprises before they are surprises, this took him by surprise! In making the presentation, I read a few of the letters out loud:

> You are a legend in your lifetime. Indeed, I can think of no living man who has given a greater service for Jesus Christ in our era than D. Elton Trueblood. And the end is not yet. . . .
>
> Cordially yours,
> Norman Vincent Peale

Thank you for being such an energetic example and for holding out such a standard of excellence for us all to follow.

> You are loved,
> Bill and Gloria Gaither

I was delighted to learn that you will be celebrating your 80th birthday on December 12.... Your lifetime has spanned the most exciting period of progress in the history of America. Your achievements in the academic and literary worlds have made a significant contribution to that progress. Thank you.

> Warmest best wishes,
> President Gerald Ford

I want to add my personal congratulations to those of countless people around the world who remember you on this special occasion.... Few Christians in our generation have had both the breadth and depth of vision and insight which have marked your teaching and writing. I am grateful to God for the ways he continues to use you to build up his people.... With the warmest affection and admiration, I am

> Cordially,
> Billy Graham

One of my happiest experiences on a recent visit to North America was making the acquaintance of Dr. Elton Trueblood, someone I have long admired for his writings and Christian faith and practice. Being with him physically only enhanced this admiration.... Now I hear that Dr. Trueblood is about to have an 80th birthday.... I send him love and good wishes....

> Affectionately,
> Malcolm Muggeridge

With joy and admiration I send you an 80th birthday greeting.... Few have accomplished even in a long lifetime what you have by uniquely combining your talents as a student, teacher, husband, father, author, preacher, minister and philosopher. I join a host of friends in wishing you Happy Birthday and expressing appreciation for your years of servant-leadership to Christ and His Church. May God bless you with many more years of fruitful service in His kingdom. Kindest personal regards.

> Sincerely,
> Senator Mark O. Hatfield

Upon turning eighty, the man who had expressed his feelings through the written word in the past, wrote one more book, *Essays in Gratitude,* a collection of "I Remember" essays first published by *Quaker Life* magazine. The opening chapter of this volume is a beautiful piece, "The Blessings of Maturity." In this essay he shares the joy of old age, of making "plans without being hectic," and how he is learning to "savor each step of the journey." The word *savor* has special appeal to Elton in his ninth decade.

"I shall not travel long distances to speak, except under circumstances which give reasonable promise that a real difference can be made," he wrote. "Realizing the limits of my energy, I propose to use what remains as wisely as possible and, in any case, not to waste it. . . . I may travel a little, but I shall go by train when I can arrange to do so; and, if I fly, I shall try to avoid close connections. Running through an airport to catch a departing plane seems to me a foolish act, especially for a person more than eighty years of age." When Elton is pressured to travel south to speak these days, his standard response is, "No, I am tired of running through the Atlanta airport with my tongue hanging out!"

At his mature age, Elton loves the feeling of liberation. He is liberated from the struggle to "get ahead" or "to build a reputation" or to "establish a home." "Suddenly, I realize," he writes, "that, for the first time in my life, I do not have too many duties. . . . I am enjoying the clock, rather than fighting it. For many men and women in middle life this kind of freedom is never experienced. It is a particular joy of maturity to be able to produce, but to produce without strain."

In mature age, as in youth and his middle years, Elton's model has continued to be Samuel Johnson. Elton wrote, "I have now lived longer than did the scholar from who I have gladly learned for many years, and this I recognize as an unearned blessing."

One recent cold and icy day, I returned to the Yokefellow office after a round of racquetball with my wife. As I walked into the office the door was ajar, and there was a trail of blood from the couch to the lighted bathroom. "James, is that you?" came Elton's familiar voice from the bathroom. "I have just had a terrible fall." Soaking some towels in cold water, I placed them on the back of his head to slow the flow of blood from a rather large cut. He had walked out of the front door of Teague Library, and not sensing how icy the brick walk had become, he fell straight back, with the back of his head hitting the step into the library. I wanted to take him to the hospital, but he did not want to bother. What he did was a typical reaction for the Johnsonian professor. He sat on the couch, leaned his head back on the cold wet towels, and proceeded to recount some memorized verses of poetry. "Perhaps I should learn a new language," he pondered out loud. "You know, James, that when Samuel Johnson had a stroke, to make sure that his mind was still operating in good order, he learned the Dutch language." Even in pain, Johnson was acting as model! Finally, after nearly two hours he felt strong enough to walk back to his home, Virginia Cottage. Not five minutes after he had walked in the back door, the garage door opened, and the Trueblood car pulled out, with Elton sitting in the passenger seat. I knew what had happened. Virginia had insisted that he go to the hospital to be checked!

The next day Elton walked into the office for coffee with a new bandage on the back of his head. "James, take out your calendar," he ordered with a twinkle in his eyes. "Mark the date February 16, 1994, as the day when I need to go and get another tetanus shot!"

Elton's life has been relatively free from sickness or injury. He has been hospitalized only three times, all three occuring after he was seventy-nine years old. Two of these were for hip replacements. Following his second hip operation the doctor told him to be sure and use a walker for a few weeks so that he would not put his full weight on the new joint. It was not easy to make Elton use such a device, but Virginia kept insisting. Once while I was at the Trueblood house during this recovery time, Elton decided to walk over to Teague Library. From the kitchen, Virginia told him to be sure and use the walker as the doctor had instructed. Elton consented to take it with him, but as soon as he was out of the door he carried it over to his library! When he returned home he carried it back. Elton is not a very good patient.

Upon the release of *Essays in Gratitude,* a copy was sent to David Firth, editor of the *Friend,* the Quaker magazine of London Yearly Meeting. The book was reviewed by Firth and served as the impetus of an excellent editorial about "the grand old man":

> We lack in British Quakerism a Grand Old Man; or for that matter a Grand Old Woman. Though there have been charismatic giants in our past, and though we still have any number of Remarkable Old Persons, the revered Friends who might today have aspired to the title Grand seem to have preferred to retire modestly to their farm or their books; they do not stay around to gather glory.
>
> In America, on the other hand, such Friends exist. These thoughts come to me on reading a book of *Essays in Gratitude* by D. Elton Trueblood. Now Elton is a Friend on whom the title does sit. He is rather Grand, and at the age of 81 he would not deny being Old. Indeed in this book he counts "The Blessings of Maturity" in a most moving and comforting introduction. . . . Elton sets great store on the friendship of people from whom he can learn, and his life has inevitably brought him in touch with more than his share of interesting figures, including more than one occupant of the Oval Office. But his methods are charming: "It came to me as something of a discovery," he writes, "that many of the persons with whom I should like to be acquainted are approachable. . . . The conviction of the approachability of people who are leaders has . . . led to morning coffee with the Archbishop of Canterbury in London and to afternoon tea with Radhakrishnan in Madras. Why not? These are persons, too, and they may be as eager for friendship as anyone else." So on a visit to Britain this summer it was Lord Caradon at the Lords, Malcolm Muggeridge at home, Bishop Stephen Neill in Oxford; while back in 1958, on embarking on the Britannic at Liverpool his first act was to scrutinize the passenger list, which resulted in several hours spent on deck with the noted classical scholar Edith Hamilton and the even more noted theologian Paul Tillich. . . .
>
> Inevitably there is a flavour of the orotund after-dinner speaker, of the "it has been my very great privilege." But that is the normal privilege of the Grand Old Man. Anyway, it has been *my* very great privilege to meet Elton on three occasions which remain happily in my memory. Two of them were in a Fleet Street pub; but I hasten to add that Elton had invited me to lunch at the Cheshire Cheese because of its association with Doctor Johnson and its proximity to his house. Samuel Johnson is one of the most revered and most

quoted figures in Elton's pantheon, and one of his many books is a collection of Johnson's prayers; so it was with a sense of occasion that we sat at a table directly under the Doctor's portrait and a commemorative brass plate marking his favourite seat.

The other occasion was on Elton's home ground, in the charming little temple, or rather the Teague Library, which he inhabits on the Earlham campus. Here it was the very great privilege of my wife and myself to be shown Elton's prize squashes (a pumpkin-like vegetable). Noting our genuine amazement at the luxuriant leaves and enormous fruits, he disclosed that his historical researches had led him to plant them on the site of an ancient compost pit.

Was this canny ruse the throwback to his farming origins, as grandson of hardy Midwestern settlers? To me this passage seems very American, and very enviable: "The life which I experienced in my Iowa childhood . . . was unusual because of the almost perfect combination of the work ethic and high educational standards, united by Christian commitment. . . . We had no reason to complain because each one of us was needed if the agricultural venture was to succeed. I cannot remember, in my boyhood, sleeping beyond five o'clock any summer morning."

Throughout his life, "the Grand Old Man" has been a public person. As a writer, lecturer, professor, and minister, his schedule of places to go and things to do was constantly filled. One day, in a rare moment of outward emotion, he came into the Yokefellow office and shared a poem of remembrance and gratitude that had been sent to him.

The words in the poem touched Elton, who, for a moment, looked as though he was remembering some past times in his own life. The poem is entitled "Can You Come Home for Christmas?" A portion is printed below:

I'm writing to you somewhat soon
    About a certain, special date;
Strange thing to do, right here in June,
    But Christmas plans just will not wait . . .

The papers praise your civic worth;
    The people join in warm acclaim
(I somehow knew, before your birth,
    That multitudes would sound your name).

Your calendar is always filled
    With such important things to do;
But I'll admit that I'd be thrilled
    To get one special gift from you.

No packages, no presents fine;
    No fuss or flurry, no ado;
No frilly, fancy place to dine:
    The Christmas gift I want is *you.*

> Can you come home for Christmas, Joe,
>   And maybe spend a day or two?
> It is a lot to ask, I know:
>   The gift I really want is *you!*
>
>   Love,
>   Mom

At the top of this poem written by Thomas Carruth, Elton has scribbled, "Really good," and has underlined "The Christmas gift I want is *you.*"
On that morning in the Yokefellow office, with tears on his cheek, Elton
candidly expressed the price one pays for being a public person.

On November 1, 1957, Elton wrote in his diary about "a decision" he
had made. "For many years I have been conscious of a tension in my life,"
he began.

> On the one hand I felt the need, with strict loyalty to logical consistency,
> to explore erroneous and shoddy thinking, particularly among students. On
> the other hand I have felt the demands of compassion for these same persons.
> The difficulty is that loyalty to the former conception sometimes gives the
> impression that the latter is lacking. In some cases it seems necessary to
> choose, because insistence on logical rigor will have at least the appearance of
> a lack of love.

In a reflective mood—Teague Library, 1983

Now, nearly 57 years of age, I have determined that in the remainder of my life, I shall try to err, if I err, on the side of tenderness. Perhaps I have done the service requested of one in maintaining sharpness of mind, and my future role is that of being obviously loving as well as really loving. At least the experiment is worth trying.

As one studies the life of Elton Trueblood, this shift of emphasis is detectable. Although he never abandons his strong concern for clear thinking and logical rigor, he does, as he has grown into a time of remembrance and gratitude, make the move toward combining this concern with the "warm heart." This shift is noticeable in his writing, but in his speaking and personal encounters the move is most discernible. In reading the early sermons Elton delivered (for example, "The New Apologetics," which was his first sermon at Woonsocket Friends Meeting) and then hearing him speak in recent years, one realizes Elton has shifted from complexity of discourse to a profound and loving simplicity. In a most recent sermon, Elton chose as his text 1 Cor. 14:1 – "Make love your aim." His entire message focused on "caring as the supreme work of persons." He pointed out the fact that *love* is used forty-seven times in the Gospel of John, twenty as a verb and twenty-seven as a noun. In John's first letter, he noted *love* appears twenty-five times. In conclusion he said, "I want to use the time that I have left to care for as many as I can."

This message, which was not simplistic yet profoundly simple, is in stark contrast to the tough thinking and strong debating style that had marked Elton's earlier career. In 1957 he had made the decision to err on the side of tenderness and to be more loving, and in the more than thirty years since, one can see how this tenderness of concern has grown. What seems to make Elton's care and loving concern for persons so meaningful is the fact that he has come to this place through the fire of tough mindedness and impatience for sloth. The simplicity of his message of love and

Author James Newby with Elton Trueblood, 1989

caring would not be nearly as profound had he not struggled long and hard with tough and complex philosophical questions. I am reminded of the question asked of the theologian Karl Barth toward the end of his life, concerning the one truth he would like to share with others. His response: "Jesus loves me this I know, for the Bible tells me so." Perhaps a profound simplicity is the fruit of arduous study that passes through the maze of complex thought. This seems to be the case in the life of Elton Trueblood, as well as in the life of Karl Barth.

As he concluded his chapter "The Blessings of Maturity," in *Essays in Gratitude*, Elton made a special point to write about thanksgiving, the one thing, he believes, that can never be overdone. "I find that the one thing which I want to put into practice in my own life is the conscious and deliberate habit of finding somebody to thank." Earlier in this essay he wrote about the very sad habit that many in older age practice of "indulging in continued complaints about other people." The antidote for this, Elton believes, is to focus on gratitude. "The person to thank may be the driver of the bus, the teller at the bank window, the church janitor, the policeman on the beat, the mail carrier, the clerk in the grocery store, the telephone operator, and many more. In this fashion, gratitude can become a way of life. The greatest blessing of maturity is that gratitude may transcend the simple occasion, to become both habitual and continuous." In Elton's life, this has occurred.

THE ENCOURAGER

Therefore encourage one another, and build one another up.

In a 1980 interview for *Christianity Today*, entitled "A Life of Broad Strokes and Brilliant Hues," Richard Foster concluded with this question: "In your autobiography you speak of the importance of living life in chapters. What chapter do you see yourself in now?" Elton's response: "This chapter is one of encouragement."

Actually, throughout Elton's whole life, in every one of his chapters, there has been the strong element of encouragement. It is really the centerpiece of his personality. Daily, letters come to him telling about how through his writing, speaking, or personal encounters he has influenced lives. For the writing of this volume, literally hundreds of people have shared their "Trueblood experiences" with me, most about his special encouragement and sense of humor.

Harold Cope, former president of Friends University and now retired in Sandy Spring, Maryland, told about the time in 1947 when he traveled with Elton to Louisville, Kentucky. At the time, Dr. Cope was employed at Earlham.

> Elton had to make a speech in Louisville, and I offered to drive him there in order to have a chance to visit with him. We were supposed to be there for

a 6:00 P.M. supper, and he would be speaking at 7:30. We started out at 1:30 P.M. and everything was going fine until we were about five miles from Greensburg, Indiana. We had to stop on the highway because the telephone company was repairing the phone service because the poles had been damaged by a mild tornado that had gone through the area. We waited for about half an hour for the road to be cleared, but when I tried to start the car it wouldn't work. What was I to do? Here I had the speaker of the evening, and my car wouldn't run!

I talked to the phone repairman who had his portable phone. He helped by calling all three of the garages in Greensburg but got no answers. However, he indicated that certainly one was open and offered to take me there. Elton decided to stay in the car. We did find one open and the attendant brought me back in his pickup truck. He gave me a push, and the car started, and so we drove back to his garage.

Upon getting out of the car the garage man said, "You have a blown head gasket." He indicated that he could tell by the way the engine was firing and by looking at the exhaust. We asked if he could repair it, and he replied, "No, your engine is too hot."

At this point Dr. Trueblood took over! He asked, "Are there any trains or buses in this area, because I have to get to Louisville to make a speech." The man said, "No." Elton looked around outside the garage and saw some cars and said, "Could you rent us one of those cars?" "No, I am not in the rental business." Elton said, "Well, will you sell us a car?" The garage attendant responded, "Yes." Then Elton in his characteristic way, said, "Well, you know when a person buys a car he needs to try it out. So, what we'll do is try it out on the way to Louisville and let you know when we get back whether we want to buy it."

The man's response was, "All right, I'll fix your car!" While the car was being fixed, Elton and I walked into town, got a bite to eat, as we knew we would miss the supper. When we came back the car was ready to go.

We arrived in Louisville by 7:00 P.M. Elton was calm and collected, acting as though this kind of thing happened to him all the time. He was master of situations like this.

Perhaps Elton's oldest living friend is Keith Conning, whom he met while a student at Johns Hopkins. Mr. Conning shared some experiences he had had with "the encourager":

In the early 1930s I was a freshman at Johns Hopkins University. There I met Elton Trueblood, the leader of a luncheon group that was called "The How To Be Religious Though Intelligent on Wednesday Group." Since Elton had also invited those who had registered at the university as atheists or agnostics, it was a stimulating experience to meet each week, to study, dissect, and reassemble our thinking. The experience of those years showed me that Christians have no need to apologize for their faith and need never be on the defensive intellectually.

Later, as a Presbyterian minister I found this was a secure foundation on which to stand. For example, I remember one time when I was calling to make a door-to-door survey in Detroit. It was a bitterly cold afternoon. At one home I introduced myself as the minister of the neighboring church. "You're wasting your time here," the lady at the door replied, "We're atheists." Harking back to college days, I answered, "There are so many varieties of atheists. What denomination do you belong to?" The lady replied, "Maybe you'd better come in out of the cold." She opened the door wider, and we had a fascinating conversation such as we had at Johns Hopkins. Elton has influenced my ministry to be positive and confident. For this I am truly grateful.

David Kingrey, a Quaker pastor from Whittier, California, wrote about his first experience with Elton and to what it led. Often people have said "Be careful when encountering Elton, it may change your life." For David Kingrey, this has been true:

> Elton spoke in my home church, West Milton (Ohio) Friends Meeting when I was a junior in high school. After the worship service, as I was walking down the outdoor stairs, Elton called to me and said that he wanted to meet me. Sheepishly, I turned back, and he walked over to me. During that encounter, Elton invited me to come to Earlham College to study under him. I was so impressed that Elton wanted to be my teacher that I made the decision that day to attend Earlham. During my seven years in the college and the School of Religion, Elton was my professor and my encourager—truly my mentor. To him I am indebted for guidance into the ministry.

James Turner, a Nazarene pastor, had this to say about his teacher:

> To know Elton Trueblood is to know a great teacher, a great philosopher, a great writer, a great humanitarian, and a great Christian, but also a great friend. In an interview with Elton, I think our second time of meeting, I asked, "Who is Elton Trueblood?" and with a gleam in his eye and without hesitation he said, "Your friend." I have found that, over the years, delightfully true. I have found much comfort in the shade of this great oak. I doubt a day has gone by, since I met Elton, that he has not in some way, benefited my life. I could not repay my indebtedness to him, but I have acknowledged the debt often.
>
> You are not in the presence of Elton long before you realize something stirring in your soul. Only one who is dull could go into his presence and come out the same. Without considering himself great, he challenges you to greatness. He will say, pulling a book from his shelf, "If you cannot be great yourself, you can walk with the greats." In handing you the book, somehow you feel morally obligated to read it.
>
> I met Elton in a time when it would have been easy to blend in with mild Christianity. Struggling against the stream of complacency can cause you to relax or become cynical, both of which will render one ineffective. I asked Elton in our first meeting, "Sir, I am young [now he tells me I am middle-aged]. If you had one thing to say to me, what would it be?" I shall never forget his words, for they were like manna to my spiritual and mental faculties. "Jim," said he, "deliberate mediocrity is both a heresy and a sin. God has called us to excellence, and neither he, nor we, shall be satisfied with less."

From "down under," a letter from John E. Mavor, director of the Department for Mission and Parish Services of the Uniting Church in Australia, had this to say:

I have just greatly enjoyed reading the autobiography of Dr. Elton Trueblood entitled *While It Is Day.* It is some years since the autobiography was
published but it was still very special for me and a great delight to read.

As a young minister, Elton Trueblood's writing was very influential on my
ministry. I conducted many camps for young people and some of his great
ideas in books, such as *The Company of the Committed,* I shared *with thousands of
young people* in this part of Australia where I live.

On May 5, 1987, Edmund Fuller, the esteemed book review editor for
the *Wall Street Journal,* wrote his last column, entitled "Closing the Book
on a Reviewing Column." In it he shared part of a recent speech Elton
delivered in North Carolina concerning education and — one of his favorite themes — choosing one's own companions. For a man who had given
his career to literary pursuits in an age of video, in the same though somewhat different way than Elton, Fuller found Elton's words encouraging.
Edmund Fuller wrote,

> Recently, at Guilford College, not far from us in North Carolina, my wife
> and I heard a notable talk about education and faith by the elder statesman of
> American Quakers, Elton Trueblood. He laid special emphasis on one aspect
> of the printed word. Transcending time, space and languages or origin, it gives
> us extraordinary freedom to choose the intellectual company we will keep, to
> select those with whom in spirit, we will walk. That is a privilege. Moreover, to
> those who can see it so — a minority, Elton Trueblood asserts — in the highest
> sense it is a duty, in at least a due proportion of our reading time. Paraphras-
> ing Joshua, "choose you this day whom you will read."

All of the testimonies to Elton's encouragement would fill its own volume this size. Suffice it to say that he has made the Scripture passage from
Thess. 5:11 his own life's operating principle: "Therefore encourage one
another and build one another up."

PROFESSORIAL HUMOR

*He possesses "a mirth consistent with tender compassion for all that is frail, and
with profound reverence for all that is sublime."*

As he encountered the young man on the walk in the heart of the Earlham campus, Elton immediately sensed this student's embarrassment. He
had been one of over one hundred in Elton's philosophy class where one
of the most important requirements was a paper per week for twelve
weeks. This young man had not turned in one! "Well," said Elton, "You
know that you are going to fail the course. But tell me, why didn't you turn
in at least one paper?" The response came slow and deliberate, "Dr. Trueblood," the student began, choosing his words carefully, "I have such a
high standard of excellence that I could not bear to produce and then
submit to you any of the poor stuff of which I knew I was capable."

Elton loves to tell this story. The usual response is "With an answer like that I hope you passed him." "No," replies Elton, maintaining his strictness with regards to academic excellence. "He still failed the course."

It seems strange that a serious writer like Elton Trueblood would have such a delightful sense of humor, but he does. He loves a good joke or story and will keep a dinner party or audience laughing if you give him the stage. Some of his best stories come out of his own experience as a college professor or from his colleagues in the same profession.

The following story about an absent-minded colleague actually occurred. Elton relates what happened:

> I was called late one evening by a well-known writer and scholar and asked if I would be his guest at breakfast the next morning, since I was leaving the afternoon of that day. I readily agreed and met the professor at 7:45 in the winter darkness of Harvard Square. When we finally found a restaurant open and went in, the professor, looking sheepish said, "Now I have a terrible confession to make." "Oh, that's all right," I answered, "I have some money." "It's worse than that," he replied. "I have a habit of getting up early, while my wife is still in bed, to get my own breakfast and this morning I forgot and did it."

Some of Elton's best stories come from the age of the telegram. He has often shared the following example:

> George Fox, the founder of Quakerism, well-known to the reading public through his famous *Journal,* has been the subject of much laborious biographical research since his death at the end of the seventeenth century. Recently, at a scholarly meeting near Swarthmore College, there was some argument as to the exact date of the death of Fox. Finally the question was settled by a telegram from a Harvard scholar who wired to say that George Fox died on such and such a day. The Western Union operator called when the telegram arrived, said she had a sad duty to perform, and read the telegram in her best voice of condolence.

Stories that have come from Elton's children have a special place in his heart. One out of the "Kids Say the Darndest Things" variety was told by Elton in this way:

> I took our third son, aged five, to Los Angeles by train. As we stopped near one station, he noted the men working on a siding. "What are they doing?" the boy asked. "They're repairing the track," I replied. "Why are they doing that, Daddy?" "They do that to earn money to support their families," was the best I could muster at the moment. "Now don't kid me, Daddy," the boy answered. "You know they couldn't support their families doing that." "How might they support their families?" I asked, really interested by now. "They could write," he said with finality.

On another occasion Sam was asked by his father to help him weed the garden. In the midst of this toiling work, Sam stopped his hoeing and said to his father, "Dad, just because gardening is your hobby doesn't mean that it has to be mine, too!"

Concerning gardening and humor, Elton wrote one of the best pieces of humorous writing on the subject ever written. The following was discovered in his diary. It is entitled "On Gardening."

Having been a practising gardener for almost six years, I am now ready to tell the truth about gardening. This is rarely done. The person about to begin has little opportunity of learning the truth because hardened and veteran gardeners have joined in a conspiracy to delude and entice new members of their fraternity.

There are a few real joys in gardening, but they are largely overshadowed by the hard work which the production of flowers and lawn entails. The trouble is that one who has a garden can never rest with a clear conscience. Always there is some work, be it pruning, spading, hoeing, seeding or watering which cries out for you. This is not work which it would be *desirable* to do, but work which you *must* do if you want to have any standing with your wife and neighbors. Neighbors who have bowed their necks to the Yoke of slavery are highly contemptuous of those who rebel.

While I write these words, I am conscious that I am using stolen time. Even as I write the weeds are growing, the crust is hardening over the tiny seeds, the rabbits are feasting on new shoots and the snails are building up their population enormously. All this I could bear, but I find it very hard indeed when the writers in the garden magazines go out of their way to rob me of peace and leisure. Just when I hope that I can slip away for a set of tennis I notice the list of "things to do this month" which some urban editor gets paid for writing. I can picture this man sitting cozily in his city apartment, telling me each month what I *must* do. There is no month of the year in which the up and coming gardener can relax. If it isn't bulbs that require planting, it is grass that requires cutting or hedge that requires clipping or manure that requires spreading.

Of course you will say to me that I might hire a gardener and let him worry. But it is not so simple as that. The average hireling gardener is no doubt a good fellow, but he wants to be directed. He wants the boss to do the brain work while he provides the muscle. But this is wholly wrong. I do not mind in the least using my physical strength and I am never so happy as when spading, providing I am not, at the same time, worried by some other work that cries out for a worker. What I so greatly resent is the constant necessity of thought. How hard it is, for example to know *when* to move the soil. If it is moved when it is too wet it bakes into clods that will not melt all summer. If we wait too long it is so hard and dry that it is almost impossible to handle.

Now the trouble is that I use my brain at my regular work and when I get out of the study I want to relax intellectually but this is precisely what the successful gardener cannot do. It is therefore a great mistake for college professors to own gardens, since their two kinds of work are then too similar. In fact, gardens undoubtedly detract materially from the literacy and scientific production of college faculties. How can you think about the problem of monetary reform or atomic structure while you are worrying over the control of fungus growth?

You will no doubt say, dear Reader, that I am a foolish man to write as I do. If I present this matter in its true light, I cannot expect any respite from my unhappy labors, for no one will purchase my garden. Dear Reader, you are right. That is why men have not had the courage to say this before.

"I am still a farmer at heart," Elton has often said. As with most gardeners, there is always more produce grown than can be consumed by one family, and so he gives vegetables away to his neighbors. One of his neighbors at Earlham is Tom Mullen, dean of the Earlham School of Religion. Elton always takes him vegetables from his garden, and on one occasion he asked him, "Tom, why don't you put out a garden? It is wonderful exercise, and then you could enjoy the fruits of your own labor." Tom responded, "Elton, it says in the Bible that it is more blessed to give than receive. If I put out my own garden, it would take away your opportunity of becoming more blessed by giving me your vegetables!" Each summer Elton loves to tell visitors this now familiar story.

Some of Elton's best humor comes from his trips to England and Scotland. He enjoys reciting the epitaph on the Scottish tombstone: "Consider friend as you pass by, as you are now, so once was I. As I am now, you too shall be. Prepare, therefore, to follow me." And then with characteristic good timing he tells about "the wag" who scribbled underneath this epitaph: "To follow you I am not content, until I know which way you went!"

During the energy crisis a few years ago, Elton wrote down the words on a sign outside a British petroleum station: "We can *fuel* some of the people all of the time, and we can *fuel* all of the people some of the time, but we can't *fuel* all of the people all of the time!"

I have recently taken up the game of golf, a game that Elton tells me he gave up long ago because, he says, "It was destroying my confidence." He enjoys repeating the story about a colleague at Stanford who went to Scotland to play golf on the old course at St. Andrew's. After a rather poor drive on the first hole, his colleague confessed to the experienced caddy that he was having some back trouble. "Sir," said the caddy, "I have been working here for forty years, and I have yet to meet a golfer in the best of health!"

In London, Elton tells of walking past a church, and on the bulletin board out front was this message: "If you're tired of sin come on in." Below someone had scribbled, "If not, call 922–5506!"

As an octogenarian, Elton is often asked how he has lived so long. His response: "Choose your ancestors with care." When asked about his life pattern, he says, "I am more productive in the morning hours than at any other time." And then with a smile he'll add, "I know God loves night people too, but I don't think he understands them!"

The best story to come from his book titles relates to *Alternative to Futility* and was told to him by a bookseller in Montreat, North Carolina. He said that a woman once entered his store asking for the book by Elton Trueblood entitled, *Alternative to Fertility!*

As a graduate of Johns Hopkins University, he tires very quickly of people who refer to his alma mater as John Hopkins, leaving the *s* off of *John*. When this occurs he will tell the story about the learned professor from "The Hopkins" who spoke in Pittsburgh. In his introduction, his host made the common error, saying that he was a professor at "John Hopkins University." Without a word of correction, the professor stood and thanked his host, saying, "It is wonderful to be here in Pitt_burgh!"

As a strict disciplinarian on time, Elton can hardly stand to sit through a whole program of announcements, special music, etc., that takes the bulk of an evening before he is introduced to speak. A story about President Eisenhower in this respect is often shared after he has had to endure such a long and difficult evening. The former president was asked to speak at some occasion and had to sit through the kind of preliminary activities described above. When it finally came time for him to be introduced, the host said, "And now General Eisenhower will give us his address." The former president stood and said, "My address is Gettysburg, Pennsylvania. Good night." And he left.

Winston Churchill, like Eisenhower, is one of Elton's favorite statesmen. During a 1982 trip to England, he shared with the Yokefellow tour group why Churchill was buried at Bladon instead of in the floor of Westminster Abbey as the queen requested. Churchill told the queen, "Your Majesty, no one walked over me in life, and I will not allow anyone to walk over me in death!"

Because of his life on the college campus, Elton knows about the difficult work of the development department, especially at a small liberal arts school that is not tax-supported. Whenever development officers or the president of an institution are in his audience, Elton is likely to tell the story about a former president of Smith College who was speaking to a group of elderly Smith alumni, many of whom had written the school into their wills. Following his especially inspiring talk, one elderly woman asked the president, "Sir, what can *we* do to help Smith at this time?" The president's one-word response: "Die."

Elton's favorite fund-raising story centers around the concern about how often one should ask for money in a given period of time. He tells about the urbanite who was visiting a mink ranch. After the tour, the owner of the ranch asked if there were any questions. Immediately the city-dweller's hand went up, and he asked, "How many times a year do you skin them?" Seeing the humor in the moment, the rancher responded, "Well, we used to do it twice a year, but we found it made them nervous!"

Much of Elton's humor is spontaneous, such as the time we were together in Chicago for a large Yokefellow gathering. He had just concluded his speech and was making his way to the book table at the opposite end of the meeting hall. Two young women were responsible for the sale of books, and as I have heard him do countless times, Elton asked them how the sales were going. On this particular occasion he asked, with a smile, "How are we doing, girls?" To this inquiry one of the women, obviously a strong feminist, said, "Sir, we are *not* little girls!" Taken by surprise, Elton asked her, "Don't you like being called a girl?" "No," she replied, "not unless you like being called a little boy." With a broad smile Elton responded, "Of course I don't mind being called a little boy! Doesn't it say in the Bible that we must become like little children in order to enter the Kingdom of Heaven?"

Elton loves to tell of humorous events when the "jab" is on him. There was the time when he was speaking at Buck Hill Falls, Pennsylvania, and Sebastian Kresge, the founder of the Kresge stores and foundation, happened to be in the congregation. Not being one to miss an opportunity to find financial resources for Earlham or Yokefellows, Elton told Kresge after the worship service that he would love to come and visit him in his home. To this the elder Kresge responded, "I would love to have you come, but remember, I am not the one who gives away the money!"

One time when Elton and Virginia were visiting in the Elizabeth City area of North Carolina, Elton decided that he would call one of the Truebloods listed in the telephone book. Since this was the area in which the Truebloods settled when they migrated to America from England, there were many still living in the vicinity. He chose a Trueblood at random, telephoned, and when a voice on the other end said, "Hello," Elton responded, "Hello there. This is your cousin Elton." There was a long pause on the other end of the line, and then the other Trueblood said, "You sound like a white man to me!" Of course, as was the common practice in slave times, many of the slaves would take the names of their master, which were kept through the succeeding generations. When Virginia Trueblood would tell this story, she would say, "It was the only time I saw Elton speechless!"

One of Elton's favorite lines is "Now I know what they will do with me in hell," and then he fills in the rest depending upon the disagreeable situation. For example, if there is one thing that he cannot bear, it is long meetings. Often he has said, "I know what they will do with me in hell. They will put me in a meeting that never ends!"

As one who has given over ten thousand public speeches, he knows what organized groups are like before the introduction of the speaker— there is usually a long list of announcements! During one meeting, after a particularly tedious time of one announcement after another, Elton leaned over to me and said, "Now I know what they will do with me in hell. They will put me in a meeting where there is always one more announcement before I speak!"

On another occasion when we traveled together to Indianapolis for a meeting at the Lilly Endowment, we had a very difficult time finding the right street due to a lot of road construction. We could see the interstate highway from every direction, but we couldn't get on it. After about twenty minutes of going back and forth on various streets trying to find the entrance ramp, I pulled over to the side of the road and in frustration just looked up at the expressway trying to gather my thoughts about what to do next. The silence was broken when Elton said, "James, now I know what hell will be like. We will always be able to see the right road, but there will be no way to reach it!"

He enjoys telling about the woodsman who loved his old axe so much that he wouldn't even think of getting a new one. "I've had to replace the head twice and the handle three times," the woodsman would say, "but I will never get a new one!"

During a recent gathering at Earlham College, I saw Elton making his way through the crowd to greet me. I could tell by the twinkle in his eyes that he was anxious to share his most recently acquired anecdote. He began, "An advertisement in a local paper read in part, 'This Sunday the guest lecturer at Christ Church will be Edgar Jones, A.B., B.D., D.D., Lit. D., LL.D.'" And then with characteristic good timing, he sprung the punch line: "Topic — *Humility!*"

At another time he was speaking at a large gathering of prisoners in a federal penitentiary and had taken his daughter, Elizabeth, along. At the end of the meeting, Elizabeth, forgetting for a moment where she was and anxious to go home, turned and asked the man next to her, "How do I get out of here?" The response from the prisoner: "Lady, I wish to God I knew!"

Elton Trueblood's sense of humor does not detract from his profundity but combines with it to make his personality that much more powerful. I can say of Elton as Macaulay said of Addison, that he possesses "a mirth consistent with tender compassion for all that is frail, and with profound reverence for all that is sublime."

DEAN OF AMERICAN RELIGIOUS WRITERS

Always I am a bit surprised by what has been written, for I have become in some sense an instrument.

Elton Trueblood is the "dean" of American religious writers. Although he is no longer writing books himself, he continues to encourage others to write. Clayton Carlson of Harper & Row, San Francisco, has said, "We receive about ten thousand unsolicited manuscripts each year, and Elton Trueblood is responsible for a large number of them!" Everywhere Elton travels he encourages people who want to write. He is one who knows about the power of the written word and the difference it can make in the lives of those who write, as well as those who read. This appreciation, coupled with his gift of encouragement, produces many manuscripts from people who might never have written without his encouraging word.

On one of his many visits to Washington, he stopped at the headquarters of the Church of the Saviour on Massachusetts Avenue. When he walked in, he noticed Elizabeth O'Connor, secretary of the church and author, lying on a couch. "Elizabeth, what's wrong?" Elton inquired. "Oh, Elton," said Elizabeth, "I just can't complete this book." In a voice that commands respect, Elton said, "Elizabeth, get up and take thy pen in hand!" As Elton tells the story, Elizabeth O'Connor rose and completed the manuscript.

The popular author and speaker Keith Miller is another Trueblood writing student. He tells about how Elton convinced him to come to the Earlham School of Religion to study with him.

> He was the keynote speaker and I was a lay witness at the first week of conferences at Laity Lodge (Texas). I was visiting with him between sessions and said, "I would sure like to study with you" (one of those off hand complimentary remarks one makes to a speaker).
>
> He pulled out his little black book and said, "School starts the 26th of September. Can you be in Richmond by then?" That was on June 7th. I didn't know what to say. But Elton turned to me and said, "You *were* serious weren't you?" I had been but had no idea of quitting my work. Besides I had no money to move and go to school while supporting a wife and three children. I told him I would pray about it and see about the funding possibilities.
>
> Within ten minutes a man walked up to me (who knew nothing of my conversation with Elton). This man . . . was president of a company. He said that he and his wife were tired of putting money in buildings and would like to support conferences like the one we were attending. He said if I ever wanted to go into this sort of work they would like to help financially. And that was how we got to Earlham. They helped with our move and expenses.

Elton wrote the foreword to *A Taste of New Wine,* and, as the cliché goes, "the rest is literary history."

My wife, Elizabeth Newby, is the daughter of migrants and lived for the first fourteen years in the back of a truck. Sensing that Elizabeth might have a story to tell and a book within her, Elton encouraged her to write. In 1977 *A Migrant with Hope* was published by Broadman Press, all of it being written in Teague Library while I was a student in the Earlham School of Religion. As repayment to her writing teacher, Elizabeth edited a number of his addresses and essays, and Broadman published these in the book *A Philosopher's Way.*

In 1978 he helped Jeb Magruder with his book *From Power to Peace.* Magruder wrote Elton,

> I am most grateful for the time you took to read the galleys of *From Power to Peace,* and particularly appreciate your astuteness and understanding of where I have to go. As I have reflected over the past few years, I realize that the social concerns smouldering since prison need an outlet. Personally, I do not believe this outlet can be found at the corporate level, even in a Christian organization. Instead, I need to immerse myself in the direct needs of people and believe the tools I gain with both the M.Div. and M.S.W. will allow me to channel my energies in this direction. Again, my thanks for your encouragement and support.

Richard Foster's *Celebration of Discipline* includes another of Elton's forewords. In the year that *Celebration* was published it was the only unsolicited manuscript that Harper & Row accepted. It has had incredible success in the religious world of the 1980s. To date it has sold close to 450,000 copies in the U.S. alone.

Richard Foster has shared how Elton encouraged him to write. He was attending a National Pastor's Conference in Dallas, Texas, where Elton was a speaker. Dr. Foster had stayed on an extra day with his ministerial colleague at the time, Ron Woodward, and ran into Elton in the hotel lobby. He described what happened next:

"He called us over and first he had me read the first paragraph of a speech he was preparing to give at some college — out loud of course. Then he turned and asked me what book I was working on.... I mentioned that while I was writing a few magazine articles, that I did not feel ready to write a book. He then said to me, 'Well, that is fine but soon you *must* write a book.' That comment triggered something important in my mind and I went home and dashed out the outline of what is now *Celebration of Discipline*. I sent a one-page summary of the book to him, and he responded with some very helpful comments."

A beautiful example of teamwork in the house of Harper comes in a story Elton tells about working with Harry Emerson Fosdick and their mutual friend and editor, Eugene Exman. Fosdick had written his autobiography but could not reach consensus with Harper on an adequate title. In desperation, Mr. Exman telephoned Elton and said, "Elton, I know you are good with titles, can you help Dr. Fosdick find one for his autobiography?" Elton told his friend that he would try.

One week later Elton called Mr. Exman and said that he had a title for Fosdick's book. "But," he added, "it will cost you lunch at the Twenty-One Club." Mr. Exman quickly agreed — a small price to get a good title! At the New York club, Elton kept Dr. Fosdick and his editor in suspense until they were all having coffee after lunch. Then, when the moment was right, Elton told them the title. "I knew that the title of an autobiography would be best if it could come from the author's own words," Elton recalled. "And so I began to go through the best writing that Harry Emerson Fosdick had done, which I soon realized was his hymn, 'God of Grace and God of Glory.' I went through each line carefully and at first selected, 'The Facing of This Hour' but then jumped down to the final line and realized it was much more powerful." The final line, which eventually became the title of Fosdick's autobiography, *The Living of These Days*.

In his autobiography, Elton writes about the task of writing and the joy he experiences by doing it. "The very art of writing can be remarkably creative. When I sit down with paper in front of me, I know in general what I want to say, but I seldom know the details. As the ideas are expressed in written form, however, they begin to grow and to develop by their own inherent logic. Always I am a bit surprised by what has been written, for I have become in some sense an instrument."[1]

Elton has never dictated into a machine or used a word processor. His writing has always come page by written page, all in longhand and all with a favorite pen. "This," he jokingly tells people, "is how God intended." A recent survey of the back closet of Teague Library shows evidence of

Elton's style. It would take a small truck to haul away the piles of yellow legal size pages filled with his handwriting!

"Each author must learn at what time of day he operates most efficiently," he writes. "Being a morning person I make it a rule not to write after noon. Sometimes I find I can revise in the afternoon or evening because that can be done when my energy is not at its peak, but on the whole not even this is part of my practice."[2]

Elton shares with his readers his filing system for ideas before the actual writing of a manuscript: "I empty one or more manila folders in the collection of thoughts, quotations, epigraphs, etc. Day after day I transfer notes from my breast pocket notebook to the appropriate folders. Later, when the division into chapters has become fairly clear, the notes are divided accordingly, each potential chapter having its own folder."[3]

In his *Life of Johnson,* Boswell wrote about his subject's work as a helper of potential authors: "There was, perhaps, no man who more frequently yielded to the solicitations even of obscure authors, read their manuscripts, or more liberally assisted them with advice and correction."[4]

In this way, Elton has been like his mentor. It is a task at times arduous, but as one who knows the joy of publishing a book, he wants to pass this joy to others by sharing the secrets of his own literary life and style. As the dean of American religious writers, he considers it one of his important ministries.

A FIRE LEFT BURNING

They gathered sticks, kindled a fire, and left it burning.

He stood tall and erect as I sat down, concluding my introductory remarks. It was the 1988 annual banquet of Yokefellows International, and the great Earlham College dining hall was packed. Some even had to watch by way of video hookup in the small dining rooms off the main floor. "Four score and seven years ago," Elton Trueblood began, "I was a little boy." The room erupted in laughter and applause. These were the gathered faithful who had come to hear their leader share his life story. Although he was eighty-seven years old, he spoke without a note for most of an hour. His topic: "My Pilgrimage."

Elton divided his message into three major parts — his time on the East Coast, his time at Stanford and the West Coast, and his time at Earlham in the Midwest. With love and affection he recalled his teachers and the influence they had on him. He spoke about Willard Sperry, Bliss Perry, and Alfred North Whitehead at Harvard; he reflected on the influence of Arthur O. Lovejoy and Rendel Harris at Johns Hopkins and the wonderful relationship he had with Rufus Jones at Haverford. Each name mentioned and each place to which he referred was spoken of in a tone of tremendous gratitude. It was a beautiful occasion, and all present will not soon forget the warmth of that evening together. For forty-five minutes we sat at the feet of our beloved teacher.

For Elton, the past is only important as it serves as prologue to the future. His message to those gathered under the Yoke that eventful evening was not in any way meant only to focus our attention on the past but also to learn from his pilgrimage so that we can more effectively minister in the future. "If we are not advancing, we are declining," he often says, quoting Whitehead. "There is no such thing as a holding operation."

All who have been inspired, encouraged, renewed and "turned on" by the dynamic message and personality of Elton Trueblood know there is a price to pay for such an experience. The payment is not to him but to the world in which the Order of the Yoke is called to serve. Elton can rightly be termed a ministerial "fire starter."

Above the large fireplace in the Earlham dining hall, these words are inscribed on a long and wide wooden beam: "They gathered sticks, kindled a fire, and left it burning." It is a direct quotation from the log of Robert Fowler, who was the captain of the Quaker sailing vessel *Woodhouse*. Before the ship left England for America in the late 1600s, it docked on the south of England for repairs. Because the repairs took several days, the Quakers on board left the ship to go into the surrounding communities and share the Christian message. In recording what took place, the captain wrote, "The Ministers of Christ were not idle, they gathered sticks, kindled a fire, and left it burning."

In his late eighties, Elton speaks with a sense of finality. He is fond of quoting the words of Stephen Grellet: "I expect to pass through this world but once. Any good, therefore, that I can do, or any kindness I can show, let me do it now. Let me not withhold or defer it, for I shall not pass this way again."

Passing this way *once* is probably enough for Elton. He has kindled many fires and left them burning.

EPILOGUE

THE FINAL CHAPTER

Vernal flowers, however beautiful and gay, are only intended by nature as preparatives to autumn fruits.

——*Samuel Johnson*

The writing of this biography began in one chapter of Elton Trueblood's life and is now concluding in another. The decision to move to the Meadowood retirement community near Lansdale, Pennsylvania, was not an easy one. After all, Elton had been in Richmond and at Earlham for forty-two years, coming in 1946 and leaving in 1988. What finally convinced him that he should move was the fact that he would be close to his children. Sam, the attorney and the youngest son, lives just a few miles away, and Arnold, the builder, is a short fifteen-minute drive. Elizabeth, in northern Maryland, is sixty miles to the south, while Martin, the eldest, lives in Williamsburg, Virginia. As he anticipated the move from his beloved Earlham, he shared his feelings in verse, a poem he has called "Rest."

> This place, my settled home for forty years,
> In which my little children learned to play,
> I now prepare to leave, not without tears,
> And spend my future life another way.
>
> My books and flowers I sadly leave behind;
> The roses I shall no more prune and tend,
> But all of this will be retained in mind
> Until my earthy life shall reach its end.
>
> The garden where the lonely now can rest
> Is harder than all else for me to leave;
> But children far removed from our midwest
> Will give me ample reason not to grieve.
>
> So now I go with joy to Meadowood
> Where friendships quite unknown will soon begin;
> The life I have before me will be good,
> For I shall dwell nearby to kith and kin.

The Religious News Service conducted an interview with Elton by telephone as he prepared for his move:

"Today I've been cleaning out my desk, and that's nearly enough to kill a man," said the Rev. D. Elton Trueblood from his office at Earlham College in Richmond, Ind.

Going through personal possessions to prepare for a move can be a daunting prospect for anyone, but Dr. Trueblood might make a special case for exaggerated language. After all, this is the desk of an 87-year-old scholar who has taught at the same school for more than 40 years and who has produced 36 books on topics ranging from history to philosophy, autobiography and religion.

In a telephone interview from his library, which contains 2,000 volumes he is donating to the college, the noted Quaker philosopher confessed that he was "nearly broken to pieces" because he is leaving the school where he has spent so much of his life and career.

"Though Earlham is a real paradise, I am 600 miles away from any of my children," said Dr. Trueblood. He said he is going to live in Lansdale, Pa., to be near his four children, 13 grandchildren and five great-grandchildren.

"Remember, I am four score and seven years old," the scholar noted. "Although I'm very well now, I'm not stupid enough to think I'll always be."

In an "editorial opinion" in the Richmond paper on the Sunday before his departure, the headline read, "City To Miss Trueblood." The editor said,

Richmond may be losing a great resident but his memory will have a special place here forever.

D. Elton Trueblood's life touched so many people, in so many ways, that his impact on the city and its residents can never be measured.

Despite the dozens of books, thousands of lectures, and countless other appearances, perhaps his most telling contributions have been one-on-one in the privacy of his library on the Earlham College campus.

His 42 years in Richmond, preceded by stops at Stanford, Harvard and other prestigious universities, have been a special gift to the city—a gift that won't leave with him.

Throughout the world, Trueblood, 87, is known as an accomplished author, speaker and theologian. In many ways he is better known thousands of miles away than across town.

His efforts in Richmond have been extensive, though, on a variety of levels, not the least of which is his library, where he has received thousands of students and friends as well as strangers. Also significant has been his work with Yokefellows International, which he founded, and the Yokefellow Men's Lunch every Thursday in Richmond.

That Trueblood has chosen to leave Richmond after all these years is less significant than the fact that he chose Richmond in the first place. He's moving to Meadowood, located in suburban Philadelphia, to be closer to his four children who live in Pennsylvania and Maryland.

More important was his decision 42 years ago to come to Earlham and Richmond. He will be missed, but not forgotten.

On January 5, 1988, a feature article was written about Elton in the *Indianapolis News* entitled "Earlham's Mr. Chips," a title given to him by Earlham's communication director, Peter Smith: "He is our Mr. Chips. . . . The best way to describe him is as *the* charming elder statesman." Stressing the sweetness of old age, Elton told the reporter, "My mind works better now at 87 than it ever has. I can memorize faster. . . . The terrible mistake of most older people is to quit. What you don't use you lose. Why not learn a new language like Greek after 70? It *is* possible."

In April 1988, Elton was called an "exemplary citizen" by the mayor of Richmond. The proclamation noted that he had "indelibly imprinted the city of Richmond in the minds of many world leaders."

Not to be outdone, the mayor of the city of Indianapolis, William H. Hudnut III, honored Elton by giving him a "key to the city." In his letter, the mayor said, "Your Capital City recognizes you as one of the leading citizens in the state of Indiana, and we salute you from afar for all your wonderful deeds of ministry."

Moving day was May 31, 1988, a hot and humid Memorial Day in Indiana. A grandson, Jonathan, was there to supervise, while a group of volunteers loaded a rented truck. Elton sat in the living room of his home, Virginia Cottage, as piece after piece of furniture was removed and placed on the truck. He looked lonely sitting there as people were buzzing all around him. No doubt his thoughts were on the wonderful memories of seventeen years in that home on the Earlham campus. The picture of Virginia Trueblood, after whom the house was named, was still hanging over the mantle. He had decided not to move it with him but to leave it as a reminder to all who stayed there (it was to become an Earlham guest house) of the beautiful woman of the house who had been such a gracious hostess for so many years.

It had not been the same since Virginia's death in September 1984. I had been in the office when the telephone call came from St. Vincent's Hospital in Indianapolis informing Elton that his wife had just died of a massive heart attack. She had been taken by helicopter from the hospital in Richmond to Indianapolis just two days before. Elton had visited her at St. Vincent's the previous day and had felt encouraged by her progress. Plagued by heart problems for years, however, Virginia could not bounce back again as she had done for so much of her life. Now she was gone, and Elton felt a tremendous void in his life.

On that warm September afternoon, he called friends one by one to share the sad news. He telephoned Virginia's two children, Dindy and Henry, and then called his own four children. The pattern of his announcement of her death was the same in each call: "I have sad news; she's gone." With this said, Elton would break down in tears, apologizing to me and the children for doing so. The word of Virginia's death spread throughout the community, and soon the small Yokefellow office was filled with concerned friends. There was my wife, Elizabeth; Tom Mullen, the dean of the Earlham School of Religion; Wayne Carter, pastor of First Friends Meeting; Robert Pitman, loyal secretary to Elton and dear friend of Virginia; Mrs. Cutter, a cousin; and Carrie Campbell, the faithful Earlham student who had cooked the meals for the Truebloods and who had been a close companion to Virginia. We had gathered together in remembrance of a wonderful woman and out of love and concern for Elton. It was a time of thinking about how things were and, in the back of our minds, how things were going to be.

I am sure that Virginia was on Elton's mind as he sat in the nearly empty living room that last day in May 1988. As I stood there next to him, we saw the "George Washington" desk from Teague Library being lifted onto the truck. If there is a piece of furniture that exemplifies the Trueblood contribution to the written word, it is this desk. After seeing it safely into the truck, Elton wanted me to walk with him over to the library and "sit for awhile." As we walked the familiar brick walk between his house and his study, the grand old man was going over his list of things he wanted me to be sure to remember after his departure. It was a sad and slow walk, one that I had made countless times with Elton Trueblood, but this time it had a sense of finality.

With the desk removed from its familiar corner, Teague Library looked strangely barren. The books were still on the shelves, the pictures were still on the walls, and the walnut paneling was still intact. With the removal of the desk, however, and the eminent departure of the life that had for so many years sat behind the desk, the library no longer exuded that unmistakable spirit of vitality.

The place over the fireplace where the Seth Thomas clock once ticked was also bare. I suggested that I should hang a picture of Elton to fill the void, and I did. Quietly we sat for some minutes reflecting on the joys and sorrows we had shared there together. It was a "last thing," for both of us realized that the likelihood of being together again in Teague was not good. After about an hour I left, leaving Elton alone with his thoughts. It was at Teague, on the leather couch, that he spent his last night as a resident of the Earlham community. The next morning at shortly after 6:00 A.M., Elton as passenger, with his grandson Jonathan Trueblood driving the truck, departed Richmond for Meadowood.

As I write this it is Saturday night, and I am seated behind Elton Trueblood's "George Washington" desk at his new home in Meadowood. As has been his practice in recent years, Elton has gone to bed by 8:00 P.M. Before retiring for the night, he graciously helped me pull out the hide-a-bed where I will sleep. It has been six weeks since the move, and he has told me that Meadowood already feels like home. "There is a clublike atmosphere here," he has said. "Everyday I sit in the library, and every evening I dine in the dining room."

Elton's apartment is small, with one bedroom, and has been beautifully decorated with mementos of his many travels. Right in the middle of the living room is his beloved desk, behind which are double glass doors exposing a beautiful view of the Pennsylvania countryside. When I arrived this afternoon, I met him as he was leaving the apartment of a neighbor. He is still encouraging and building up a fellowship. Tomorrow I will attend the first Meeting for Worship at Meadowood, planned and led by Elton Trueblood.

On the wall to the right of his desk is a picture of an old oxen yoke that hangs just outside the Yokefellow Institute in Richmond—a gift from a dear friend. On the wall to the left of the desk hangs the only citation of the scores he has received. It is the Upper Room Citation, presented to him in Indianapolis in March 1974:

D. Elton Trueblood
Chosen to receive the annual Upper Room Citation in the year
Nineteen Hundred and Seventy-Four
for notable contributions in worldwide Christian fellowship.
Born in Pleasantville, Iowa
Graduate of William Penn College, Harvard University
Johns Hopkins University

Professor:
Guilford College
Haverford College
Harvard University
Stanford University
Earlham College
Chief of Religious Information Agency
and Advisor to Voice of America
Founder of Yokefellow Movement
Author of stimulating books

D. Elton Trueblood
Committed and disciplined disciple of Jesus Christ,
teacher of the young, faithful and articulate interpreter of
the Society of Friends, lucid writer, designer and
motivator of Yokefellows, architect of new and fresh
approaches to the inner light, faithful exponent of the
Christlike life in a troubled world. . . .

Here at Meadowood, Elton Trueblood's life is one of relaxed reflection. In the evenings he loves to sit on his patio and look out over the countryside, and during the day he writes letters of encouragement and makes calls on his fellow residents. He is still the philosopher, and I find him grateful for the opportunity to have more time to think and pray and reflect on life. Sam, his lawyer son, stops to see his father as he drives from his home in Lansdale to his office in Norristown. Elton greatly looks forward to these visits. He also accepts a few engagements, such as a recent invitation to speak at the George Washington Chapel in Valley Forge. He is finished, however, with engagements that require a great deal of travel.

He now enjoys the opportunity of remembering events and people in his life that have been meaningful. Where in his early and middle years he was always preparing for the next speech or outlining the next book or planning the next class lecture, he now has much more time for reflection.

In Plato's *Republic* we read about a conversation between Socrates and Cephalus. Socrates is reported as saying, "There is nothing which for my part I like better, Cephalus, than conversing with aged men; for I regard them as travelers who have gone on a journey which I too may have to go, and of whom I ought to inquire whether the way is smooth and easy, or rugged and difficult.... Is life harder towards the end?" The old man replied to the inquiry of Socrates by saying, "Old age has a great sense of calm and freedom."

Elton Trueblood is enjoying this "sense of calm and freedom." As I conclude this epilogue on a Sunday afternoon, he sits behind me on his new patio, looking out over the trees along an old fence row that borders the Meadowood property. He is gathering the autumn fruits of his lifetime of nurture and cultivation. He is at peace.

Notes

Preface

1. James Boswell, *Life of Johnson* (London:Oxford University Press, 1934), 2:446.

1. 1900–1922

1. George Fox, *Journal of George Fox*, ed. Rufus Jones (New York: Capricorn Books, 1963), 525.
2. D. Elton Trueblood, "I Wish I Had Known: John and Agnes," *Quaker Life* (December 1984) :29.
3. D. Elton Trueblood, *While It Is Day* (New York: Harper & Row, 1974), 3.
4. Ibid., 8.
5. Clare and Ethel Trueblood, *Footprints* (privately published, 1979), 5.
6. Trueblood, *While It Is Day*, 20.
7. Ibid., 21.
8. D. Elton Trueblood, *Essays in Gratitude* (Nashville: Broadman Press, 1982), 108–9.

2. 1922–1933

1. Trueblood, *Essays In Gratitude*, 110–11.
2. Trueblood, *While It Is Day*, 26.
3. Trueblood, *Essays in Gratitude*, 113.
4. Trueblood, *While It Is Day*, 126.
5. Ibid., 39.
6. Trueblood, *Essays in Gratitude*, 116.
7. Trueblood, *While It Is Day*, 127.
8. Clare and Ethel Trueblood, *Footprints*, 32.
9. Ibid., 33.
10. Trueblood, *While It Is Day*, 33.
11. Ibid., 150.
12. Ibid., 33.
13. Ibid., 41.

3. 1933–36

1. Trueblood, *While It Is Day*, 42.
2. Ibid.
3. Ibid.
4. Trueblood, *Essays in Gratitude*, 21.
5. Trueblood, *While It Is Day*, 127.
6. Ibid., 43.

7. D. Elton Trueblood, *The Essence of Spiritual Religion* (New York: Harper & Row, 1936), 136.
8. Ibid., xi.
9. Trueblood, *Essays in Gratitude*, 56.
10. Thomas Kelly, *A Testament of Devotion* (New York: Harper & Row, 1941), 18
11. Richard M. Kelly, *Thomas Kelly: A Biography* (New York: Harper & Row, 1966), 91–92.

4. 1936–1945

1. Trueblood, *While It Is Day*, 45.
2. Ibid., 46.
3. Trueblood, *Essays in Gratitude*, 52.
4. Ibid., 52.
5. Trueblood, *While It Is Day*, 47.
6. Ibid., 68.
7. D. Elton Trueblood, , *The Predicament of Modern Man* (New York: Harper & Row, 1944), 18.
8. Ibid., 29.
9. Ibid., 34.
10. Ibid., 53–54.
11. Ibid., 66.
12. Ibid., 76.
13. Ibid., 96–97.
14. Ibid., 97.
15. Trueblood, *While It Is Day*, 51.
16. Ibid.
17. Trueblood, *Essays in Gratitude*, 36–37.
18. D. Elton Trueblood, *Foundations for Reconstruction* (New York: Harper & Row, 1946), 10.

5. 1945–1954

1. Trueblood, *While It Is Day*, 150.
2. Thomas E. Jones, *Light on the Horizon* (Richmond, IN: Friends United Press, 1973), 181.
3. Trueblood, *Essays in Gratitude*, 44.
4. Ibid.
5. Ibid., 129.
6. Ibid.
7. D. Elton Trueblood, *A Philosopher's Way*, ed. Elizabeth Newby (Nashville: Broadman Press, 1978), 122–24.
8. Trueblood, *Essays in Gratitude*, 134.
9. D. Elton Trueblood, *Alternative to Futility* (New York: Harper & Row, 1948), 13–14.
10. Ibid., 28–29.
11. Ibid., 57.
12. Ibid., 62.
13. Ibid., 69.
14. Ibid., 73.
15. Ibid., 100–103.
16. Ibid., 124.
17. D. Elton Trueblood, *The Common Ventures of Life* (New York: Harper & Row, 1949), 36.
18. D. Elton Trueblood, *Basic Christianity: Addresses of D. Elton Trueblood*, ed. James R. Newby (Richmond, IN: Friends United Press, 1978), 38.
19. Ibid., 43.
20. Trueblood, *Essays in Gratitude*, 85.
21. Trueblood, *While It Is Day*, 108–9.

6. 1954–1956

1. "Dr. Trueblood to Start Full-Time Federal Religious Duties in April," *Palladium-Item* of Richmond, IN (March 9, 1954).

2. Trueblood, *While It Is Day*, 133–34.
3. Ibid.
4. Trueblood, *Essays in Gratitude*, 48.
5. Ibid., 49.

7. 1956–1966

1. Trueblood, *While It Is Day*, 141.
2. Ibid., 73.
3. D. Elton Trueblood, *Philosophy of Religion* (New York: Harper & Row, 1957), xiii.
4. Trueblood, *Essays in Gratitude*, 41.
5. Ibid.
6. Ibid.
7. Trueblood, *While It Is Day*, 104.
8. Ibid., 115.
9. Ibid., 115–16.
10. Ibid., 120.
11. Wilmer A. Cooper, *The ESR Story* (Richmond, IN: Earlham School of Religion, 1985), 7.
12. D. Elton Trueblood, "Plain Speech," *Quaker Life* (January 1962): 14.
13. Trueblood, *While It Is Day*, 75.
14. Ibid.
15. Trueblood, *A Philosopher's Way*, 42–43.
16. Trueblood, *While It Is Day*, 77.
17. D. Elton Trueblood, *The Humor of Christ* (New York: Harper & Row, 1964), 9.
18. D. Elton Trueblood, *The Lord's Prayers* (New York: Harper & Row, 1965), 9–10.
19. Trueblood, *While It Is Day*, 77.
20. D. Elton Trueblood, *The People Called Quakers* (New York: Harper & Row, 1967), ix.
21. Ibid.

8. 1966–1972

1. D. Elton Trueblood, *Robert Barclay* (New York: Harper & Row, 1968), ix.
2. Trueblood, *Essays in Gratitude*, 65.
3. Trueblood, *While It Is Day*, 81.
4. Ibid., 153.
5. D. Elton Trueblood, *The Validity of the Christian Mission* (New York: Harper & Row, 1972), ix–x.
6. D. Elton Trueblood, *The Teacher* (Nashvile: Broadman Press, 1980), 74.
7. Trueblood, *While It Is Day*, 98–99.
8. Ibid., 99.
9. D. Elton Trueblood, *The Future of the Christian* (New York: Harper & Row, 1971), 72–74.

9. 1972–1980

1. Bill Moyers, *Listening to America* (New York: Harper's Magazine Press Book, 1971), 31–32.
2. Hibbs, Ben, ed., *White House Sermons* (New York: Harper & Row, 1972), 213.
3. Ibid.
4. Ibid., 214–16.
5. Abraham Lincoln, "Meditation on the Divine Will," in d. Elton Trueblood, *Abraham Lincoln: Theologian of American Anguish* (New York: Harper & Row, 1973), 44.

10. 1980–

1. Trueblood, *While It Is Day*, 64.
2. Ibid., 65.
3. Ibid., 66.
4. Boswell, *Life of Johnson*, 4:121.

Bibliography

Boswell, James. *Life of Johnson*. London: Oxford University Press, 1934.

Cooper, Wilmer. *The ESR Story*. Richmond, IN: Earlham School of Religion, 1985.

Fox, George. *The Journal of George Fox*, ed. Rufus Jones. New York: Capricorn Books, 1963.

Hibbs, Ben, ed. *White House Sermons*. New York: Harper & Row, 1972.

Jones, Thomas E. *Light on the Horizon*. Richmond, IN: Friends United Press, 1973.

Kelly, Richard. *Thomas Kelly: A Biography*. New York: Harper & Row, 1966.

Kelly, Thomas. *A Testament of Devotion*. New York: Harper & Row, 1966.

Moyers, Bill. *Listening to America*. New York: Harper's Magazine Press, 1971.

Trueblood, Clare, and Ethel Trueblood. *Footprints*. Privately published, 1979.

Trueblood, D. Elton. *The Essence of Spiritual Religion*. New York: Harper & Row, 1936.

_____. *The Predicament of Modern Man*. New York: Harper & Row, 1944.

_____. *Foundations for Reconstruction*. New York: Harper & Row, 1946.

_____. *The Common Ventures of Life*. New York: Harper & Row, 1949.

_____. *Philosophy of Religion*. New York: Harper & Row, 1957.

_____. *The Humor of Christ*. New York: Harper & Row, 1964.

_____. *The Lord's Prayers*. New York: Harper & Row, 1965.

_____. *The People Called Quakers*. New York: Harper & Row, 1967.

_____. *Robert Barclay*. New York: Harper & Row, 1968.

_____. *The Future of the Christian*. New York: Harper & Row, 1971.

_____. *The Validity of the Christian Mission*. New York: Harper & Row, 1972.

_____. *Abraham Lincoln: Theologian of American Anguish*. New York: Harper & Row, 1973.

_____. *While It Is Day*. New York: Harper & Row, 1974.

_____. *Basic Christianity: Addresses of D. Elton Trueblood*, ed. James R. Newby. Richmond, IN: Friends United Press, 1978.

_____. *A Philosopher's Way*, ed. Elizabeth Newby. Nashville, Broadman Press, 1978.

_____. *The Teacher*. Nashville: Broadman Press, 1980.

_____. *Essays in Gratitude*. Nashville, Broadman Press, 1982.

Books by Elton Trueblood

The Essence of Spiritual Religion. New York: Harper & Row, 1936.

The Trustworthiness of Religious Experience. London: Allen and Unwin, 1939.

The Knowledge of God. New York: Harper & Row, 1939.

The Logic of Belief. New York: Harper & Row, 1942.

The Predicament of Modern Man. New York: Harper & Row, 1944.

Dr. Johnson's Prayers. New York: Harper & Row, 1947.

Foundations for Reconstruction. New York: Harper & Row, 1946.

Alternative to Futility. New York: Harper & Row, 1948.

The Common Ventures of Life. New York: Harper & Row, 1949.

Signs of Hope in a Century of Despair. New York: Harper & Row, 1950.

The Life We Prize. New York: Harper & Row, 1951.

Your Other Vocation. New York: Harper & Row, 1952.

with Pauline Trueblood *The Recovery of Family Life.* New York: Harper & Row, 1953.

Declaration of Freedom. New York: Harper & Row, 1955.

Philosophy of Religion. New York: Harper & Row, 1957.

The Yoke of Christ. New York: Harper & Row, 1958.

The Idea of a College. New York: Harper & Row, 1959.

Confronting Christ. New York: Harper & Row, 1960.

The Company of the Committed. New York: Harper & Row, 1961.

General Philosophy. New York: Harper & Row, 1964.

The Humor of Christ. New York: Harper & Row, 1964.

The Lord's Prayers. New York: Harper & Row, 1965.

The People Called Quakers. New York: Harper & Row, 1966.

The Incendiary Fellowship. New York: Harper & Row, 1967.

Robert Barclay. New York: Harper & Row, 1968.

A Place to Stand. New York: Harper & Row, 1969.

The New Man for Our Time. New York: Harper & Row, 1970.

The Future of the Christian. New York: Harper & Row, 1971.

The Validity of the Christian Mission. New York: Harper & Row, 1972.

Abraham Lincoln: Theologian of American Anguish. New York: Harper & Row, 1973.

While It Is Day: An Autobiography. New York: Harper & Row, 1974.

The Encourager. Nashville: Broadman Press, 1978.

The Teacher. Nashville: Broadman Press, 1978.

Essays in Gratitude. Nashville: Broadman Press, 1982.

Books about Elton Trueblood

Newby, Elizabeth, ed. *A Philosopher's Way: Essays and Addresses of D. Elton Trueblood.* Nashville: Broadman Press, 1978.

Newby, James R., ed. *Basic Christianity: Addresses of D. Elton Trueblood.* Richmond, IN: Friends United Press, 1978.

———, ed. *The Best of Elton Trueblood, An Anthology.* Nashville: Impact Books, 1978.

Index of Persons